Love Letters
from a
Desert Rat

'Alex and Nan'

Love Letters
from a
Desert Rat

'Alex and Nan'

Edited by Liz Macintyre

The
History
Press

This book is dedicated to my wonderful family, friends and pupils and to Jeanne and Andy who guided me through difficult days.

Also to my parents, Alex and Nan and all their generation for an inspiring example of quiet courage.

When this war is over, it will be enough for a man to say, 'I marched and fought with the Desert Army.'

Winston Churchill, speech to the men of the 8th Army
Tripoli, January, 1943

For the growing good of the world is partly dependent on unhistoric acts; and that things are not so ill with you or me as they might have been, is half owing to the number who lived faithfully a hidden life and rest in unvisited tombs.

George Eliot
Middlemarch, 1871

First published 2008

The History Press Ltd
The Mill, Brimscombe Port
Stroud, Gloucestershire, GL5 2QG
www.thehistorypress.co.uk

British Library Cataloguing in Publication Data.
A catalogue record for this book is available from the British Library.

ISBN 978 0 7524 4706 3

Typesetting and origination by The History Press Ltd.
Printed in Great Britain

CONTENTS

MAP

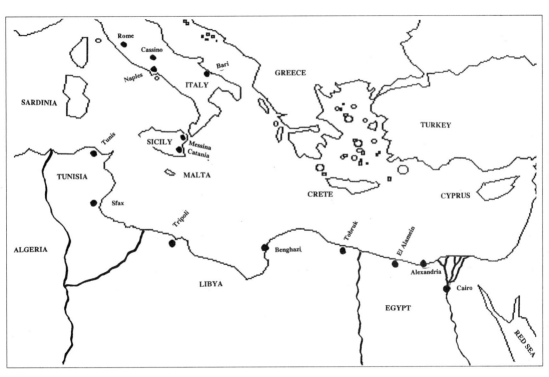

Alex's travels with the 8th Army.

INTRODUCTION

Seventy years ago, in the Albert Ballroom in Glasgow, Alex Macintyre met Nan Smith. Nan had recently returned from a holiday to Bangor, Northern Ireland. Dancing every evening, her feet were in great need of a rest and in fact she was only at the Albert to chaperone her younger sister. When Alex asked her to dance she explained, 'No – sore feet'. He didn't take this as the final answer and asked again. Nan, by now fired-up and with plenty of fighting spirit, relented and they danced together for the first time.

At the end of the evening Alex offered to walk her to the bus stop, and from then on she was his girl.

They were two young Scots people – a lather in the building trade and a shoe shop saleswoman – both in their twenties – planning some day to marry and settle down in a very ordinary way. But this was 1938 and their lives were determined by events far beyond their control. By 1939 and the outbreak of the Second World War, this young couple in love faced up to partings and even sorrow – the 'toil and tears' promised to the British people by Winston Churchill.

In 1998, sixty years after the Albert Ballroom meeting, my wonderful mum, Nan, died. She had told me to 'Look after your Dad's things', so I lifted down the small suitcase and the box of letters stored at the back of the wardrobe.

I decided to write Alex and Nan's life story for my own family. I wrote down details about Alex as Nan had told them to me – his Glasgow childhood, his drunken father, his career as a wartime driver and mechanic. She had spoken about all his hobbies – the photographer who spent hours in his own wee darkroom in our flat – his project to build a TV set over many months in our small kitchen. Most bizarre to my mind was his scheme to breed canaries! He had even gone so far as to build nesting cages in their bedroom before the scheme was abandoned. Even Nan had her limit.

I knew they had been married in December 1940, just before Alex left to fight in the Second World War. She briefly mentioned that he had been with the 8th Army all through the desert campaign, Sicily and Italy, but little more. This was the missing part of my Dad's life story.

Liz Macintyre.

So for the first time, I read the wartime letters of Alex, my Dad of whom I had no memories, and they immediately captured my heart. I began to transcribe the letters to computer for others to read. This became 'Mum's Book' – the idea of bringing Alex's remarkably well-written letters to a wider readership.

This is the family story behind *Love Letters from a Desert Rat: 'Alex and Nan'*. The story is told as Alex saw it at the time. These are his own words.

Enjoy.

Liz Macintyre, 2008
www.lizmacintyre.co.uk

Certain views expressed by Alex are of their time and these have been retained in the book. They are opinions expressed during wartime when he saw the best and worst of humanity.

❧1940❧

Romance – journey to war – new surroundings – marriage proposal –
Nan's reply

3 September 1939: Britain and France declare war
on Germany

January 1940: Food rationing introduced

Spring 1940
'The Stagger Inn'
Leeming RAF Station, Yorkshire

My dear Nan,

In the first place I must apologise for my first note. I have managed to buy some ink since then and it does make a difference. I can spell better.

Well Nan, we are getting on pretty well with the job down here, so good in fact that there is a man going home tomorrow. He will post this letter for me in Glasgow. So far I have not received any reply from you, but I should like you to reply to this little letter. You see Nan it is very lonely down here, miles from anywhere and I am writing this sitting in a small hut on the moors, with the aid of a paraffin lamp. I am being left in peace to write this for once.

You will have noticed that I am no letter writer. I just can't put on paper all the things I should like to. The only gift I seem to have is that of the GAB.

I am keeping well and I hope you are too.

You have no fear of me breaking my promise as I look on you as my girl and am looking forward to being home and seeing you again (believe it or not).

How are you enjoying the blackout?

Well goodnight Nan.

Yours faithfully,

Alex

May 1940: Churchill becomes British Prime Minister – German armies enter France

June 1940: Rapid German advance through France and around 320,000 British and French troops are evacuated from the Dunkirk beaches, northern France, back to the UK. Italy, led by Benito Mussolini, declares war against France and Britain

22 June 1940: France surrenders to Germany

July/August 1940: German bombing on towns and cities – the Battle of Britain

*Enrolled at Arbroath, 12 September 1940
Roswallie Reception Station, Forfar
16 September 1940*

My dear Nan,

Here I am again, with a little more news this time.

Well, I have arrived and had my first day, also all my kit. Here it is: 2 pairs boots, 3 shirts, 2 uniforms, coat, 2 gym suits, 3 pairs socks, razor, soap and a lot of brushes etc.

The food is pretty heavy but quite good. We are sleeping in an old mill, on the floor of course, and here's a bit of news I have just got: <u>All leave has been cancelled.</u>

How am I getting on? Well I think I'll better stop meantime.

Please turn over I've started again.

The first month up here is spent in drilling and PT, also rifle drill. As far as I understand we don't get any driving until after the first month is past. We rise at 6 a.m. every morning including Sunday. Have to get downstairs, be washed, shaved etc. and get back up to make our beds, and back down again for breakfast at 6.45.

After that, we have the Barrack room to brush out, rifles to clean and polish our own buttons etc. and down for parade at 8.10, fully dressed including puttees. After that, the day's work begins. (Ha ha.)

Well Nan, I'm in the Army now and it really isn't too bad. The life is pretty rough but I've had worse. Did you go near Mother in Glasgow or Hamilton? Write and let me know, as Mother is not much of a writer. She can't put it all down on paper. As you know, that seems to be a hereditary trait in the Macintyre family, although you must admit I'm doing not too bad so far with this letter (do I fancy myself?)

Now I come to the most important part of my letter and it is a confession: <u>Nan, I'm broke.</u> I came up with what I thought was sufficient, but I made a mistake. I never expected that I would have so many things to buy, certainly they are small things, but they add up to quite a lot. Dusters, boot polish and speaking of polish, I go through about two tins a week. The old Army game of 'Polish and Spit'. An hour a day is taken up with polishing boots. Oh! And just when I remember, don't think I am hinting for polish Nan, because by the time postage is paid it is cheaper and <u>safer</u> to buy 1 tin up here at a time.

__Now to get back to the money business. I wonder if you could send me up 10/-? I just want 10/- not £10 and just for this first week. I am asking you to do this as you have more experience of this type of thing than Mother. That's that.

Now for yourself. How are you keeping Nan? Is the chin still up? How are all the Smith family? Did you get any reply to the letter to McDonald's? And another thing, do you know anybody close to you who has a phone? Some of the chaps phoned their girls on Saturday night and I was quite jealous. I could get out to a phone after 7.30 at night if you could let me know a number.

That's all my news meantime so cheerio and God bless you.

Yours always,

Alex

Xxxxxxxxxxx

21 September 1940

My dear Nan,

Here I am again. Well I must say I enjoyed that phone conversation. It was a real break.

Well, I think I am beginning to get used to this kind of life – that is to say if you can call it life.

My own section are quite a decent lot of chaps, but the administration is the worst out from the Lt. Colonel right down. These men are here just to train recruits. They are all Englishmen and talk about swank. One of them got a sore face coming back from a dance one night and as he can't identify anybody he is making everybody suffer.

Still, enough of this mournful talk. Just you wait until I am an Officer myself (ha ha).

And how are you keeping now Nan, and all our friends?

We are CB (confined to barracks) this weekend, the result of the second injection. I am feeling sore myself just now but I can take it. (Oh yeah?)

Well Nan, sometimes I get depressed but when I do I just think of you, and my spirit rises again. When I do get these moods, it's the thought of you that keeps me going.

By the way Nan, how is my letter writing progressing? Any improvement?

I suppose I must finish off this letter now and get some more work done. Get my bed made etc.

Whatever happens, keep your chin up.

Yours always,

Alex

Xxxxxxxxx

September 1940: Italian Army attacks British-controlled Egypt to gain control of the Suez Canal. British forces drive the Italians back and advance into Libya

4 October 1940

My dear Nan,

This is just a wee note to let you know that I have not forgotten you. The reason that I haven't written sooner is because I am writing this in bed and the bed is in hospital. I have been here since Tuesday; although the MO (Medical Officer) won't say what is wrong, he says that I am a very lucky man.

When I arrived here I was put to bed and, believe it or not, my temp. was 103. There is, however, no need to worry as I feel not too bad now. You remember how I was on Sunday? Well, I seemed to get worse instead of better on Monday and reported sick again. I was sent here on Tuesday morning to have my vein attended to, and felt so bad that I passed out when I got here. I have a terrible pain across my chest when I breathe and I also have been very sick. The first thing I got here was just tossed onto a bed and told to stay there.

I am really not ill and could be a lot worse off than I am here.

As soon as I get any more news I'll let you know, but in the meantime don't worry and keep your chin up. Everything will turn out for the best. God bless you and again don't worry.

All my love,

Alex

7 October 1940

My dear Nan,

The MO has just told me that so far as he knows, he can do no more for me here. He has brought my temp. to normal and expects that I will be fit to travel in a day or two. He says that I will be going to Edinburgh Castle by ambulance on Monday. I think that the first thing I have to get is an X-Ray exam when I arrive at Edinburgh. So far, I am feeling quite well and the only bother I have is the pain in my chest when I take a deep breath.

I am beginning to enjoy this enforced rest. I get all my meals in bed and I fairly enjoy them and I can get all I ask for, within reason of course.

I am the only Scot in this place just now. All the rest are Yorkies and do they complain about the least thing? They want orange juice, mouthwashes, beef tea, Horlicks and goodness knows what else and they get them too. Some of them have been going round these hospitals for months now and having the time of their lives, and they still complain.

Good luck and always keep that chin up.

Yours always,

Alex

Gunner Macintyre
53rd A/A Driver Training Regiment
Dreghorn Camp
Edinburgh
28 October 1940

My dear Nan,

Here I am again and in case you don't notice I am using a pen. I got your very welcome parcel today and thank you very much. I am hoping to get this letter finished tonight, that is if Jerry allows it. He knows this place is here and is trying hard to get it. He has been over quite often this week night and day, but the bombs have been dropped a good distance away. He did come pretty near one morning and we had to get into the trenches in the wood. This was at 3.30 in the morning and the trenches were about a foot deep in water, and it was coming down heavens hard, so you can guess how it felt.

Here's some good news. The Weekends have started proper. Four men are going tomorrow and another four men go every weekend from now on. If any one of these men fail to return all leave is stopped and we all suffer.

Good Heavens there's the bombs again and no warning. I am just going to write on until the lights out. On second thoughts I think I'll stop just now and continue later on.

Well Nan, the lights are on again. The bombs were far away and I am quite safe.

I may not manage to get to Glasgow on Sunday as I may be on guard at the weekend. I will try and get that present for you tomorrow in Edinburgh and post it. It won't be much but it will always be a little reminder.

I was on the lorries twice today – the Big 7-ton fellows. I had the wee fellows first, but they were too easy, so they put me on to the Big fellows. They are really massive vehicles but with a little practise I should not find them any way difficult.

Well Nan, I'm afraid I'll have to finish now and get to bed so goodnight and good luck and 'Here's to the next time'.
Meantime cheerio,
Alex

PS Give all the family my regards and all your friends who are my friends.

Dreghorn Camp
8 November 1940

My dear Nan,
Well Nan I arrived back OK and in the middle of another warning. We had some night on Monday, a right big raid which lasted 4 hours with plenty of fireworks.

We had some more equipment issued today. All the full pack including water bottle etc. All the canvas has been treated with anti-gas preparation and therefore we must not Blanco them, neither must we polish any buckles as they would reflect light and be seen by the enemy. Thank goodness that's something we can keep dirty!

The weather here is still the same (raining). I would have written last night but as you have just seen old Jerry said NO. He really seems to be after the ships in the Forth. The *Hood* etc. Jerry certainly got some welcome last night.

Here's something else. Tell Freddie that I have had 5 shaves from one of his type of blades.

Well, I'm afraid that's all this time and I'll just finish by sending my best regards to all the family.

Well Nan if this letter seems short you will understand that it is because I haven't very much to write about. I think that the main thing is that we have each other, and nothing else really counts. I'd better stop as I am getting too sentimental (ha ha).
Cheerio and God bless you,
Yours always,
Alex
xxxxxxxxxx

Dreghorn Camp
12 November 1940

My dear Nan,
Thanks very much for the surprise parcel. 'You are a one you are.' I don't know if you will get this letter before the end of the week or not but I am trying to catch the post. I am afraid that this letter is going to be the same as the last one: very short and to the point.

I'm sorry Nan I'll have to finish meantime.

This is me back with the rest of the news (joke).

We had a concert by the Royal Artillery Band this afternoon and it was quite good although it was Highbrow. I think that most of the audience was asleep before the finish, but we all woke up when they played the 'King' (National Anthem). The Colonel was greatly pleased with, as in his own words, 'a very attentive audience'. I doubt he must have been sleeping too!

Give all the family my regards and tell them that I am burning the candle at both ends. I don't think I'll do myself much harm though, because the candle is very small, isn't it? (Cheek.)

Well Nan, God bless you.

Cheerio meantime,

Alex

xxxxxxxx

Nottingham   *Marriage proposal*
December 1940

My dear Nan,
You will notice that there is no address. I have arrived at Nottingham. We are leaving here again on Wednesday morning for Southend and so far I get 7 days' leave. This doesn't seem so good as it seems at first, for at Southend we are being issued with fresh kit for overseas. Frankly the leave I am getting is Embarkation Leave. I can't tell you where I am going but it is certainly out East and well out too.

I don't know how this little note seems to you but in any case, don't let it get you down. Remember the old 'Chin'. I will send you word from Southend if I am coming home on Friday or Saturday. Could somebody meet me at the Station as I expect I will be carrying full kit? I might need a wee hand.

Well Nan, here's another thing. If you want to be Mrs Macintyre before I go away you had better make your mind up (ha ha). However Nan, apart from joking, if it would make you happy, and if that is what you want, then let me know when I see you. I will leave it to you. Think it over well, and I will do whatever you say, whether yes or no.

Please don't make any mistake Nan, because all I want is to see you happy. I don't think I'll say any more, I'll just let you use your own judgement.

Tell the family I was asking for them and keep all my love to yourself. Cheerio meantime.

Yours always,

Alex

xxxxxxxx

PS This doesn't seem much of a love letter Nan, but it is the best I can do, and it really does express my feeling.

Again cheerio and God bless you.

Alex

Southend-on-Sea
December 1940

My dear Nan,

Above is my new address. We only stayed in Nottingham one night and then came to this 'Ghost Town'. We are billeted in some of the houses which have been left by the owners who were evacuated a while ago. There are streets upon streets of empty houses here, also shops and cinemas etc.

Did you get a surprise at the tone of my last letter Nan? I thought that as we had been speaking before on that subject, I should mention it again. I won't say any more about it just now as I think one can't just put down what one wants to say on paper. I know I am giving you rather a large responsibility, but you see Nan, I know you, and I know that you will do what you think is best.

There is one thing I never thought of. Is it possible to do what you may want at such short notice? You see I don't know the least thing about that business, as you have realised before, and I also think that I have said enough so far about it, as there is no use in talking about what may happen, until you write and tell me what you want Nan.

A rumour has just come in that we are going East for at least 3 years, so it is only fair to tell you in case there may be some truth in it. You see Nan, I am being very fair, and I am not trying to make your mind up for you. Just that we both know how we feel about each other, and that I just want you to be happy. (It has taken me about an hour and a half to get this far) but Nan I just can't write.

(I'm feeling better now)

Will you let me know Nan what you want so as I can make any necessary arrangements?

Please excuse this unusual scrawl but I am writing a very unusual letter (ha ha).

Well Nan, how are you keeping yourself and how's the 'Old Chin'? Have you got that job?

There seems to be so much to ask you and so much to tell you, and yet I can't get it down in this letter. Perhaps the other business has made me excited eh? Somehow I think it has and I won't rest until I get your answer. This is the Truth. How is the rest of the family? Well Nan, I'm afraid this will about finish my letter except for my usual goodnight wish.

I love you Nan, and may God bless you and yours.

Goodnight Nan.

Yours always,

Alex

Xxxxxxxxxx

Nan's reply

85 Shields Road
Glasgow
16 December 1940

My dear Alex,

Many thanks for your welcome letter, it was waiting for me when I went home at dinner time and was I happy to see your handwriting again. I missed writing to you last week Alex, somehow there's so much I want to say and I felt before I started into the good work this afternoon I must get a wee letter off to you.

I must say Alex dear I was surprised to hear you were going overseas so soon but well life is full of surprises and we must just 'put a stout heart to a steep hill' and as you always say Keep the Chin up. You have managed along well so far and I know with your wee Nanny's earnest prayer and good wishes you will be successful right through.

Yesterday (Sunday) I had written a wee note to your mother saying I would be out to see them and mother suggested coming with me for company getting home in the blackout, so Alex I was delighted and we both set off about 1.30. Your Uncle was at the window watching for me and your Mum had the door open so Alex don't say we didn't get a good welcome. They were delighted to meet mother and Alex you should have heard the tales that were spun. Your mother is so cheery and took to mother right away. We had a wee talk in the bedroom together just your mother and I. Alex, I will never forget the kind words she said to me. No girl could have had a warmer feeling towards anyone than I had yesterday for your mother. I will tell you all about our visit when I see you but no matter what turns up we have both to rest content that she has no worry about either of us and she knows we were meant for each other. I left her feeling heaps brighter.

Well Alex, I must get down to that big answer and responsibility as you call it. Your wee Nanny's answer is, Yes Alex dear, we have stuck to each other and loved each other dearly in good weather. Why can't we be good partners in stormy weather?

With your love Alex I know I will carry on and keep the home fires burning and you Alex will help the rest of your men to bring the peace and joy we are looking forward to one day sharing, and as far as I can read from the papers the old Italians have had a good whacking.

I hope you don't mind me taking the liberty of writing to Ewan asking him if he can manage to be our best man. Margaret will be my bridesmaid and already is helping me with anything I suggest. Don't worry Alex about any excitement, apart from a bit of ragging, I'm sure everything will go through without any fuss. I will do my best to arrange matters but there are some things I will have to see you about and can't manage until I hear definitely if you are coming. I do hope they allow you time for travelling. I will speak to Mr Munro later about getting a few days off and during these precious hours we will enjoy seeing each other and have a wee time to our two wee selves.

The family at 85 are asking kindly for you and looking forward to seeing you soon.

I am writing this in wee bits between seeing customers so I hope you follow all I say.

Let me know if there's anything I can do for you here and I am only too pleased to do it. Meantime Alex I will carry on and only hope Ewan can do the necessary. Mother will have a wee cup of tea ready for us on the Night of Nights and I'm sure everything and everybody will get along nicely.

I hope this finds you well Alex. Your wee Nanny is in the pink and has been given a wee bit [of] extra strength to get on with the good work. I will count the days till I see you and no matter what happens keep your usual cheery self and give us that big smile – you know the one I like.

Till then here's all the best and Nan will love you till the moon turns tartan. Pearl and Jessie are busy dressing the window and making a good job of it too. They send their good wishes.

Cheerio Alex dear. With all my love and a tight hug and kiss.

Yours forever,

NAN

xxxxxx

Alex and Nan married in Glasgow, 20 December 1940

Southend on Sea
25 December 1940

My dear Nan,
Here is your first letter from your husband and my first to my Wee Wife.

Well to start with the train was 5 hours late on getting to London, and I had to stay there all night. Of course, we were taken to a large hostel and given a good bed and a good breakfast. The train didn't arrive till midnight so it couldn't get to Southend until about 12 o'clock today. My pass was stamped in London, so I had no trouble at this end.

I'll send you £24 and that gives you £28. After you pay Fred £25 you should have £3 left to start our house (ha ha) and maybe buy that locket for yourself. I don't know how the allowance will go this week because of the holiday delay.

We had our Christmas dinner today with the Officers waiting at the tables. Roast Pork with baked spuds and apple stuffing etc., pudding and plenty of Beer. It was all right too. We are all having a holiday today – no Parades etc. so I am taking the chance to get my kit all tidy again. That's all my news meantime, Nan, except that I will try and catch up on some sleep (crude). I am not there to give you a right goodnight but just wait until the 'next time'.

Tell everybody that I was asking for them and don't forget that all my love is for you and you only.

I'll just close by wishing my 'Wee Wife' goodnight and God bless you. Cheerio meantime.
Your loving husband,
Alex
xxxxxxxxx

PS Do I spell 'husband' right?

27 December 1940

My dear Nan,
Thank Margaret and Fred for the surprise parcel they sent me. The scarf is the very thing I needed. I put it on as soon as I opened the parcel.

There is no definite word yet dear of moving. Just the usual rumours. I can tell you one thing though. We have finished with all our issuing of kit etc. All jags and vaccinations have been finished also and we are running around doing practically nothing. Just waiting for something to happen.

How are you keeping Nan, are you taking care of yourself? Nan dear, you have no idea of how much I am missing you. I used to miss you a lot before we were married, but it was nothing compared with what I feel like now. The thought which is in my mind all day is 'How soon will it be when I see my dear wife again?' That is exactly how I feel Nan. I know it sounds sloppy but any way there it is. I don't believe I really loved you until we were married and parted. If I loved you before then Nan, it is 10 times stronger now. I think I'll better stop now as I am getting too sentimental (ha ha). Never mind Nan, it does me good to say these things sometimes.

I'll just say Goodnight dear and may God keep you and all your friends safe from harm.

I am keeping well dear, and you have nothing to worry about so far as I am concerned. I may see you sooner than you expect, at least I hope so. (Ha ha.)

Please mind dear [to] remember the 'Old Chin'. Mine will never go down anyway.

Well dearest again I'll say goodnight and God bless you. Give my regards to all at 85 and tell Dad to watch his horses as beef is very scarce now (ha ha). Good night dear.
Yours always,
Alex
Xxxxxxxxx

30 *December* 1940

My dear Nan,
Here I am again and I believe there is some more news this time. First of all we are definitely moving from here very soon, possibly at the beginning of next week. It is rumoured that we are moving to Scotland, namely Kilmarnock. All leave is cancelled at present.

However Nan, there is also a chance of getting leave when we move from this place, and like you I am hoping for the best. Please don't build up any hopes, dear, on this story, as I wouldn't like you to be disappointed in any way Nan.

Here is something else Nan. I will be writing as you know fairly regular, but don't be surprised if my letters suddenly cease. You see Nan, if we don't get any leave we will not be allowed to write home and tell when we are leaving as that would be giving information away and would perhaps entail extra danger.

What happens is this. We write a letter home and it is collected from us, and they are kept back and not posted until the ship is at least a fortnight away on its journey. So you see dear that if my letters do stop don't get worried and thinking all sorts of things. You'll know what has happened won't you? If there is any way I can get to see you before I leave, I'll find that way.

Thanks very much, Nan, for replying to my very impudent letter; I think you know the one I mean. But honestly dear I was worried. I don't mean for myself but for your sake Nan, because I couldn't think of you going through a thing like that without me being near at hand, and also with home-life facing such a future, as it may be called upon to face in years to come.

Nan dear, this world is mad at present so why should we wish to bring sane life into it: just to go mad with the rest? I know this is not my usual tone in my letters to you dear, but at times I really do become very serious (not often sez you) and this is one of my unusual moods of serious writing. Does this letter not remind you of my first letters to you? Very serious and abrupt?

Nan dear, I am really longing to see you again, if only for a short time, and I am hoping and praying that I will get the opportunity before I go away from this country. (My mood has changed, Nan.) When I go to sleep at night I just say to myself 'God keep my wee wife safe and well' and I often wonder how you are looking at that time, who you have been talking to, and what subjects you have been discussing. Sometimes my chin comes down and then I remember the photographer's remark about keeping the chin up and I just say 'Alex, practise what you preach' then turn over and close my eyes. (I'm getting sloppy again.)

That was an awful nice thing you did for Mother, Nan, but I'm not surprised, as it is just what my wife would do. You see it was that fine nature that attracted me from the very beginning and it really made me come to love you.

It was really nice of Freddy to take you to the Panto, and when you told me about it, I remembered our night there last year. Remember how we wanted your Mother and Dad to see the show too? I wish I had been there with you Nan. However, you and I will just have to wait and hope for that time to come again soon, when we will always be together.

I was very pleased to hear that Mother had gone to see you because I wanted you two to be good friends. My Mother and my wife together is my whole life, Nan. You understand don't you?

How am I doing now at my letter writing – 4 pages already, not bad eh?

Meantime I say Goodnight dear and God bless you. See and keep well and look after yourself because I need you an awful lot now.

We are getting better grub now and not before time too. It has been terrible down here but there was an awful row last week, and it helped a lot. The officers themselves caused it too. How's the money business coming along Nan?

Tell them all at 85 that I am hoping to see you all again soon.

Goodnight again Nan and God keep you safe.

Yours always,

Alex

Xxxxxxxx

⟨1941⟩

News of embarkation – brief reunion in Glasgow – Durban, South Africa – first impressions of Cairo – hospital, leg trouble – wedding anniversary – sandstorm

Southend-on-Sea
January 1941

My dear Nan,

I'm afraid I will be getting no more leave. To put it down in plain hard facts it looks as if I am going abroad without seeing you again. There is however a chance of seeing each other again and until I am actually on board our ship I will not give up hope.

I love you so much dear and I really am taking the idea very hard. But there is nothing either of us can do about it so I suppose we'll just have to be brave and patient, to keep our spirits high and hope that our parting is not to be too long and that when we do meet again it will be for ever and that there will be no partings to spoil the happiness that I think we both deserve.

Well dear Nan, so far I have been writing in a very sad strain not in the least like my usual letters, but you understand me and you know that I like to say what I am thinking. I also know that my wife is a very good listener. I know that I am asking a lot from you to be brave dear, and wait for me, but I know that you will do it to the best of your ability.

I thank God every night and ask him to protect you dear from any harm. Perhaps I am selfish because I pray that you are kept safe for me, but God knows that you, Nan, are my whole life and that without you I have no thought of life. To me dear you belong and I belong to you in every way, both in mind and body. You may smile dear but there are times when my thoughts bring a lump to my throat. Right now I believe my heart is as heavy as it has ever been. The last time was when I walked down Shields Road and hadn't the courage to look up at your window and wave back to you. At that time my heart was very heavy, as the thought of parting was hard, and as then so it is now.

Again the thought of parting and again the sadness. I know that I preach about keeping the chin up but at times like these our emotions are just a wee bit too strong and then when I do think I become rather depressed.

Nan, I don't want you to get the impression that I am going about in a sad frame of mind. I am the opposite. It is just that I like to tell you all I can and that I love to have my wee chat with you.

I am writing this on Saturday afternoon and I am sitting alone in the Billet. The rest of the chaps have gone out but I made an excuse so I can have my wee talk in private. I was determined to write my wee letter this afternoon.

Well dear I think I'll say cheerio meantime and may God bless you and keep you safe always.

Nan, always remember that I love you with all my heart.

Yours always,

Alex

January 1941

My dear Nan,

I have some definite news for you. I expect to move from here on Tuesday or Wednesday of this week. The advance party left at 6 o'clock tonight and are going a 12-hour journey by train to the point of embarkation. If all goes well I am going to try and phone you. It seems very funny because if I do phone I will be speaking to you before you get this letter. I know that it will cost a lot of money but I think it is worth it just to talk to each other for a few minutes. Dear Nan I hope I can manage because I am looking forward to it so much.

Honestly, I think leave is out of the question now Nan and I myself am resigned to the fact. I'm afraid, dear wife, that it will be a very long time before we see each other again. I know that I have always been optimistic about this matter up to now Nan but I wanted to sort of prepare you for this hard blow. I am feeling rather dumped myself right now at the thought of a long parting but I console myself with the thought that Nan will be waiting for me when I return, because God will be good to me and keep my dear wife safe and well. The way I feel just now I don't think I could live without you. You are my whole life Nan because you have given me the greatest happiness I have ever had. This perhaps sounds strange when I think of our parting but then a little sadness can't dull the happiness and as you said yourself we will always have memories.

Dear Nan, nothing can ever destroy the thoughts of these happy days or the thoughts that they bring to us both. These were the few days in my life when I really lived and for that reason I will never forget them or could I ever forget the happy smile on my dear wife's face. It may be as I said a long time before we meet again but I will always be thinking of you no matter where I go and you will be the same as you are now, the main thing in my life.

Nan, I think of you all day and everything has just to wait until after I have had my little dream and my little gossip. After I have attended to these things I go and see what can be done about the war.

That is my idea of a joke.

I am going away from here and as far as I know going abroad perhaps for a very long time but come what may remember that your husband loves you and all you stand for – freedom and a home life – and it will be for those things that he will do his job to the best of his ability. Always knowing that his dear wife will be careful and be waiting for him on his return, which we both hope will not be too far away.

Well dear I have come to the end of our wee gossip and will phone tomorrow if possible. If not I will just write again. Meantime cheerio and good luck and as always may God bless you.
Yours always,
Alex

30 January 1941

My dearest Nan,
First of all I am still at Southend-on-Sea, and still can't say when I will be moving. The rumour is now 'Next week sometime'.

Nan, I am hoping and praying that I see you at least once more before I go abroad. Nan dear I want you so much too. How I wish all this awful tragedy was finished. Why can't we be allowed to live our own lives our own way? All I am living for is to return to my home and my dear wife, and the thought of not seeing you, for perhaps a very long time, is about as much as I can bear.

Dear Nan, if anything should happen to you, I'm afraid it would be more than I could stand. Maybe I'd better stop talking like this, as I may get to thinking of the worst instead of looking on the bright side and keeping the Old Chin high. In any case, I wanted so much to let you know how strong my love for you has grown, and how much you mean to your husband. We haven't been allowed a very long period of married life Nan, but as long as I live I shall never forget our honeymoon at Largs. I always picture you as how happy you were and looked when we walked that day to Fairlie. How pleased you were, when you were pointing out the various places you knew and which were connected with your childish years. Oh Nan, how I long to take you back there again, and how proud I would be, when I walked along the same road again with the girl who means everything to me, a man who is proud to be your husband, Nan.

How I long to hold you in my arms dear, give you a wee pat and say 'Hello Fat Nannie' once again. If I could only see that nice smile that you used to give me when I said that. Will you ever forget the twin beds at Largs, Nan? I know I won't.

Please excuse me not saying anything about your parcel dear but you see I started this letter this morning and have been adding a bit now and then between parades etc. It is now 2 p.m. and I have just received the parcel now. If you excuse me I'll just see what's inside (ha ha).

Well, I've seen, Nan, and thanks very much again. I must however say something about your parcels dear, and that is <u>don't send me any more meantime</u>. If I wasn't here to receive it, I don't expect I would ever see it. Things go astray in the Army, and as I am now an 'Old Soldier', I want to make sure that nothing meant for me goes into the hands of anybody else. I will be quite content with your letters dear, because they tell me all I want to know.

It would be a great day, Nan, when I see you again and I would be quite content if it was only for a little while.

Well Nan how am I doing at writing you a real love letter? I never thought that the day would come when I would put down on paper what I have written. I used to think that any man who wrote a girl letters like this was mad. Well, I suppose I must be a wee bit mad myself now and if it is of any interest to you, I like being this way (ha ha).

Now for some news. I have none. (Ha ha.) I know this news about leave will depress you dear but as you said yourself we will always have memories. I have got to the stage now that I am just taking things as they come, and hoping and praying for the best. My one earnest prayer is that I may see you again soon, and that thought is in my mind day and night. I am getting sentimental again.

You spoke in your letter about food being hard to get in Glasgow. Is it really scarce, Nan? Did you try and get some rations with that old card of mine?

Tell everybody at 85 that I am keeping well and feeling in the pink. Goodnight dear and I will keep praying that I am allowed to see you again before I go abroad. Meantime cheerio and 'Here's to the next time'. Remember the Old Chin Nan. God bless you dear wife.

Yours always,

Alex

PS You don't need to address me as Gunner now just Driver Macintyre A.

Alex's Diary

12 February	Arrived in the Clyde much to my joy; got off unexpectedly and made for home and wife
13 February	Found Nan very ill and had to have her removed to Victoria Infirmary. Doctor to operate tomorrow
14 February	Went to Infirmary / Nan going to theatre / Have prayed
15 February	Saw Nan again and everything going to be alright. Nothing else matters
16 February	Said goodbye to my folks and to Nan. May God keep them safe till I return
17 February	Left Glasgow at night in convoy

Letter written on ship

25 February 1941

My dear Nan,

My main thought is of your health and I'm just hoping that by now you are home and forgetting all about the Ward 12A business. It will be a long time before I have any word from you Nan and I hope all is well. No pain and no worry and speaking of worry, please don't worry about me. I know it will be hard but remember we have been very lucky so far. We always have our trust in God and I don't think we have regrets. Certainly this present madness causes thoughts but even that would not affect our faith.

Now Nan, I can't tell you where I am at the present time although I have left the country. Frankly, even if I was allowed to do so, I couldn't because I don't know! Sounds Irish, doesn't it?

The food and accommodation are fairly decent and I am feeling fit.

I promise to try and write a longer letter next time but it is very difficult writing a letter to a second person. What I mean is, writing a letter to my wife and knowing that someone else will read it first. However, your letters to me are not censored so you can write in your usual style and I should enjoy them Nan.

Please take care of yourself Nan. Although we may be very far apart, our thoughts are always with each other. We can always see the same sun and moon and when you realise that, we may be saying and thinking the same things at the same time. So it doesn't seem too bad does it Nan? Perhaps it won't be long until this madness of war is over with people living their own lives and in peace.

Tell Ewan that I was asking for him. Tell Torchy (Margaret) that she should really think a lot of him. He is worth it all.

God bless you all and remember the 'Old Chin'.

Yours always, Alex

Xxxxxxxxxx

PS Tell Fred to prepare himself for a hiding at darts!

[Note: Nan had injured herself lifting a pail of sand at work.]

March 1941: 'Clydebank Blitz'

April 1941: British air-raid casualty figures are over 6,000 killed, nearly 7,000 injured

April 1941: Hitler sends troops to support his Italian ally in 'North Africa' – countries of Egypt, Libya and Tunisia

German General Rommel leads his Afrika Corps troops against British forces

From Durban, South Africa
Received May 1941

My dear Nan,

Here I am again. You can rest assured that I am well and feeling fine. I can say that we have made our first call at a port since we left the Old Country. My first sight of the land was very beautiful and reminded me very much of some parts of our own Scotland. We were entertained by the natives with their little boats which to me looked very frail. They came right out to the ship and dived into the water after any money which was thrown to them. The natives really are wonderful in the water. I will even go so far as to say that they are almost as good as myself. (Sez who?)

Before I write any more Nan, perhaps I will better explain why I am only using the one side of the paper. As you will understand, this letter will be examined before posting and any wording which may be thought to give away information will be <u>cut out</u>. If I was unfortunate to have some sentences on both sides, the harmless part would be destroyed along with the part cut out and I want, if possible, my letters to get to you as I write them and as interesting as I can make them. It will be a long time before you get this letter, so the talk of natives etc. will be of things that happened weeks ago and should not be considered dangerous information.

We have crossed the Equator and had our visit from Father Neptune, who held his court on board our ship. Another fine experience for me. The trip was quite interesting. I am sorry it could not have been made under different circumstances.

Are you back at work yet Nan? I suppose you will feel rather strange for a while, but the whole business will just be a memory.

I have often thought how strange it was that I happened to be near at hand when it all happened. It has made me think quite a lot since I left you that night. I still think that it was a blessing in disguise and that I was meant to be there at that particular time. I don't think I shall ever forget the sight of that white arm waving to me from the Infirmary bed.

Well dear wife, there is so much I could say, but as I already have said, I don't like the idea.

Where we are would suit you fine Nan, fine and warm. In fact, it is too hot for comfort. I could enjoy a real good fall of snow, believe it or not. Perhaps it may not be very long before I am back enjoying Glasgow weather again. At least I am hoping that it will not be too far distant. As for enjoying Glasgow weather, I mean that. It would be very nice right now. It could be as cold and wet as it liked to be and I would still enjoy it. Seems strange doesn't it Nan? Still it's a strange world and at the present time mad also.

I wonder when it is all going to end and when people will realise that there are more things in life than creating instruments of murder and destruction. The earth could be made a beautiful place and the human race have the power to do so. It is my sincere wish that this present madness will end soon, and that good will come out of it. I think that my wish is also that of all decent-minded people.

Are you going to Church yet Nan? What I mean is, are you fit yet? I added that last sentence, because the first one seemed strange by itself. I haven't been to Church myself since I left Southend. We had services on board ship but somehow or other they seemed out of place and I didn't go. It didn't seem to be the correct atmosphere. There was an impression of something lacking, something I can't just describe.

Well dear Nan, the worst thing to contend with here so far is the heat. Remember the sun at Dunoon? Well, I know now that it was not warm then, just nice and cool, compared with this heat. It is a crime to go without a topee on. Everything is warm, and as for myself I never lost so much sweat before. My body is continually pouring with sweat, even with no clothes on. The drinking water is warm and flat. We are being issued with minerals, lemonade etc. Also quinine and lime juice. Of course, I don't suppose we will always get them, but I won't worry until that time comes.

Well Nan dear, this is the end of my letter at last (again says you) and I am quite pleased that I managed to say so much, when I was tied down to so little.

May God always be with you and may he always protect my loved ones that I have left in His care. Above all my Wife, that one person who means everything to me.

Good night dear and 'Here's to the next time'.

Your loving husband,

Alex

Xxxxxxxxxxx

PS I've forgotten your birthday date again. Please send it again will you Nan?

May 1941

My dear Nan,

We have had four days' leave at Durban and it is the most beautiful place I have ever seen. The planning is very modern, reminding the visitor very much of advanced American ideas. Transport facilities leave very little to be desired, operating as they do on fine broad streets. If this is a sample of colonial cities then the sooner we leave Scotland and settle here the more satisfied I would be. Frankly, the place has got me Nan, and I would not mind coming back when all this trouble has come to an end. I did not dream that the towns of our colonies were like this and it is an experience I will never forget.

I will now and try to tell you about the people.

You must realise that I saw them from the eyes of a visitor in uniform and things may be different in peacetime. Everybody looked after us very well and we were given concerts, dances and invitations to their homes by people we met in the streets. All transport was free for us. The town has some great canteens. Here is the menu of the first meal I had: 2 eggs, 2 sausages, bacon, mashed potatoes, tea, bread and butter, fruit salad and ice cream. I even helped myself to apples, grapes on the table while waiting for the meal and the whole meal was not even costing 1/-! I had some lovely trips from folks and visited the Zulu native reserve. We went one day and arrived in time to witness a ceremonial dance, which reminded me of scenes I had seen on the films.

I had my photograph taken while on leave and the photographer promised to send them to you. He told me to 'Keep my chin up'. Funny, how that phrase always crops up, isn't it?

And now Nan dear what of yourself? You must have had a hard time during that raid on Glasgow. I hope you remembered what I always told you and not let the noise worry you. Noise is terrifying but it won't hurt you no matter how dreadful it sounds. My thoughts have always been for my wife and her people and how they have fared. I hope it won't be too long until I get word from you. It's really impossible not to worry.

How are you getting on for food Nan? Now don't be telling me you are getting plenty because I know that it must be scarce back home.

Everything is warm here including the drinking water and I never thought I would lose so much sweat and in the end think nothing of it. It did make me feel rotten at first but now the sight of my own body glistening with sweat, or those of my mates, doesn't affect me in the least. It is surprising how we get used to things in life, which at first seem to set us a hard task, even the bleak-looking future for yourself and the folks at home may become easier as time goes on, and may end sooner than we may at the present time dare to think.

Remember that it is always darkest just before the dawn.

I'm afraid I have come to the end of my talk at present. Paper is very scarce and I am using the last of my stock.

Remember to 'Keep the Old Chin up' and everything will come alright in the end.

God bless you dear wife. Tell all our people at home that they must not worry too much.

Your loving husband,

Alex

April – December 1941: German troops besiege Tobruk (Libya) – a vital port which supplied the Allied forces in North Africa

June 1941: Clothes rationing introduced in the UK

14 June 1941   The first 'Green Envelope' letter

My dear Nan,

Well here I am with another system of correspondence. These 'Green Envelopes' as they are called are another new idea for us fellows out here. They will not be censored, providing we play the game, and not try to get any military information through. We are put on our honour, and there is no doubt that all the men will respect that position.

To begin with, I am still well, and feeling pretty fit. The heat doesn't bother me very much now although I will never get used to the flies. They are in [their] millions everywhere. I must mention the food. Plenty of Eggs and Onions. We never get meat without onions and practically every break-fast consists of 2 eggs. The only change from the eggs will be some beans instead. I don't want you to get the impression that we are being fed like Lords, as we certainly are not, but taking it all over the food is no worse than we had at Scotland. Certainly we have to exist some days on 'iron rations' but there is always some food going when we get back to Base Camp. In case you don't understand the term 'iron rations' it means Bully Beef (*tinned corned beef*) and Biscuits and water if you have any. In any case things could be a lot worse than they have been up till now.

I am now doing very little actual driving except for a very special convoy now and then. I have been given the job of assistant mechanic for the

Section and I can assure you that I am kept very busy indeed. I am held responsible for all the lorries being in condition for running at any time. Altogether there are close on twelve vehicles ranging from M/Cs to the seven-tonners and if you have any idea of Army drivers you will realise that there is quite a lot of work to be done. Still, Nan, the work is interesting and far better than full dress parades etc.

You will also be interested to know that I am now wearing that 'Wheel and Crown'. I have also been at Cairo, although it was not a leave but just a call we made there one day. Speaking of Cairo it did <u>not</u> give me the impression of romance as some novels say it has. My opinion is that although the centre of the city has some fine buildings the largest part is composed of ugly, dirty and smelly streets. Not at all romantic. As for the natives, they are the most dishonest race I have ever come across. Their main object in life is to see how much money they can swindle you out of and as for their other customs well, they don't seem to have changed since the days of the Bible. The tall Arab is still seen riding the very small ass and of course wearing his very long robes. Still seeing all these things is indeed a truly great experience and one that should remain in my memory.

I have had all your letters up till March 25. I have had none now for the last month but they must be lying around somewhere. I have received both cables you sent dear and as they are the latest news I am very happy. It makes a big difference to know that everybody at home is well and that everything is OK. I hope that you are not too busy at the shop, and not risking your health too much. Whatever you do take care of yourself as I couldn't bear to have anything happen to you now. Dear, you have no idea of how much you mean to me now. I always think of you at nights and it may seem odd, but on a Sunday my thoughts are with you and everybody at 85. I picture you in Church with Margaret listening to Rev. Brown, and I say a wee prayer myself.

Have you seen Mother recently Nan? How are all the folks at 85? And my good friend Ewan, God bless him. Is May still as cheeky as ever? Or has she met someone to quieten her now?

Please don't be worrying about me out here as everything is OK and it may not be awful long before we are together again.

There is one matter I must mention dealing with the war itself, and that is the fact that Jerry can be stopped. We could have licked him in Greece if we had had air support, and there would have been no need for these awful days on Crete. Our Army itself man to man is superior to Jerry. We only require the equipment, that's all. I am telling you this because people at home are being told by others that the German Army is unbeatable. This is just a form of propaganda, so don't believe it, Nan. We will get him and very soon too.

Well dear, I think that is about all for the present, except that I must tell you that I have sent you a small gift I bought up in Palestine. It is a butterfly brooch made of silver and done up very finely with coloured silver wire. It is a very nice wee gift and I hope you get it all right. It was because the colours were like those in your floral frock that I bought it. I do hope you get it Nan dear.

Cheerio again dear wife and always remember that I love you, whatever may happen, and always remember about the old Chin. Tell Fred to practise his dart playing as I may be wanting a game soon and that I am right hot now. Tell Dad that I hope his arm is not too sore these days and tell Mother to try and not worry too much.

Good night Nan dear and the best of everything in life. May God bless you all.
Your loving husband always,
Alex
xxxxxxxxxxxxxxxxxxxxxxxxxx

26 June 1941   *Hospital*

My dear Nan,
Here I am again with some surprising news and I don't want to alarm you. I have been practically forced to notify you that I am in Hospital, and that I will be a patient for quite a while yet. I had no intention of telling you, but as there is a chance of you being notified by the Red Cross, I thought that it would be best to let you know the whole story myself.

To start with, do you remember my bandaged legs, when I was home last? Well some thing went wrong with my left knee and it started to give me some trouble out here. I had a small operation about 7 weeks ago in one of the British Hospitals out here. I was only in a fortnight before I was back on duty again.

On way back from Palestine we stopped one night at one of the Australian camps. I didn't feel too good that night and I had to be removed to the nearest hospital the next morning, which was an Aussie camp. Well Nan, I came in on the 12 June, and I have had another operation on the knee, which was rather a nasty job. The only thing was to remove the part of the knee affected. I will be as good as gold again in about 2 months. Wounds take a lot longer to heal out here than they would back home. It won't be too long before I am fighting fit again.

Now don't get any ideas Nan. My leg will be all right apart from a scar and in that I consider myself very fortunate indeed.

We never intended to stop the night at this camp on our journey from Palestine. It was just a last-minute idea and if I hadn't got to a Hospital when I did I may have had a far different tale to tell. So you see, Nan dear, I still have that element of good luck with me.

I am being treated well here and I am in good hands. The Major in charge of my ward or tent as it is, is one of the finest surgeons in Australia. I am the only Scot here in the ward, but the Aussies are all good company, although some of them have some nasty wounds.

Well Nan dear that is the whole story of why I am in 'Dock' and my biggest worry is you may be thinking foolish things. Please Nan, as what I have written gives you the whole story, don't worry about me. Even now I have just been told that I can get up and go about on crutches, and that means that I am getting a lot stronger already.

I am using these Green Envelopes at present as they are about the best I can get and also have the advantage of being uncensored. The mail comes here all upset. What I mean is that I got some letters posted in March a week or two ago, and yet only yesterday I had a letter from yourself dated 27 February telling me that you were home from the Infirmary. That gives you an idea of how the letters come.

You will have got my cable by the time you read this, also I hope that wee brooch I sent for your birthday. Nan, I do hope you get it safe and that you like it. It isn't much but I thought it pretty, and the colours reminded me of Largs when you wore that frock. The colours are similar and that's why I bought it.

Well Nan, that is all my chat for the present and if you do get any word from the Red Cross you will know not to worry.

Goodbye for the present dear wife and may it not be too long before we see each other again. God bless you.

Yours always,

Alex

xxxxxxxxxxxxxxxxxx

28 June 1941

My dear Nan,

What an awful lot of letters you must be getting just now. Imagine me writing every two days? To tell you the truth, I have such a lot of time on my hands at present that I have decided to write every other day and it does help to break the drabness of the long day.

The ward of course is cheery and there are always some patients who can start an argument. Between ourselves we have some right good debates until some wag comes in with a few choice wise-cracks and the one-time serious talk becomes a subject for amusement.

The Major here is perfectly satisfied with the progress, and I can see for myself the difference almost every day. There is very little pain now, so don't be getting any ideas that I am suffering, because I really am not. I am lying in bed getting plenty of food and just having the time of my life, so what more should I want eh?

I know that so far everything at home is all right. I noticed by your P.C. that you went to McDonald's in April. You have my best wishes Nan dear.

Cheerio for the present and good luck and 'Here's to the next time'. May it not be too long distant. God bless you all.
Yours always,
Alex
xxxxxxxxx

3 July 1941

My dear Nan,
As I haven't found a nicer way to commence my letters I will just begin by saying 'Here I am again' with the addition of 'Feeling fine and coming along nicely'.

I am coming along real well now, so good that I have dispensed with crutches and can get along fine with the aid of a stick.

I managed to get to the Cinema last night! The one we have here is just a compound without any roof, boasts of four walls and a screen, and the show starts when the sun goes down. The films are 'Talkies' and it is surprising how good the reception is at times. The show does provide a couple of hours' diversion and entertainment and that is all it is meant to do, so it serves its purpose. The film last night was *Kentucky Moonshine* and I must say that although the show wasn't anything great I enjoyed myself very much indeed. I also enjoyed the little walk which was my first since I came in to this Hospital and although I felt it very tiring it proved that my leg is OK and it only needs time to heal and regain strength and everything in the garden will be lovely again.

I am writing this letter sitting in a deckchair in the shade of one of the verandas and looking now and then onto the usual expanse of sand. A soldier out here has to fight the country as well as the enemy. Its heat, sand, water and its habit of making clean wounds go septic. The last is the biggest curse discharging sores and wounds. Still we are here to do a job and that's that.

And now for ourselves, Nan. I am pleased to see by [your letters] that everything at 85 is still much the same. 'Freddy has a cold and Ewan calls and takes Margaret to the pictures.' 'Dad is sitting reading' and is Mother by any chance using the sewing machine? God bless you all Nan, and may nothing happen to destroy that peaceful picture.

Well dear wife, my usual address is still good yet as all mail is forwarded to me here at El Kantara (on the Suez).

Well again, I am coming near the end of this little chat. My watch is still going well, although I have had a new strap put on as the heat and the sweat from my body perished the old one. The strap I have now is made for the climate. It is made in such a way that there is a shield between the watch and the wrist and a cover over the face which keeps out a good lot of sand. The ring is still on too, Nan.

As soon as I am passed fit I'll let you know. I am out of touch with the other chaps so I can't tell you anything. The last I heard they were about 70 miles from here.

I will give you my present address but don't use it unless perhaps you may want to cable:

The 2nd Australian General Hospital,

Abroad

Yes Nan, that's all the address!

May God bless you. Remember the Old Chin.

Yours always,

Alex

Xxxxxxxx

18 July 1941

My dear Nan,

I am beginning to feel a little like my own self. I am still in hospital however, as my leg is not just completely healed yet. As I have told you before, this is the fault of the climate and nothing else. Back home we would take a chance but not here, the sand and flies must be treated with respect.

I have been in this hospital for nearly six weeks now and I have lost touch entirely with my Unit. I may be sent back to them and again maybe not. I am in great company here and I will be sorry to part from them as they are all great fellows. I wish I had been in the Aussie Army.

I am just thinking about this time last year when I was looking forward to my Fair Holidays. I don't know how it seems to you but to me the year has really flown.

What about yourself dear wife? Got these red cheeks yet?

God bless you all.

Your loving husband always,

Alex

Xxxxxxxxxx

7 August 1941

My dear Nan,

This is to let you know that I should be discharged any day now. I have been transferred from the Aussie hospital as the beds were required for their own boys and I am speaking the truth when I say that I was sorry to leave. I have been with these fellows since I came to the country and found them really great company.

Has Ewan gone to the air force yet or does he still come and take Torchy (Margaret) to the pictures once a week? Is May still waiting for me to 'take her home'? I hope all the newlyweds will be very happy. If they get as much happiness out of married life as we do, then they should not wish for any more. How are things going at MacDonald's Nan? Tell all the staff that I am asking for them. Yes, the whole fourteen!

I am now walking a mile or two every day and my leg is standing up to it no trouble. This country is just heat and sand. I have become quite used to the climate but I still sweat every bit as much as ever I did.

May God bless you all.

Yours always,

Alex

xxxxxxxxxxxxxxxx

25 Aug 1941
C Battery Base Depot
R.A. Middle East Forces

My dear Nan,

Well Nan, I have been discharged from hospital to the Base Camp here. I don't expect to be kept here any length of time as I may be going back to my own Unit any day, or failing that perhaps to a new Regiment. I will just keep cheery and remember the 'Old Chin'.

Some chaps out here have told me that although the food ration is not too bad back home there is quite a shortage of fags. Has Fred been reduced to smoking tea yet or can he still buy his favourite brand? Out here there is no shortage of smokes, although at times matches are hard to get in certain places.

The leg has healed up now and is giving me practically no trouble. My general health is good and although I have become used to the heat I must admit I cannot ignore the presence of these flies. Although we have quite a number of mosquitoes, which, by the way, take the place of the flies at night, there seem to be very few of the malaria type ones so at least that is something to be thankful about.

Cheerio for the present dear wife.

Yours always,

Alex

Xxxxxxxxxxxxxxxxxx

1 September 1941

My dear Nan,

I must congratulate you on sending me such fine and regular mail Nan, although they don't always come to me in rotation. For instance, I got one yesterday marked '6' and I haven't yet received any of the previous five! I expect those snaps from Dunoon will be in one of those previous five. I am certainly looking forward to that envelope. It is a while now since I've seen you dear and I want so much to see how you have been keeping since I left home.

You sent me a registered letter, Nan! It was a lovely thought on your part to send me some money Nan. It will come in right handy as I expect to be paying a visit to Cairo soon on leave. It will interest you to know that the amount you sent is equal to a week's pay out here. This is not a cheap place for soldiers. Many places put up signs such as 'Special terms for the Forces' and as far as I can make out it is a case of adding to the price! Still, I can manage and as long as I can have a smoke and a cup of tea I won't grumble.

The country itself is just a waste of miles upon miles of sand. I wouldn't mind seeing some green fields and trees. I have been promised five days' leave from here and that will be my first since that seven days last December 1940 so it should be quite a break for me shouldn't it?

By the time you get this letter I should have passed nearly 12 months away from you. I hope we won't be parted at the end of the next 12 months. I often pray and thank God for giving you to me at the very time when I needed you most and I know everything will turn out alright in the end and we will be together again.

I received your letter about your holiday at Dunoon. I was thinking back to our holiday there. The boating trips, putting and the first day you wore that frock. The frock I called an overall at first and upset poor Mother. Did you ever get the little brooch I sent to match the frock?

I am pleased to hear about Ewan and I wish him every success and plenty of 'Happy Landings'. He is a fine lad Nan. If I know Margaret right I know that she will take it all on the 'Chin' and keep smiling. If she does get a wee bit blue, tell her to take a lesson from you, and see what 'taking it' really means. Does she realise the great shock I get when I receive word of her knitting a green jumper and now a yellow one? Does she realise that if I had for one minute to visualise her in these 'Creations' I would have a complete nervous breakdown? (Ha ha.)

Your loving husband always,

Alex

Xxxxxxxxxxxx

October 1941

My dear Nan,

Here is my weekly letter, and I am sure that it will contain quite an amount of fresh news.

The snaps that you have sent me are simply great. The walking ones are especially good. What memories these pictures bring back. Our holiday together at Dunoon last year and the fine way in which we enjoyed it. My sole wish is that we will be together again when the next holiday period comes round.

If all goes well, I should have some experiences to relate, which at the present time I am not allowed to mention. I can, however, without any fear of censorship tell you that I have had a bathe in the Med, the Red Sea and the Suez Canal. As for the rest, Nan, these will just have to wait!

I am so pleased that the long-awaited brooch has arrived. I hope it wasn't damaged or broken on the journey home. There was always that chance and that was why I packed it as well as I could with the materials to hand. Well Nan, did the colours match the frock?

What do you think of the photos I have sent Nan? I must tell you that I have changed appearance again! Yes, you guessed it, the 'stache' has been removed! I am of course still very, very handsome (ha ha).

I am certain of getting '7 days' in Cairo very soon. You can tell Ewan that this will be my first leave since December 1940 when you and I had that great few days at Largs. There has been leave going in the Unit, but when it did come round I just happened to be elsewhere, either that or it was cancelled before it reached the 'M's'. Have you been receiving all my letters, Nan? I have been sending quite a number of them to you recently. At present, we are getting very good facilities for writing, so I am taking the advantage when I have the chance of writing as often as possible. However, please don't start worrying if my letters become scarce, or perhaps cease for a while.

Now for myself Nan, I am well and fit, and having practically no trouble at all with my leg. I am not handicapped in any way Nan. Actually, the only reminder is a stiffness in the morning which goes away in about a half-hour's time. Now don't be getting any foolish ideas Nan please about any permanent disability as they would be very silly. We do not sleep on feather beds and everybody feels stiff in the morning, providing of course we were sleeping during the night.

In case you forgot, we do get 'visitors' now and then you know, and they will come at the most awkward times too!

Are you still enjoying life in McDonald's, Nan, and are people still buying shoes? I always picture life at 85 being pretty much the same as it was when I left. Dad on the chair reading the paper, Mother sewing, yourself and

Margaret sewing in the parlour and being interrupted only by a discussion between Fred and Margaret. It's a lovely picture dear wife.

God bless you and all our friends.

Yours always,

Alex

Xxxxxxxxxxxxxxxxx

7 December 1941: Japanese attack the US navy fleet at Pearl Harbour, Hawaii

USA declares war on Japan and its allies, Germany and Italy

18 December 1941

My dear Nan,

Here is the long-awaited letter which I have been promising for quite a while now. I have managed to find some writing materials at last, paper, pen, which by the way comes a very long road indeed. It took me about a <u>month</u> to get this pen so I will have to be very careful as dear knows when I'll get another. Another scarcity is a watch which keeps time. My watch is perfectly sound but just happens to be filled up with sand as is the case with everybody else's. We have 'amateur experts' but I would much rather wait until I get to cleaner surroundings. It may not be very long now either as Jerry is right out of here for good. At the present time he is running and running right hard.

Your letters are so chatty and so interesting too. I have received your Xmas cards and some parcels have arrived for chaps already so I am hoping to receive mine soon.

I am sorry about the mail but I will try and make up for it now. I will manage more tomorrow as I am due a day off to look over my 'Chev'. So far Nan, I have had no trouble with the lorries apart from minor things.

20 December 1941   *Wedding anniversary*

Our anniversary dear wife and what a distance between us. You at home with your people and I out here in the Western Desert. All I can say Nan, is that I send my best wishes and that God may be with you. It doesn't seem 12 months since I stood beside you at 85 listening to Rev. Brown. My only wish is to be at home when our next comes along.

I celebrated today by having a right good wash with my water that I had been saving up for a few weeks now. After I had <u>my</u> wash, I washed three pairs of socks in what was left of my two pints of water, so that wasn't bad was it?

My best wishes for the coming year to you all. Remember the 'Old Chin' and keep those red cheeks.

Your loving husband always,

Alex

xxxxxxxxxxxxxx

25 December 1941   Sandstorm

My dear Nan,

Seems strange that I should be writing to you from here in the Desert during Christmas Day. This period of the year when one is reminded of 'Peace on Earth' and yet on looking round at present surroundings one sees nothing that is not connected with war and with destruction.

Well, dear wife, today is a very unpleasant day indeed. A dust storm has been raging since early morning, but as you have not experienced one perhaps I'd better give you an idea of what they are like. Can you try and visualise a typical March day at home, when there is rain, being blown up or down Shields Road, by a very high wind? You know the kind of days, Nan, when the rain is washing down the faces of the tenements, and perhaps bringing down a chimneypot here and there? Well, Nan, try and picture that wind carrying sand, a very fine sand instead of rain. The sun is blotted out, and it is like being in a fog. Dust is everywhere and on everything you touch. In your eyes, ears, nostrils and you can feel it gritting between your teeth. This again, Nan, is a true picture of the 'romantic desert'. Well Nan such a day is today. I am writing this sitting in the driving cab of the lorry. I have all doors, windows etc. closed up, and it really makes the best place for letter writing in such weather.

So much for my description of a dust storm, and now for news about <u>our</u>selves. Letters from home are arriving better now and I got another one last night. The snap is very good indeed and easily one of the best you have sent me. I am well and getting quite good food. At the present time I am smoking Eyetie cigarettes called Macedonia, and they are complete with the Eagle etc. stamped on them. Our friends the Italians left a few thousands lying around during their 'glorious advance'. Their chocolate tastes very nice too. I have enclosed a wrapper but I am sorry that I couldn't also send you the contents. Still you can say that you have had a piece by proxy, Nan, because I was wishing you had some when I was eating it. You can almost taste it can't you? (Ha ha.)

Grub's up Nan, so that's all for today as it will be dark soon after dinner. Cheerio meantime.

Christmas Day 1941   Christmas food

I have just finished lunch which by the way was quite a nice surprise. We had cake – baked yesterday – pineapple cubes, bread, cheese and tea. Not bad, eh? We have also been promised a Christmas dinner tonight with all the Army tradition. At least as far as possible under the circumstances. I forgot to mention that we also had two oranges with our lunch. Well dear wife today is much the same as yesterday. Still very dusty, although it is clearing a bit now and then. There was no mail last night, nor any parcels. I know that you posted your parcel early enough, but Nan it won't arrive for Christmas now. It should be here for Ne'erday and that should be even better, shouldn't it? I hope you like this way of writing, dear, in a sort of diary form. I thought that by writing this way it would make my letters more interesting. Tell me what you think of the idea will you?

So the mornings are frosty in Glasgow now? And you are taking lumps out of one coat and adding to another? I laughed when I read about the 'unmentionables' and then, of all things, an umbrella. Nothing seems to have changed much at 85 has it? Although when I read in the *Sunday Post* about queues and coupons etc. I really wonder. In this country, at least in the towns, there is no scarcity of anything. Plenty of food, clothes and petrol etc. As for petrol, it just flows, not like water out here but like water would flow back home. Nan, I hear my name being called so I suppose I must finish for today. I'll tell you all about the dinner when I start again. Cheerio meantime.

27 December 1941

Didn't have any time to write yesterday. Had a very busy day in the worst dust storm I've ever experienced. I was hopelessly lost for about four hours, but managed back before dark, and that was something to be thankful for.

Now for news about our Xmas dinner. We had steak, peas, cabbage and roasted onions followed by pudding and custard. Some nuts and fifty cigarettes from the folk of Nottingham (where this battery was first raised). That was at 4 p.m. and at 5.30 we had freshly baked jam-roll and coffee. The dinner, of course, was dished out by the Officers. I think you will agree with me that it was a great feed to get in the Desert. Our cooks really excelled themselves.

Tell all at 85 and at Hamilton that I send my best wishes for the coming year and for all time to come. Cheerio meantime dear, remember the Old Chin and keep these red cheeks. I send you all my love.
Your loving husband always,
Alex
Xxxxxxxxxxxxxxxx

PS This letter includes the chocolate wrapper.

⮱1942⮰

*His 'wee fire' – being a 'Desert Rat' – foot rot – leave in Cairo – sandfly fever
– leave to Jerusalem and Palestine – 'Tale of Woe', Tobruk story – change of
work, now a Gunner – story of his Christmas and the 276 Battery*

*January–May 1942: Rommel and Afrika Korps attack past
Benghazi and towards Tobruk*

7 January 1942

My dear Nan,
Today has been very unpleasant. A very high wind, and extremely cold,
although we must be thankful that there is no sand in the wind, at least
not a great deal of it. But Nan I haven't felt so cold since I left home.
None of us ever thought that we would get cold weather out here, and
now that we wear battle dress, coats, gloves, woollen helmets and leather
jerkins on top and still feel cold, well I ask you? Still, there's one good
point and that is that the flies have gone meantime and that in itself is a
blessing.
Well Nan, 'Here's to the next time'.
Yours always,
Alex
xxxxxxxxxxxxxxxxx

Sunday 11 January 1942   His 'wee fire'

Four days since I wrote last Nan and believe you me it was not possible to
write any sooner. I have been rather busy, dear, and between that and the
weather things have been rather difficult. I went out yesterday morning and
was completely lost for the rest of the day. What a day for dust. Couldn't
see two yards away. A fog back home is child's play compared to these sand
storms. At home one can drive by a kerb or follow tramlines, but out here
there's nothing like that, just trackless desert. However, I managed back last
night which I thought was quite good going. I just happened to get a very
lucky bearing from a star and I ran right into camp again and that was that.
Today has been a lot better, although very cold and gusty.

Well Nan, one of the lads has just brought a couple of newspapers for me from home. *The Sunday Post* and *Weekly News*, at least I think so. Just a moment and I'll make sure. Yes, Nan, it is these two papers. I must say that I enjoy these papers very much; they seem to be a link with my other life which now seems to be very long ago and ever so far away. This delivery of papers is only the 4th or 5th I have had, and knowing as I do that you send them every week I am a wee bit disappointed. However, there's nothing I can do about it, so I shall just have to be content with what I get.

I've looked through all your recent letters and there is nothing fresh I can find apart from Dad's 'brasses', Ewan's 'cold' and Mother's 'sewing machine'.

One thing I must say and that is that although I said I would look through your letters I don't want you to think that I have them all dear as that would be wrong. I keep them until I have quite a number, and then I read them all again, and after reading and digesting the contents, I gather them all together, go out and dig a hole in the desert, have a wee fire and then bury the ashes. This is something I haven't told you before dear but I always have my wee fire on a Sunday morning between 11 and 12 noon because at that time you will no doubt be in Church back home. I hold my own wee service then with all the letters.

Seems silly doesn't it Nan? But there you are, I always was a sentimental individual you know.

Cheerio meantime dear wife.

Yours always,

Alex

xxxxxxxxxxx

14 February 1942

My dear Nan,

This time I really have a little news for you. We expect to be getting our issue of K.D. etc. today – K.D. is short for khaki drill and that means shorts etc. Of course when the weather does become real warm we shall have our friends the flies back again, although I believe I prefer the flies and heat to these awful dust storms.

Nan, your parcel has not arrived yet, but I have not given up all hope.

I will mention before I finish Nan, that a year ago tonight I saw you in the Victoria Infirmary. Remember Nan?

I would like to say more tonight dear but I am sorry I haven't time so again I will say cheerio.

15 February 1942

Well dear I will continue on the subject of your illness last year. I know it is a painful memory to you as it is to me. Believe me I was worried though I did my best to hide it. These few days are days I shall never forget Nan but still perhaps I have said too much? I believe I have so would you mind if I changed the subject?

Well Nan, today has brought more word from you in the shape of newspapers. I had three lots today, but as I haven't opened them yet, I can't give you the dates. Perhaps I'd better explain why I don't open these papers Nan. You see, if I open my papers just now they will be torn or perhaps lost, and that of course would never do. I have just put your papers down behind my driving seat just the way they arrived and they should remain there undamaged until the time comes for me to read them.

No! dear your parcel has not yet arrived, but I promise to let you know the minute it does, if ever.

I have another fag packet to send you Nan and this is a real Italian brand. They are a real continental smoke and quite a nice change from the ordinary cigarette. I think I'll also enclose <u>another</u> packet this week. This is an issue fag and is made in India, and like all issue fags is a fairly decent smoke. So there you are dear, four packets and from four different countries: South Africa, Egypt, Italy and India.

I am going to try and get some stamps and I will put them inside these packets. I will let you know of course in my letters if I have sent any and you will know to look inside for them. Have you destroyed the letters with the Aussie stamps on them? I hope not as these will give you a start. I don't know anything about this game of stamp collecting myself Nan, but as some of the lads go mad about them, I shall try and get one or two on the chance that they might prove of interest to you.

You see dear it is very hard to make a letter from here interesting, so I am trying a few ideas out, to see if they will help.

Well dear, I can again say that I am still well and quite fit, although I can't say that the food is anything special. Of course, a lot of quite good meals were spoiled with these awful dust storms, which I am glad to say are becoming less frequent now. Today has been a lovely day, nice and sunny, not too hot, and still no flies, at least not enough to bother us. But they're coming, yes, Nan, they are coming, the dear little souls.

I have a day or two yet before this letter is due for postage so I will hang off, on the chance of some more word from home arriving either tomorrow or the next day.

By the way, did I ever tell you the story of my famous guard duty one night rather long ago? It has been kept up on me ever since.

My mates have just come in from guard Nan, and that means the finish of writing for tonight. I will have a wee cup of tea with the lads, which I made about two hours ago. We have a sort of large flask which keeps the tea warm for rather a long time. Where the flask came from is nobody's business, and that is that!

16 February 1942

Now Nan, here is the story of my famous guard duty. The fact is that I went out on guard at 5.30 one night and returned at 6 o'clock in the morning, so instead if doing 2 hours' duty I and my mate did 11 and a half hours!

Fact is we got hopelessly lost in the desert, so we were wandering around with rifles over our shoulders and couldn't find our camp until the dawn. Now you know why I am never allowed to forget it.

Here's something Nan, I have just received a postcard from you dated January 31.

So you are having heavy snow at home? And the weather is getting warmer out here now. What a contrast, eh?

Nan cheerio for the present and good luck.

Your loving husband always,

Alex

xxxxxxxxxxxxxxxx

7 April 1942   A 'Desert Rat'

My dear Nan,

The first thing I shall mention is the fact of the change in writing in this letter. This happens to be the first letter with my new pen. Yes dear, the one you sent me in my birthday parcel which has arrived!

It has a much finer point than my other pen and therefore just the type I like. As you know I write better when I write small, and by being thinner the pen uses less ink. That itself is a great advantage, as ink is very scarce here and the bottle I have just opened has been in my bag now for almost six months. However Nan, leave has started again and I will get one of the lads to fetch some more back with him. While I am on that subject I should be on leave myself about August or September if all goes well. That makes it almost two years without any leave now but why worry? I will have all the more credits by then and therefore should have a better time. But to go back to pens again I will use the other for airgraphs only as it writes much heavier and should therefore be more easily read. It does swallow ink you know so I think just to use it for that purpose would be the best idea.

Well dear wife, now for some gossip about ourselves. The weather is much warmer now, the dust storms have stopped and we have moved out of the heart of the desert to nearer the coast. Today, I had a swim in the sea and if all goes well we may manage to get one each week. It's a long way to travel but believe me it's worth it. The water is also a bit cold yet but it was great to get under plenty of water after such a long time. The last bathe I had was in October 1941 and since then only two showers. The second shower was when a field hygiene unit came to our area with 'mobile showers'. Yes Nan, believe it or not 'Showers Mobile Desert Rats for the use of' to use the Army style of describing. 'Desert Rats' of course, is the name we give ourselves.

In your letter (35) you mention the fact of your friend Doris being engaged to 'the chap who drank a lot' to use your own words. My but isn't he a lucky fellow? Being able to get drunk I mean. What would I do to get right 'blotto'! Just imagine drinking and drinking until you knew that one's thirst was quenched and you couldn't hold any more. All we have here is tea made from salty water and it tastes just like tea would taste if made from salty water! Put salt in your cup some day and try it Nan (ha ha). Still I'm not grumbling dear although it may seem that way, but just giving you an idea of life out here, compared to what I read of in the papers you send me of men at home with all home comforts earning 10/- a week and threatening to strike if they don't get more money (naughty naughty).

So with that piece off my chest, dear, I shall say 'here's to the next time'. Good night again dear wife.

8 April 1942

I had another dip today. As I said yesterday we are trying to let so many men go for a bathe each day. Well today my lorry was given the job of taking the men to the sea and of course when I got there I had another wee bathe myself!

So you all had a good time at the Burn's Supper and of course Piper Fred Smith would be one of the attractions. Well done Fred and I hope you make a host of good friends and who knows that perhaps one day you may meet that one Friend who will make all the difference. Of course, Fred, I could fetch you some to choose from: some of the 'veiled women from the Mystic East'. These, of course, are not my words but No! I think they just smell.

Dear me, here I am talking to Fred and I started by writing to you Nan. Sorry, it must be the sun again.

Give my regards to all at 85 including of course the Budgie and dear wee May who is always having dates. Tell them all to keep their chins up and remind them when they wonder why things are a wee bit quieter now out here, that they just don't understand this desert that's all.

So dear wife with that choice piece of advice I'll say cheerio for the present.

Yours always,

Alex

25 April 1942

My dear Nan,

The reason for this awful writing is that something seems to have gone wrong with the jolly old pen. I've had it up and down and all I can find is that the ink seems to be drying up before it gets to the point.

Certainly where I am writing is like a hot house, and also it is the hottest part of the day, round about two o'clock. There isn't a breath of wind today so you can gather that it is quite warm. I am sitting on my blankets and I am only wearing my shorts, and of course my boots and socks. Why don't I have my boots off, you will be saying? Well, Nan, I don't like my bare feet in the sand. There's many 'wild animals' around this part. Scorpions, snakes, lizards and centipedes. Some of the centipedes are three and four inches long. We have found a few tortoises in the camp and I had one myself for a pet for a day or two, but as I was unable to feed it I let it go again. Even went so far as to call it 'Joey', but I couldn't let the poor thing starve could I?

Well Nan, so much for today's picture of my 'Desert Home'.

At present I try and finish all my work before midday Nan, and if possible have my siesta period in the afternoon. Yes, Nan, that is a fact. It is so warm that everything practically stops for a few hours in the afternoon. Things start to happen again between four and five and at seven o'clock it can be termed cold. Yes dear, right cold <u>and</u> the overcoat goes on again.

26 April 1942

Sorry dear, I had to finish rather suddenly last night. I had to take supplies to an outpost and just managed [to get] back before dark. My only means of direction was a compass and naturally the journey took a bit longer.

Well Nan, to carry on where I left off which was the subject of the 'wild animals'. We are free of mosquitoes here of course. They are only found where there is water lying stagnant. They are very numerous around Arab villages and in the Suez Canal. At this time last year we were being bitten alive by them, although fortunately malaria was very scarce. You do know of course that malaria is the result of a mosquito bite? At least 'bite' is the name given which is wrong because the insect doesn't really bite, but instead pierces the skin, and sucks the blood. I have watched them very closely, Nan. I have let one land on my arm, watch it till it swelled up with blood and then fly away again. It was quite safe because we all knew that there was no malaria in that area. I understand, by the way, that the germ is carried by the female only (women again).

Well dear wife, that I believe finishes the lecture on Natural History for today!

I have had a grand mail from you. Most of your gossip is in the letter which I have before me as I write.

You say that the green envelopes take a while longer Nan, but of course they are well worth waiting for aren't they? So neatly written etc. Tut tut such conceit (pen is playing tricks again).

Now Nan, don't worry if my name is left out of the mail delivery here. At present there is some mail arriving every night, so I am left out quite often, but I don't expect something every night. That would be asking just too much wouldn't it?

It's great to read of Margaret, Isa and yourself meeting at Eglinton Toll and going to the Cinerama. And the film was all about snow? And it was snowing outside too. With so much snow your eyes were dazzled. What is snow Nan? Is it nice white cool stuff? You know dear Eglinton Toll and snow seems awful far away and ever so long ago. Certainly it becomes cold here during the night and also early morning but it never seems clean. There's always that dust over everything. It is a common saying now that when we get home again there must be a bowl of sand on the table at mealtimes, so that we can sprinkle some on our food, just to make us feel at home you know. However, at the present time the dust storms are very few and far between so that is one blessing.

Also out here, dysentery is a rotten disease. I have seen a man so bad that he couldn't walk, but had to crawl on his hands and knees. Dysentery is one of the diseases caused and carried by these damn flies. Among the others are typhoid, typhus and enteric fever. You can understand the pest these flies are, can't you? All empty food tins are burned and scraps of meals buried. Latrines, which are just small trenches, are set on fire every day and covered in again. An open latrine left uncovered for a day, say during August or September which are the worst months for flies, might put a whole camp down with dysentery. And authors rave about the Romance of the Desert? When you think of all these pleasant 'wild animals' and insects and then think of Scotland it isn't hard to believe where the 'Lure' lies is it?

I had a good laugh reading about the Girls' Association concert. It wasn't the idea of Margaret looking like Mae West but the big laugh – the thought of Margaret singing! Did the A.R.P. turn out that night Nan?

I agree with you that Freddy should get out and make new friends. Who knows who he may meet through time? I waited a long time myself but 'She' did come along. Remember her Nan? A wee girl named Smith who thought she could dance (ha ha). And I kept the poor soul waiting for half an hour the first night. And the poor soul waited too. She didn't know why then but does she know now eh? Yes dear, that half hour seems nothing now does it? You have again been waiting for me and this time for over a year Nan, and all I can do is write you a letter, and say that I love you and God bless you my dear wife (tut tut going sentimental again).

Of course Nan I like to read of your wee nights out and of how you enjoyed yourself. Sorry you didn't get the stockings though. Still never mind, just buy a pot of paint instead!

No, Nan, I haven't forgotten 11 April [*their engagement*] but I know that you will understand when I say that so much has happened within the last week or two that I just couldn't get my thoughts to run so easily as usual. My head was full of other things, by that I mean actual events happening, so I just couldn't settle down to write. Perhaps I have written on the 11th dear. I don't know.

So, Nan, I can only say Happy Anniversary now this day Sunday 26 April 1942 and with that wish dear, I must say cheerio for today.

Another day has gone, another day nearer the end, another day towards peace and remember dear that it is always darkest before dawn.

God keep you safe my dear.

27 April 1942

Well Nan today I have been rather busy. Just my luck to get a hot day and plenty of work. Still I managed most of it during the morning and kept a job underneath the lorry for the afternoon. That is the coolest place to be. You are in the shade and get any ground breeze that may be going.

I am well at present, and quite fit. I have a good appetite which never seems to be satisfied. I could do with a lot more grub, but what we do get isn't too bad. In one of your letters you mention that 'horrible bully beef'. I can assure you, Nan, that I have had a number of good feeds with a tin of 'bully'. It certainly is no use cold, but isn't too bad warmed up, and there's always a means of heating it up. The usual dinner is stew, rice and tea. Breakfast is still bacon (tinned) and midday is either cheese or herring. At all meals of course there is tea and at present we have bread and not biscuits. So things could be a lot worse and indeed they have been, dear, and so I am not grumbling. Well, Nan, I must finish meantime.

I'll let you know if I get any more mail tonight.

No, dear, no mail today for yours truly.

29 April 1942

Well, dear, something fresh has happened after all!

Know what it was? Yes, you've guessed, another letter has arrived (40) and I must say a big Thank You for the Postal Order. It couldn't have come at a better time because your poor wee man was stony broke!

I have already borrowed 20 Piastres from the Office on the strength of it (ha ha). You see, Nan, we should have been paid today and also had our fag issue too, but the stuff hasn't come up so poor me was left without a smoke, and although we have some in our canteen (which don't give tick – ha ha) I couldn't buy any.

But with my 20 Piastres I sailed arrogantly into the canteen and ordered 20 Players cigarettes and I had 15 Piastres change. After I had repaid a debt of five fags, I had to buy another twenty because my visit to the canteen must have been well reported and some of the lads came and borrowed from me (ha ha).
Your loving husband always,
Alex
Xxxxxxx

30 April 1942

The weather has been very bad indeed. Another sand storm blown this time by a Khamseen or hot wind. As if one wasn't enough without the other! It is six o'clock now, and I am in a lovely mess. You see, I have been pouring sweat all day and naturally the sand or fine dust has stuck. The sweat is still dripping yet, and some of it has dropped on to the paper. Soon dries though. You remember how we saw men on the films in tropical scenes, mopping their brows and with the bodies all glistening? Well, that's how I am at present only it isn't oil I use but the real sweat! To say the least, Nan, it is a bit uncomfortable. When I look at my body I am reminded of the proverb 'all is not gold that glistens'. Or should the word be glitters? (Ha ha.) Anyway, why worry. I glisten more (ha ha).

I almost was lost today getting to the cookhouse from my 'apartments', otherwise my little hole in the ground. The distance would be about the same as looking from your room window to the railway and I could not see it!

Give a special word this time to Margaret and Ewan. Perhaps, Nan, I may torment Margaret but at the same time I think a lot of my 'sister'. It's just my cowardice, as I can say what I like without the fear of her getting her own back (ha ha).
Again dear wife cheerio for the present.
Yours always,
Alex
xxxxxxxxxxx

28 May 1942

My dear Nan,
Since my last letter, I have had very little time to do any writing, and I suppose that you will have heard on the radio and read in the papers the reason why. I haven't managed to write a word and naturally haven't received any either.

The 'fun' has started again, and the little quiet spell we had is finished. However, dear, I have managed an hour or two this afternoon for a wee chat with you. I have taken my boots off and my feet are 'airing'. They haven't been off for the past three days and nights so they need an airing don't you think? And what a smell. Phew! My mates can't smell them, nor even their own, as they are having a nap, so yours truly is being forced to smoke more often (ha ha).

I can't give you any war news in these letters, Nan, but I can assure you that everything is OK and perhaps events may seem strange to you back home at times, but as I said before Desert Warfare is different, and I honestly believe we will have him this time. And that, dear wife, is all the shoptalk, and I will now reply to your last letter (43) which had the snap of yourself.

You really look very well Nan and I am so proud to show some of the lads your snaps. Of course the usual remark is 'What the ★★!! did she see in you?' to which I reply 'Ugh! You're only jealous'. Yes Nan, I still have that sense of humour!

I read that some of _my_ portraits have reached 85 at last. In case you don't know dear I am really a model for what the well-dressed soldier is now wearing (ha ha).

As you said in your letter, I will have numerous experiences to relate, some humorous, some sad, but Nan it is surprising how one can see humour in almost everything, apart from death itself. For myself I thank God for my health and a keen sense of humour.

I have your letter before me as I write. However dear you fairly surprised me when I read that everything had been settled about your work, before you let me know! Frankly, I wasn't worrying about you going to any of the Services, as we have been told that our wives at home will not be conscripted, but that there was a chance that they might be required for munitions or other essential work. I have been expecting word from you for a long time now that you had been forced to change your occupation, and like yourself, I never mentioned the matter either, which makes me think that we were both playing the same game. We are a funny pair aren't we? (Ha ha.) Still Nan, everything has come right and that's the main thing isn't it? Well dear, I am feeling tired now, so I will finish meantime and perhaps join the rest in a nap. We may not get a chance tonight so here goes.

Same day (evening)

Well Nan, I've had my nap, my dinner (yes we're posh; late dinners you know) and a little excitement. It is getting late already and the moon is on its way so I won't have time to say very much. I am well and not feeling too bad at all. We are being kept busy but things are going the right way at present and it helps a lot.

God bless you.

29 May 1942   Foot Rot

I am well myself apart from a little trouble with my feet. A spot of what is known as foot rot out here. It isn't painful or in any way serious just a bit of a nuisance. It is caused by sweat and sand, but I am having treatment now and I do feel a lot better for it. This trouble makes the feet feel very hot and very itchy, and does become very uncomfortable. So there you are my dear, my one and only complaint, which I would not have, if I was not keeping my boots on so long, but there you are Nan, another side of desert warfare.

I have just come back from having my lunch Nan, which was herrings (tinned), syrup, bread and tea. We are having bread at least three times a week, and lovely bread it is too, as it doesn't have to come too far from the bakery.

Well dear. I am going to have my usual siesta period. In the afternoon things are quiet, as it is very hot, and in any case we do not get much sleep at night at present because of it being a full moon. I won't manage to add any later on as I will be on sentry duty tonight, so this must be all for today.

Cheerio and God bless you dear.

2 June 1942

Well Nan, it has been a day or two since I wrote last, but I have been very busy as you will no doubt understand from the 'News' etc. Well dear a lot has happened these past few days and the most important of all is that more mail has arrived here! A dust storm is blowing today and if that itself wasn't enough the wind is from the desert, a south wind and is real hot.

I was real interested to read of Emma's 'event' *[Emma is Alex's sister and this would be the birth of her baby]* and of your views on that subject. Well dear, I am sorry to disappoint you, but the fact is that by the time I get home I shall be so old, and 'soaked in vice' etc. I won't be fit for anything but an armchair. These words, my dear, are not mine but the utterance of a well-known MP back home. Another remark was that all the Middle Eastern Forces have done was 'sun themselves on the banks of the Nile'. The poor fool!

Yes Nan, that is what that MP said, and I only wish that same person was out here in this Unit. We have now been in action almost twelve months, nearly nine of which have been spent up in the 'Blue', our name for desert. I'm afraid that we haven't had a great deal of 'sunning'. Sun we have had, yes, but I would rather be without it, when it burns everything including the body. As you know Nan, I never complain but people who talk like that just make me mad and all I can say is repeat <u>that person is a poor fool</u>, because men are really living and fighting under conditions which are far short of being ideal and at present the 8th Army are doing well too. We have stopped Jerry again and he is going back so at present we are quite satisfied. Jerry by the way is reported to train his Afrika Corps in hot houses in Germany so as to have them used to the heat!

Well dear we have had an increase in our pay again, which amounts to 6*d* a day as from March 28. As I understand it the army will pay half of my allowance to you and give me the half to myself. It all boils down to the fact that you will draw the same money and I will draw an extra 3/6 per week.

My, my I feel like a 'bloated capitalist'. Ha ha.

So Nan with that witty? remark I shall bring this letter to a finish. Cheerio, dear wife, good luck and God bless you all.

Yours always,

Alex

PS The reason for the letter being crushed is that I left it to take a drink of water and the wind blew the whole lot out into the sand. Still, I have managed to collect it all (ha ha).

9 June 1942

My dear Nan,

Perhaps I should tell you about myself as owing to the present 'fun' you may be worrying about your wee man. Well dear wife I am well, the weather is rather warm, and at present the food is very good considering the present conditions. And that, Nan, is all I can tell you about things at present. I will leave it to the radio etc. to give you all the news from the Western Desert.

I will now take another glance through your letters. I read how you intend to do a bit of dressmaking with your frock. This reminds me to say once again how pleased I am that you are now in McDonald's and to know that you are so happy there. I knew that you wouldn't go to any of the Services dear, being my wife (has its good points after all eh?) (Ha ha.) Still, Nan, all's well that ends well.

The next item tells me to expect a parcel from yourself, and as the story seems a bit mixed between a blue case and something about confetti, I really don't know what kind of parcel to expect. By the way Nan, where did the confetti come from? And who was married in December 1940? What!? Myself? Dear me what a memory! Never mind dear wife our time shall come again, and perhaps not too far away either.

And now Nan, you speak of sending me some warm clothing before the cold weather comes again. It certainly is a nice idea on your part dear, but I can assure you that I have plenty of warm things in my kit. Then of course we wear battle dress also and coats and jerseys. So you see Nan, you could only send me what I already have, and I am sure you understand that it wouldn't make much sense now would it? Still dear thanks very much for the kind thought, but how dare you speak of washing my socks etc? I can wash, patch, darn and Oh! almost anything myself. The idea! As if I couldn't look after myself without depending on my wife (ha ha).

I read that Ewan is expecting leave very soon. Lucky fellow. Tell him if he can get me some leave to 85 then I'll do all his exams for him. Yes, a dozen times over. My last leave was December 1940 and dear knows when the next chance will come again. As I said Nan, lucky fellow.

That gossip dear, finishes my talk for today, although I should like to reply to people who do not think America is doing enough. Perhaps they haven't got going in the actual fighting, but I can assure you that the USA is practically feeding the Middle Eastern Force and that itself is quite a big job, don't you think?

10 June 1942

Well, if it isn't that man again!

I was on sentry duty last night which brings me back to the other story of when I was lost and had to do eleven hours instead of just four. Nan did I ever tell you exactly how that story <u>finished</u>? Well dear, we wandered about that night for eleven hours, although trying to keep within a certain area, because the other camps round about also had sentries out, and well you know we didn't relish the idea of landing in someone else's lines, and perhaps causing a little 'inconvenience' (ha ha). But to get on with the story Nan. After about eight hours we thought we should try still another direction and we came upon some lorries. There was no way of identifying them, but in any case they gave us a certain amount of shelter from the cold wind. The first thing that struck us as being strange was the fact that they were not guarded, so after bemoaning the fact of <u>us</u> doing sentry duty while the drivers of <u>these</u> lorries didn't, we sat down with our backs to the wheels and the wind and tried to snatch a few hours sleep. It wasn't a great success so when dawn came and we could sort of see things, we had a look around, and here is the greatest laugh (now, not then). We had been sitting down against our own lorries!

When the tale was told in the camp next morning I had rather a pleasant (?!) time. Someone suggested that 'When Macintyre goes on guard he should draw 24-hour rations'. However, I ignored them all and got my own back when some of the 'wags' were lost themselves the next night!

Your letter 46 asks if my watch is still keeping time. Well Nan 'tis a sad tale. The poor wee watch reposes in a box in my pack. You see the leather strap rotted away a long time ago so the watch was tied up in a safe (?) place in the lorry. It was there for a long time until one day quite recently. We had to move quickly and my watch was forgotten until too late. I found it two days later under a load of ammo' – only about four tons that's all! Naturally, it wasn't going, and was showing scars of its encounters, but a closer examination showed that although 'battered' it can be repaired. So it stays in the box until I can once more get to another 'big city'. And that, Nan, is the story of my poor watch. It has had quite a tough time being buried in water, then sand and now under a load of ammo'.

Well dear wife I must say Cheerio.

20 June 1942: Fall of Tobruk – German forces take around 30,000 prisoners

7 July 1942

My dear Nan,

Well Nan, today I have just seen a paper and I can read of the sensation the battle in Libya has caused at home, and of the supposed defeat of the 8th Army. I say 'supposed' dear because an Army which has made the enemy fight every inch and then stop him completely cannot be called defeated, can it? However Nan the same Army is still fighting and will continue to do so.

First of all dear I am sorry to tell you that your last letters have been lost. I can't tell you where but just 'somewhere in Libya', so it now means that I will just sort of start from scratch again. Although I have lost a few things I hung on to all my personal items, and you will be pleased to know that I still have the purse with the wee coins etc. and all the photos etc. so I haven't just done too badly have I now? Another thing Nan, is that we still have our equipment such as guns, lorries etc. and that itself was quite a feat I can assure you.

I have sent two cables from Egypt and also an airgraph as I knew that you would be a little bit anxious. For myself dear I can assure you that I am well at present, and not in any way suffering although I won't deny the fact that I feel rather fed up as we all are at having to come back all that distance. Still Nan our day must surely come back along and perhaps who knows it may be quite soon, providing of course our so-called 'Leaders' don't make any more damn mistakes.

This may not pass the censor dear but it is the truth, and the thoughts of all the men out here, who are beginning to wonder if we do possess any real Generals. Certainly Nan, all men can make mistakes, but men who play a game with lives can't afford to, and the sooner this is realised the sooner will this war be over. I know this is not my usual style of writing, but are you surprised? I'm sorry I had to go back to shop talk Nan but I had to express my feelings so there you are.

The last letter from you Nan was 47, but I'm afraid that I can't remember all the news it contained. So much has happened and so quickly during these past few weeks.

Nan, I may not manage to buy a small gift for your birthday in October. While I am on the birthday subject Nan, I am going to give you a surprise. I remember the date too! 19th October (ha ha) and if I remember correctly I was in Palestine this time last year where I bought your small brooch, which gave you so much pleasure.

May God keep you safe. Good night dear wife.

8 July 1942

Well Nan, as I haven't got your letters I think the best I can do is to try and describe my present surroundings.

I won't be giving away any secrets to say that we are now out of the desert and in the fertile part of Egypt, and now I am going to surprise you Nan by saying that of the two I prefer the sand of the desert. Certainly there we had sand and dear knows what, but at least it was clean, whereas where we are now is rather filthy, in practically every respect. Up to the present Nan, we haven't managed into town, but there may be a chance of it being placed within 'bounds' very soon. I hope that I may manage to get the remainder of our snaps developed in the town and send them all home in my next letters. I can only wish that my snaps give you as much pleasure as these photos from home gave me. By the way Nan, did you receive a photo of myself on a motorcycle or has that letter also been 'lost in transit'?

And now dear, for immediate surroundings. The combination of plenty of water and heat means that during the day we are pestered by flies while at night we are bitten alive by mosquitoes. Altogether Nan a very unpleasant place. We also require a very heavy guard, not to watch for Jerry, but to protect our camp from the natives who would steal everything we have if the least chance was given them.

I have just been told that I may get to town tomorrow night but we must go straight to the pictures, and come right back. Also we have been told that there are no pubs but just in case there may be a mistake we shall find out for ourselves (ha ha). Of course, if we find a pub then I'm afraid we just won't manage enough time to get to the cinema (ha ha). In any case, it's sure to be a rotten film! And so Nan, with these few attempts at cheerfulness I must say goodnight.

10 July 1942

Yes dear we were allowed into town, and as I said we did find beer on ice, so the pictures were not visited. Anyway the film wasn't very good (ha ha)!

I made a few purchases such as soap etc. and have also managed to have my watch repaired. I had a few nice cold beers and a good feed and here is a nice titbit of news for you Nan, which has given me a pleasant surprise.

After all these months in the desert, instead of losing weight I have become heavier by over a stone. All right Nan, don't laugh, but it is an actual fact. This time last year I was 10st 2lbs and now I am 11st 5lbs so there you are, and no doubt about it. Of course dear, having swallowed so much sand I'm not surprised!

The latest news on your postcards was that Margaret's 'calling up' has been cancelled for the present. I can only hope that she is forgotten all about for the duration.

I stopped writing there just now Nan, to unload some more mail. There may be some for your wee Man.

Well Nan, there was some more mail for me.

I have heard some of the other lads receiving letters from lads at home who want to come out East. Certainly dear, no doubt these countries are very interesting, together with the strange customs of the various peoples. I know that for myself, although I may be termed an Old Timer, I still find native life a source of great interest.

Did I ever tell you about an Egyptian funeral, dear? Where the 'doings' is drawn by horses usually covered by <u>white</u> cloaks, while the mourners all walk behind, the men folk looking very solemn and dabbing their eyes, and the women throwing their arms up into the air and wailing. All very moving and very impressive, but here is the actual fact Nan. These <u>poor relations</u> of the deceased are really just engaged for the occasion. In fact, [they are] paid professional mourners. Oh, it's a great country is Egypt as for that matter is the East.

12 July 1942

Well Nan I will try and give you all my gossip on 'current events' (ha ha).

It is surprising Nan how many humorous happenings I can relate which took place when we withdrew from Libya, with just that hour or so in front of Jerry tanks. Don't think we ran away Nan. Oh no, we fought the rearguard action, all the way down, against aircraft too, for as you know the planes always come through first to try and blast a way for the following land forces. Even during these days dear, we had many laughs and jokes.

I have just received some snaps and so the first one is enclosed. Yes dear, that very young-looking blonde is your wee 11st 5lb man! The sun does bleach hair you know! If you are surprised at some of the expressions Nan, just remember that we had beer that day, and we were very thirsty (ha ha).
Yours always,
Alex
Xxxxxxxxxxxxxxx

14 July 1942

My dear Nan,

I have had the parcel you posted during April, and it was intact with all the contents in perfect condition. The socks, handkerchiefs and foot powder are ideal things to send dear and I must thank you for your very nice, sensible thoughts. In my letter card I sort of criticised you sending cigarettes, Nan, which I do know had been gathered by Mother and which I am sure must have given Mother a lot of pleasure. It seems strange dear but the fact is that I would be far happier if they were given to perhaps Fred or some other lad at home.

The main news is the fact that we are now out of the Desert at present, and the surprising fact is that if it were not for the pleasure of these visits to town, most of us would rather be back in the Desert again! We have sent far more men into 'Dock' since we came here with illness, fevers etc. than ever before, due to the damper atmosphere. Up to the present, Nan, I have managed to escape the more serious complaints but my body is a mass of insect bites, mostly mosquitoes and, dear me, they itch! It makes me want to scratch and scratch, and if one does, the skin breaks and then provides a meal for the flies and a septic sore results. What a country! However, Nan, I still weigh 11st 5lb and so I can't complain, can I?

15 July 1942

During these last few days Nan, I have managed to do quite a few wee jobs, among which was the watch repair (the most important by the way), plenty of 'baths' (in bits), plenty of nice cool drinks, mostly beer and a visit to the cinema, the film being a damn war picture called *Flight Command* with Robert Taylor. Anyway we clapped and cheered all through the show, so it must have been quite good (ha ha).

When I was in town Nan, I looked around for some thing for your birthday in October but I haven't come across anything which could be called a product of the country, such as the brooch I sent last year. All the goods in the shops are from America, so Nan, if I can't come across any small gift which is truly Egyptian, I thought I might be just as well to try and get perhaps some stockings, or something similar as we may not be here long. Still Nan, I'll make sure first before I send you a gift from Egypt perhaps made in England (ha ha).

And with that Irish remark dear I'll finish for today as I have some work to do now. Good luck dear wife. Remember the 'Old Chin' Nan because something tells me that it may not be so very long now.
God bless you all at home.
Yours always,
Alex
xxxxxxxxxxxxxxxxxxxxx

2 August 1942   *Leave in Cairo*

My dear Nan,

At last I have an interesting subject for a letter. Since I wrote last I have had a leave in Cairo, the first by the way since December 1940. Only for 48 hours, but in my opinion long enough at the present time as it is very, very hot in town, and sight-seeing is really quite a task. However Nan, I had a very pleasant time, and also spent a lot of money (ha ha).

To start with, Nan, I had plenty to eat and drink (?), supped ice cream practically all day (between meals of course) and consumed an innumerable number of milkshakes. I stayed at the Hotel Moderne, where I had early morning tea in bed, went to the films, visited the various sights of Cairo, went to a dance, went to a few pubs, went shopping, spent the hottest part of the day in a swimming pool in the centre of the town, visited the Palace, zoo, museum etc., etc. Frankly Nan, I went everywhere I could in the short time I had. Perhaps you are surprised that I haven't mentioned a visit to that great mystery of Egypt, the pyramids, but you see dear, I have already seen them quite often and to examine them thoroughly I would need at least one whole day and well I just didn't have the time, and that's that.

So Nan, perhaps I'd better start so you can follow me for the next two days! I go by train and I arrive in town during the forenoon. The first thing that catches my eye is a big sign on the platform which says 'Beer on Ice' (In Bounds to H.B.M. Forces) and so here I spend the first of my Credit. After having satisfied my thirst (of curiosity only) I walk into the street and therefore to choose from the words of authors I stand at the 'Gateway to the Mystic East'. However to use <u>my own words</u> I entered into the 'Gateway' from the station by fighting my way through a host of touts offering any-thing from a hotel reservation to a real diamond (?) bracelet. Holy men were offering to tell my fortune 'just for a few piastres, George', others selling me their sisters for 'one night of love', tripping over a few boot blacks who just wouldn't move out the way and closing my ears, hardening my heart to all cries of 'backsheesh'!

Well Nan, after all that I managed to stand quite aloof though a trifle dusty at the so-called 'Gateway' and looked forward to my adventure.

The first place I go to is my hotel, where I arrive eventually safe and sound. There I pay for two days of bed and breakfast with early morning tea, procured by simply pressing the ever-present button, which in turn brings the 'garcon' complete with white robe, red sash and red fez. After the usual argument about terms I at last agreed to pay his price which has now come down to the fixed price which I knew a fortnight before, and now go to my room, which has twin beds (memories of Largs – ha ha), French windows, shutters, wash hand basin, 'h and c' (just a matter of form) and a hard floor. After settling down, the next thing on the programme is a shower, which I succeeded in having by the simple method of standing with one leg in the bath and the other on the floor, the shower pipe seeming to have a slight bend. It is near lunch time, so I go out in search of food. In the vestibule I sit down in a basket chair and have my boots polished for 1 piastre. May as well start by living as a gentleman of leisure!

After about half an hour I find the Services Club, which has a bar, restaurant, reading, writing rooms etc. and there I have my lunch. First was sherry, soup, then grilled steak, eggs (3), chips, runner beans and of course tea, bread and real butter. Afterwards I made my way to the bar (perfectly steady I assure you) and order one bottle of beer and lemonade and wander into the lounge, sit down and have a smoke while sipping a nice cool shandy. I think this is army life at its best!

I am very warm but the inner man is now well soaked so all that is required is a nice shower or a swim. That's it! A swim. Just across the road is a 'Gardens' and in these grounds is a pool, so after crossing the street by dodging a few trams, buses etc. I arrive at the Gardens and after paying 5 piastres for the hire of pants (returnable), I immerse myself in nice cool water for about two hours and Nan there I shall have to leave you for today as it is about time I had some work done!

Still the same day

Here I am again Nan, with another hour to spare so I am taking advantage and adding a bit more just in case. Perhaps at this stage I should say that I bought some more presents, and it may seem strange dear but the fact is that I did not buy anything for my wife. I know that you will understand when I say that the parcel which I have already sent you will make up for your being left out this time. Well Nan, I have bought three brooches of silver with a gold heart in the centre. Yes dear three of them, and the buying took me about two hours. I just had to try and get them cheaper! They are at present in the front of my present lorry (a 7-tonner this time). And now I suppose you will want to know why I bought three brooches? Well Nan dear I thought it would be a nice idea to send the three 'Graces' one each to my mother, your mother and our Aunt Nellie.

I may not manage to post them off for a while, as I have got to wait until I can find a suitable tin box or boxes. At present I am not sure whether to send them separately or all in one parcel.

Sorry, Nan, but I'll finish now. I thought I had an hour but I hear someone shouting my name, so it means Goodnight.

4 August 1942

Well Nan, I will try and finish today as I didn't have time to add any yesterday. Now! Where was I? Oh yes! The brooches, and I have managed to get one tin box, so dear after a bit of thinking, I've decided to send them all in the same box, and after thinking very hard again I've decided to address them to yourself as it would look better, because of you being my wife. Perhaps it would be even better if the three 'Graces' were together when the little box is opened. What do you think, eh? The box is very small and I will be lucky to get a card inside. I will try and post it off as soon as possible, and I only hope that it arrives safely and intact, together with the parcel already posted to 'Wee Nanny' for her birthday. So now that I have spent some time on that subject Nan I'll go back to the Cairo visit, and again where was I?

Yes I remember now I left you in the pool (ha ha).

Well after spending a nice time I went outside to the refreshment bar (soft) and had some iced milkshakes. After that we went into the recreation room and had a game of billiards for an hour, and from there to the writing room for a bit of a doze (ha ha).

Waking up, I realise that I am hungry again, so here goes for another meal, which was similar to the last only that instead of meat I had chicken. By the time the meal was finished, it was early evening, and to end quite a nice day I visit the Cinema Metro, which by the way is the finest cinema I have ever been in. We have no places at home that can be compared with it. It is air conditioned, so much so that entering from outside it is quite cold. Yes dear <u>cold</u> and even at the end of the show it is quite cool. The film by the way was a real good show, the big picture called *Come Live with Me* with James Stewart.

Well dear I must finish now as I am enclosing another picture and I must watch the weight. I will continue the 'Adventure' in my next letter.
Yours always,
Alex
Xxxxxxxxxxxxxxxx

10 *August* 1942

My dear Nan,
The first news I have for you today is that I have sent off the small parcel for the 'Three Graces'. I have packed the brooches in a small tobacco tin, stitched it up in canvas (a very slow job for me), tied it up with paper and string and finally registered it. So if it does not arrive don't blame me!

Well Nan, I started to write this letter three hours ago, expecting to have a quiet time, but as the Fates have deemed otherwise, I shall have to change my mind and finish very soon. It is becoming dusk but I shall tell you about my next day in Cairo at the first chance I get. So with this dear wife I'll say goodnight.

11 August 1942

I have received an airgraph from Canada, yes dear, from Ewan, and he tells me that he had a good crossing of only <u>eleven days</u> and that although he has only been away three weeks, he wants [to go] back to Glasgow again. Poor Ewan, he'll soon get used to it.

I had a trip on the boat of <u>eleven weeks</u> not days and by the time you get this letter it will be almost two years since I left home. Of course dear, the first five years is always the worst (ha ha). Yes Nan, almost two years since I saw you and to lapse into a bit of sentimentality, I do miss you an awful lot. Still never mind Nan, it can't last for ever, and is bound to end some day.

I am on guard at present and as we have a kind of guardroom full of men – you can guess at the noise. At this time of the day we have no flies but their absence is taken over by mosquitoes and bugs. As I have said time and time again, what a country!

We have come out from the desert, which between you and I, I much prefer to our present position. But I suppose that the brass hats thought the 10 unbroken months in the sand was enough and decided to give us a rest. But if this is what is termed a rest Nan, they must have funny ideas.

Well dear, I was intending to continue my story of Cairo tonight but perhaps it would be a good idea to try and get an hour or two of sleep (insects permitting). In any case the light is not too good, and if I do burn the whole candle I'll get.....? (Ha ha.) The first remark has come this minute and looks to me to be just a beginning, so to keep peace I'll say Cheerio for the present dear wife and 'Here's to the next time'. Goodnight Nan or rather Good morning.

12 August 1942

Well dear, I shall try and go back to the story of Cairo and the first item was the Palace which was really very large and very 'Royal', so much so that it is forbidden to walk on the same side of the road as the Palace. When we arrived there the band was playing outside and had attracted quite a crowd. All very interesting and especially when you realise the colours of the girls' dresses, and the dress of the guards which is a white uniform and a red fez. With the usual brilliant sunshine you can see Nan that it is quite a nice picture. Next to the Palace is the Museum, and it is reckoned to be the finest of its kind in the world. Nan, the exhibits are all of the body and cover every known disease of every part of the body, even to skin troubles of the tongue and eyes.

The final morning was spent at the Zoo. It is vast in size being 17 miles round the wall and all the animals are in the open in natural surroundings. I really enjoyed myself, the only thing lacking to complete a lovely time was your company. I know how much you would have enjoyed it dear, but I can assure you that I had you on my arm all day long although only in thought.

Of course I left you outside later in the day when I went to visit the famous or perhaps notorious cabarets, such as the 'Sweet Melody' etc! In my opinion there wasn't anything famous about them unless [it was] the high price charged for drinks. To me, they are just low dens and like all these places they smell.

And that Nan, finishes the story of my 48 hours in Cairo. I hope I have done well so as to give you a picture of the place. I really have tried hard.

Give my regards to everybody at home, and a special word to Margaret, and to the girls with you in McDonald's, who when they make you happy make me happy too.

Cheerio Nan, remember the Old Chin.

Alex

Xxxxxxxxxxxxxxxxxxxx

23 August 1942   Sandfly fever

My dear Nan,

I want to explain why my writing is a bit scrawly. You see dear, I am just recovering from a bout of fever, to be exact sandfly fever and my hand is apt to be a bit shaky. The insect is much smaller than a flea. You don't feel them bite so the first thing you do know is that you feel shivery. Just imagine a bad dose of flu and there you have 'sandfly'. Temps. range from 102 to 105. It usually lasts about four or five days before it sort of wears off. The fever is similar to malaria only that it has the good fact of not being a permanent illness. So Nan, there you have the best I can do in describing 'sandfly' and also my excuse for a rough letter (ha ha).

And now for your letter 56 but I hear a lot of talk now and somehow I have a feeling that I am not going to be left in peace as long as I expected to be. However, I'm deaf to rumours (ha ha) and I'll just continue to write until I hear a nice sweet voice calling my name, and after the noise has subsided, I'll just ask if anybody is looking for me nice and quiet like you know. Always the gentleman, that's me!

The first thing you mention in your letter is that news from here isn't too good. Nan, I can say how disappointed we all were to be forced back again.

Well dear, I hear a nice quiet voice bawling so it means cheerio for the present. Risking a bit of trouble Nan, I'll take time to tell you that I will have a 'fire' sometime today. God bless you.

26 August 1942

I haven't been able to add anything the last three days. Between this, that and the other I just haven't had the time that's all.

So you had a long lie until 10.30 eh? Oh you lucky people, with your long lie on a Sunday morning. Speaking of resting Nan, in the cities in this country most of the shops close at noon. This is due to the heat and apart from a few people who go bathing, the population stay at home and have their siesta. It is not until about 4 o'clock that people come on the streets and up till then the streets look like that postcard showing 'Aberdeen on a flag day' – empty.

And so dear back again to your letter, which goes on to the story of Uncle Bob meeting you at the park gates. I used to do the same thing myself with some of the many pretty girls who fell for me in my youth (ha ha). Of course, I didn't fall myself. Oh no! That came at a later date when I thought I was past that childish stage (ha ha). Still dear wife apart from the teasing I do love you very much, and I thank God for bringing you into my life at such a time. A time when I needed your love most.

Sorry Nan, I'm away again (ha ha) and I must come down to earth once more.

How on earth did you manage to convince Mother that she could do with some new clothes? I've been trying to do that for years but all I could get was 'Ach no, am no needing any I've plenty' and with that I had to be content. Of course these 'maidenly wiles' can always get results can't they now? Thanks Nan, it was really very thoughtful indeed and I certainly appreciate what you have done for Mother. God bless you for your kindness.
Your loving husband always,
Alex
xxxxxxxxxxxxxxxxxxxx

5 September 1942

My dear Nan,
Today I am going to reply to your letter 57 and the first thing you talk about is a 'cleaning fit' including the washing of stockings (did you use Lux?). After which you had a real good wash yourself, combed your hair, and then settled down to have your weekly chat to me. You finish by saying 'Let's pretend that we are sitting together at the parlour fire'.

Well, dear wife call it sentiment, call it anything you wish, but I often pretend myself, especially at night, and tell you all sorts of things, things which I do hope to tell you some day. Perhaps you may laugh, Nan, but you know we have some real good talks at times. I know it is all strange talk for me Nan, but it does me good to talk like this at times. I miss you very much

Nan, and I pray earnestly for the day to come when we are together again. Who knows, it may not be too long now.

Well Nan, now that I have finished that 'sloppy' talk, I'll see what else there is in your letter. You go on to talk about Tobruk and of how sorry you were to hear that it was not possible to hold it against 'Jerry'. I can assure you Nan that everybody was surprised when Tobruk fell.

As for myself I was one of the lucky few who, when we had to go back, left it too late, with the result that we couldn't make the town of Tobruk. You will notice that I said 'lucky' Nan, but at the time it did seem to be anything else but lucky. However, as we couldn't make it we got out in a different direction, by just being that wee bit in front, and so here we are still in a position to fight again.

You will be sorry to hear that a lot of the lads who were with me at Arbroath and Edinburgh and came out with me were lost at Tobruk. By lost I do not mean all killed, but either that or taken prisoner. Yes Nan, it was a sad show, but still our day must come, and come soon, and with that we must be content, and Nan, as I hear a rumour coupled with my name, perhaps it would be as well if I finished for the present. Never do to have my dear old Sarge call me twice! Would only upset the poor fellow (ha ha).

I am sorry that you only had one airgraph in three weeks. There is a chance that some of my letters never reached home, and for that matter never left the desert, but were destroyed when Jerry came through.

I have enclosed a snap of some Desert Rats and don't pass any remarks about my shirt needing a wash either, because it wasn't see (ha ha). It needed to be burned see, and it was see (ha ha).

In your letter 56, you gave me all the details of Mother going to visit Emma. It will be a nice change for her, and of course she has yet to see the wee girl Jean, or is it Jane? I never can remember names of girls, although I did have a sweetheart at one time named Jean or was it Jane? I don't know. Anyway, she was a 'beeeeeeutiful' blonde, but instead of attracting me she repelled me by eating onions, and also I didn't like her mother who chewed 'baccy' and spat! Still enough of this fooling Nan as 'Grub's up' so I must stop meantime.

Well dear, I've had my dinner which was meat called mutton (which was called a lot of other names), gravy, duff and tea but I won't be able to write any more tonight as I have some more work to do before darkness.

11 September 1942

My dear Nan,
The first thing I must tell you today is the fact that I have received 3 letters within the last few days – 58, 59 and 60. Also, I had a letter from Australia, from a chap named Andrews who was in hospital with me last year. He was

wounded at Tobruk and is now discharged from the army and working as a civvy. He hopes that he may be able to use his arm fully in about 2 years time. This reminds me that I finished 2 years myself in the army today. It seems no time since I was signing my name at Arbroath. I wonder where I'll be this time next year Nan. Who knows…?

Your letter 59 starts with a description of life at 85. This brings home to me more than anything else the curse of war because out here Nan, with so much to occupy my mind, at times I forget my home and it is only when I have nothing to do that it all comes back again. Understand, dear?

Well Nan, from there you go on to the Tobruk business and of how happy you were when my cable arrived. You know Nan, we were lucky and didn't know it at the time! That's all the news I can give you without breaking the rules of these green envelopes. So just try and be content until the time comes when I can tell you all my tales and experience. There were periods when no-one knew the day or the date. Still Nan, I was healthy in the Blue.

12 September 1942

Well dear, I have just opened up your letter again and I find that I have become a wee bit mixed up. It seems that I already have started to reply to an earlier letter! But owing to the great amount of mail, my office routine has become a trifle confused. Must talk to '<u>my staff</u>' about it. Bad for discipline, you know (ha ha).

Well dear, this letter was sent registered and I must thank you very much for your splendid thoughts and understanding. I quite understand your reason for sending it, Nan, and it is these actions of yours that make me love you so much (careful, Alex now, careful).

I liked the bit in your letter about the wee boy in church dear and I fully understand your feelings about the dream of one of our own. Like yourself, dear wife, I often look forward to that time coming. And like yourself, I would get great pleasure from it. Never mind, dear wife, these days may come again perhaps even sooner than we may expect. 2 years today I signed on the line and became one of the Royal Artillery.

2 years, Nan, and yet at times it seems just like yesterday. Just at times though dear, just at times.

So you have had another increase in pay? Fine Nan. You know I was just thinking that it would be a good idea if, when I come home again, that I stayed at home and dealt with the housework while you went out and 'earned the bread'. Let me know what you think of the idea, will you?

Your letter goes on to mention the serious news from Egypt. Yes Nan, very serious indeed when you think of the loss of men. Most of them from Britain too. It is estimated that for every three men who managed to our present positions, 4 men didn't. The Axis radio claims that the 8th Army was wiped out. That, Nan, is a lot of nonsense! Because Jerry stopped when he reached El Alamein and who stopped him? But that much-hammered 8th Army? And that Nan, is all the shop talk I will give you.

And that, Nan, finishes my reply to your letter which I admit was a very interesting and well-written letter. Of course, now that you have copied <u>my</u> style of writing, the improvement will of course be even more pronounced (ha ha).

God bless you all.

Alex

xxxxxxxxxxxx

7 October 1942 (70)   'The Novel'
                              Leave to Jerusalem and Palestine

My dear Nan,

This is the story I promised you of my 14 days to Palestine. It will be a hard job Nan, as the wonders of Jerusalem can only be understood by actually seeing with one's own eyes. However dear I shall do my best. It's getting dark now dear so goodnight and good luck.

8 October 1942

I believe I will at last manage to start the 'novel' today!

The trip started from Egypt, Nan, and the first stop was Tel Aviv. As a holiday resort Nan, it is built on the same lines as most of the seaside places at home, and all it has to offer is the usual beach, cafes and cinemas. However Nan, it is a very nice, clean and very modern town but for a soldier on leave it is so very expensive and I don't mean maybe!

The majority of us stay at hotels just for the usual 'Bed and Breakfast'. These hotels are registered with the army and are classed as A, B, C or Ds. Being as the ordinary soldier is rotten with money we all go to the class D! Bed and breakfast costs on an average 5/-. That doesn't seem much Nan, but lunch, dinner etc. have also to be bought during the day. Together with fags, cinema and odds and ends it takes easily a pound a day for a soldier in Palestine. So you see Nan, what I mean by an expensive place. To give you an instance, I bought a cake and a cup of tea late one night in one of those cafes. The cake was 6*d* and the tea was 4*d*-10*d* in all. Fancy prices Nan eh? Still I had saved some money in the desert and as I don't know when the next leave comes along I had quite a good time. The cinemas by the way cost roughly 1/9 and the trouble was that being a resort the same film was on for perhaps 2 or 3 weeks, and apart from the cafes there was nowhere else I could go at night. My time was usually spent on the beach during the day and in a cinema at night. Well Nan, after three days in Tel Aviv I decided to visit Jerusalem and it was this visit which made my holiday really worthwhile. Oh! Forgot to mention that the films I saw were: 1 *North West Mounted Police*, 2 *Nice Girl*, 3 *Meet John Doe* and 4 *Castle on the Hudson*. It dealt with Sing Sing prison and starred John Garfield.

As you can see I had a nice pleasant stay and really enjoyed myself. To make the time just perfect would be for me to have your company dear, but then perhaps that day may come soon. Who knows?

9 October 1942   In Jerusalem

Now Nan, I shall try and tell you of my visit to Jerusalem. I left Tel Aviv by bus and the run, which lasted almost 2 and a half hours, was an experience in itself. The road is very hilly and naturally the scenery is vastly different from that of Egypt which as you know is mostly sand. Frankly it reminded me very much of some of the weekends at home that I used to have when I went [on] runs on my motorbike up on to the moors. Of course, I had a very nice girl on the pillion usually too (ha ha).

Still dear, I must get back to the tale. The first place I visited was the YMCA building which is the biggest in the world, costing I believe £250,000. There is a large tower here and a grand view from the top. Both the new city and the old with the wall round it can be plainly seen and all the churches. After a cup of tea and a sandwich (a bit cheaper this time) I went for a walk round the new town, bought these small souvenirs for you and paid a visit to the 'Aussie Club'. I paid a visit to the canteen (ha ha), had a drink, a bit of conversation and then went for lunch to another part of the building and there I had soup, steak, eggs, mashed potatoes, carrots followed by rhubarb and peaches, grapes and coffee. I'm sorry if this makes your mouth water dear but there you are – I just thought you would like to know (ha ha). After a smoke and a rest I started my tour of Bethlehem and the Old City. There was a party of us and we had three cars and a very good guide. The first stop was on the hill above Bethlehem. From that place we went to the Church of the Nativity in Bethlehem. I cannot describe this place Nan or for that matter any of these churches, except to say that the sight is wonderful inside. Hanging from the roof are dozens of lamps, either of silver or gold, and some of the smaller domes have roofs of beaten gold. The church is built over what we read in the Bible as the stable where Christ was born, and the roof of the church is the shape of a Cross. Underneath can be seen the stable and the manger and this again was a wonderful sight. Then we moved back to our cars and went to the Garden of Gethsemane and saw the 'Church of all Nations' at Gethsemane. It gets that name because every nation is represented in the building which is of pillars and domes – each dome being from a different country. Inside here is a rock which is believed to be the place of Christ's prayer. Surrounded again by lamps, paintings and ornaments either of silver or of gold. From here we drove to the Mount of Olives and to the Church of the Ascension where a footprint, carefully preserved, is understood to be that of Christ. From this spot we could see all the Old City of Jerusalem and the spot in the city wall where the Golden Gates used to be. From there, dear, we drove to the Dead Sea and tried to swim in it which I can assure you was not easy, as the water being so salty was therefore very dense. I picked up a little shell for you which I shall try and send home soon.

Well Nan, we then walked through the Old City. We started out by entering the city by the 'Damascus Gate' and going through the very narrow streets until we came to what is termed the 'Road of the Cross'. We followed this road until we reached a convent which we entered and by going underneath the floor of this place we found ourselves on the original 'Road of the Cross'. We went from there outside again and followed it right up until we reached Calvary. Here we found another church – the 'Church of the Holy Sepulchre'. It really is two in one because at one part we have the place of crucifixion and at another the actual sepulchre. At the first part there is a painting which is on the actual spot and it is surrounded by a halo of pure gold. Here again are lamps of precious metals. We were able to go underneath this part also and on the roof we saw the holes in the rock of three crosses. Next was a visit to the sepulchre itself and we were allowed to enter right inside and say a prayer if we wished. Needless to say dear I prayed for you and everyone at home.

In this church there is the rock where the body of Christ was washed, they say.

I have tried to give you a picture of Jerusalem, Nan. I have done my best but it is a very difficult job to try and draw a picture of such a place.

From Jerusalem I moved by bus to Haifa. There was bathing, cinemas and cafes galore, also cabarets and 'Honky Tonks' where the girls drink coloured water and the poor mug pays 2/3 for it. What a game. It is the chaps just out here who fall for that racket, not us 'Old Timers'.

Well dear wife, this must be the finish of my letter.
I shall say Goodnight dear wife and God bless you all.
Yours always,
Alex
xxxxxxxxxxxxxxxx

23 October 1942 (74)   'Tale of Woe' – Tobruk Story

My dear Nan,
This is a letter I have been wanting to write for a long time now. We have just been told that we can tell our folks at home of our experiences in the

Desert up till the time of the 'Alamein Line'. It should prove very interesting and I am sure you will enjoy reading it. However, Nan, there were events which I do not intend to speak of even now, but it is surprising how one can see humour in almost everything.

And now for my 'Tale of Woe' which starts from Suez during September 1941. We were a long time taking part in the defence of the Docks at Suez. And as that was our main port of the Middle East you can realise that we had a few visitors over. We were kept fairly busy, mostly of course at night, when things became a bit lively at times.

From there we moved up the 'Blue'. The trip lasted ten days before we arrived at our first sight [*sic*], which was the defence of a position south of Sidi Barrani. It was our first taste of real desert and were we thirsty! This was the spot by the way where I was lost at night and did my now famous 11 hours' guard duty. Remember, I told you that story before Nan?

We did not fire there but just remained hidden until the 'push' came off. There were Jerrys over now and then who had an idea there was something doing, and tried to find out this position. As you can see Nan to fire at these planes would be just what Jerry wanted. The push started in November 41 under General Cunningham. Instead of going forward we moved to the Mischeifa railhead. Yes Nan, a railway in the desert which had been laid down by the Army Railway Unit. It was only a single track but it meant a big difference in time for our supplies. The intention was to extend this line right to Tobruk if possible but at that time it had stopped at Mischeifa. It seemed strange at first to see engines running along the desert with the old markings of LMS and SR still showing.

Well Nan Mischeifa was growing into a very large base of supplies with everything an army needs. Petrol, food, ammo, clothing etc. and as usual our 'friends' were beginning to pay a few calls. Jerry had a hard job, as there were no buildings etc. and the materials were just being dumped on the sand and of course well spaced out. The only dump which was fenced in was naturally the food dump (ha ha).

We stayed there for five months and we did have a very busy and exciting time. As at Suez, Jerry came over mostly at night, but even though he dropped a lot of stuff he did no damage. A single line is a hard target at night even with flares, especially when we were putting up a lot of stuff at him, which the papers called 'intense A/A fire'.

As I said we were busy there as once the guns were in all the lorries went out every day to work on the dumps or elsewhere. We had trips up the line which at times lasted from three to eight days away from camp. We were there for the winter months, five altogether and it was there that we had our worst sandstorms, when it took about 2 hours to reach camp after a day at the dumps, which could be done normally in ten minutes or less.

Well Nan, after a time the railway was pushed up to Fort Cappuzo and as we had made a good name for ourselves we moved up to the railhead there.

We didn't stay there very long, although long enough to have our worst experience up to date. I won't say any more about it Nan, except to say that we left some of our lads there when we left that place.

Our next position was a place called Belhammed which lies between El Adem and Tobruk. I was in Tobruk often for supplies etc.and visited the dentist there where I left one of my teeth (ha ha)!

We were there when the fun started in June 1942 and it was hectic while it lasted. If you remember it was at El Adem that Jerry first came through, so you can judge for yourself what sort of time we had.

Well Nan, as you know things went wrong and we were left in a very awkward position. So bad that we had everything ready to blow up our guns and get out the best way we could. At one time I had visions of Stalag VX these few days (ha ha)!

It was thought it would be hopeless to try and get back and it was decided the best idea was to make for Tobruk. At that time Jerry was past us, and things did seem bad. However, we took a chance and pulled up our guns during the night and moved out just before dawn. We couldn't make Tobruk so we just said 'Well, here goes' and headed East. At that time we thought we were unlucky, but as events proved we were very fortunate as Tobruk fell two days later.

You see Nan, at that time we thought the same as you people at home and that was that Tobruk would never be taken. Why it fell so easy is as much a mystery to us even yet. Well dear we got through as you know to Fort Cappuzzo once again although don't ask me how. We fought what might be termed a rearguard A/A action all the way down because as you know yourself Nan, Jerry's way of fighting is to send his planes ahead to blast a road for his land forces. We stayed there until Jerry caught us up and we moved down through Halfaya Pass across the desert back to Mischeifa railhead once again. But Jerry was coming fast and we couldn't hold him anywhere in the desert. So once again we pulled up the guns and got moving.

Here again we were lucky as we were the last out, and we had been told that one enemy column was past us on one side while a faster column had even gone past Sidi Barrani on the coast road and they were making for Mersa Matruh. The trouble was that we were also thinking of going to the same place (ha ha). However, before the two columns could meet outside Mersa Matruh we were inside (how's that eh? Ha ha) and during our stay in Mersa we again had a very unpleasant time, between the usual bombing, strafing etc. The enclosed photo shows how near were some of the dive bombing near misses. Yes Nan, these are some of our guns and men, and the fires are where Jerry hit the petrol dump, where some of our lorries were, and was taken just after that attack had finished.

Well dear wife, before I finish I should like to remind you that during these nine unbroken months in the desert, I managed to write you all these letters you so much like, also send cables etc. and gather fancy cigarette packets for your interest, and even draw an etching (ha ha). I spent hours at that drawing, and many more playing Ludo. Yes Nan, four men playing Ludo for hours on end. Funny, isn't it?

Well Nan, I still have a few minutes left, so I am sure that you now have an idea of desert warfare. We managed back with all our guns and only had to leave one lorry behind. Of course all the wagons weren't going but still what could be pulled was pulled, and the one we left behind we left burning.

24 October 1942

Well Nan, here I am to continue my story of the Desert. We again managed out of Mersa Matruh. From there we came right down and handed over our equipment to fresh troops, who still had to sample the 'Lure of the Desert'.

And now dear, you have my 'Tale of Woe'. It is not by any means a complete story, but then to give it all to you would take me days and I could really write a book.

As I said at the start Nan, there are many incidents which I do not want to remember, but during all that time, I never lost my sense of humour. When we came back down, I had practically half my lorry loaded up with beer (ha ha). Where it came from is a military secret (ha ha).

Also the story of when we were playing a football match against South Africans at Mischiefa on our football ground. Our goal nets, by the way, were some camouflage nets we found. Well apart from the usual look-outs most of us were watching this great international match, when we heard a plane. Well Nan, as I told you Jerry didn't come over during the day as a rule but mostly at night, so we never even bothered to look up until our spotters yelled 'Junkers'. And then we scattered (ha ha). We weren't so bad as we manned the guns, and the rest had their own 'holes' but the 'visiting team' and supporters couldn't find a decent hole (ha ha). However after some excitement caused by keeping Jerry off his target, the railway line – his bombs missed by the way – the match was resumed, but we lost.

I intend to do a spot of shopping today. Namely, try and buy some more stockings for the little parcel I have ready for you.
Cheerio dear, good luck and God bless you all.
Yours always,
Alex
xxxxxxxxxx

October–November 1942: 8th Army defeats German forces at El Alamein and then pursues Rommel and Afrika Korps westward back across North Africa – through Egypt, Libya and into Tunisia

3 November 1942

My dear Nan,

I must thank you for the good mail I have had these last few weeks. I have replied to them all and as I had quite a lot gathered together, I had my fire last Sunday November 1st.

I am well but being pestered by a few flies, even though the weather is becoming cooler, especially at nights. By the way Nan, we should be back to battle dress soon, for the winter months. What a country! Roasted by day and frozen by night. Pestered by flies by day and by bugs and mosquitoes by night. Not to mention various other companions such as ants, etc. who seem to have a preference for the insides of my ears. Then of course we have the various troubles like malaria, dysentery, etc.

I don't know whether you have read it in the papers or not Nan, but after this war no British people can stay in Egypt. Sort of 'Egypt for the Egyptians' idea. I don't think you need me to tell you what I think of the idea. They can ★★!!★ have it (ha ha).

Well Nan, I could give you ever so many stories about life here. For instance, how the small change is being hoarded up so much that shops and cinemas can't give us change of even 5 piastres. Of course, shops will always give you an <u>article</u> in place of change. What a racket! It is so bad that it is now a criminal offence to be in possession of a lot of small change. Troops stationed at home are lucky as there are at least some honest folks there. Out here, there are none. And that dear wife is my tale of woe for the present.

I noticed that one of your letters was practically filled with Margaret leaving for the services. You wrote me a nice cheery letter dear, but you see I know you so well that I could read between the lines. I could see that although you were writing to me, the feeling about Margaret was uppermost in your mind. Am I right, Nan? I know the very close bond between you all so it must have been a wrench to see her going away from 85.

I have had an airgraph from May who assures me that she has now taken over the job of looking after my wife, although as she says some people think it's my wife who looks after May!

It's great to see that we still have a sense of humour. I often wonder what we would be like without it and also who has the hardest job. You at home or myself out here in the romantic East.

We have longer nights now and if I can get a light I should manage to write some more. It becomes quite dark about 5 o'clock now. It's the start of the long winter nights again. We'll have to try some more etchings again (ha ha). Either that or make a Ludo board again and play for matches. Dear me, almost forgot that there is a war on (ha ha). Must be these flies driving me crazy.

6 November 1942 Change of work

I had a bit of an argument about a month ago with our sergeant and I threw up the driving of lorries. I didn't get in to any trouble as it was only a personal argument between him and I. However, I was lucky as only the next day the chance of this course came up. Naturally I jumped at it.

I have been studying very hard for the last few weeks and I was put forward for the exam yesterday. Three of us were put forward and yours truly was the only one to get through (howsat!). The test lasted about 2 hours, each man being examined separately by a captain. After a lot of sweating by poor me, I was passed through.

I am no longer classed as a driver mechanic. No Nan, just a Gunner (OFC), Operator Fire Control. I can't tell you what the duty is as the whole 'caboodle' is secret. A lot of the job is secret even to us and all the lot is taboo to outsiders. No one is allowed to watch us in action. All this, Nan, means that once an OFC, always an OFC. Understand Nan? It is a very interesting trade and can be gone into very deeply. It is the subject of electricity and radio and I am sure you know yourself that all the theory can be very deep. Anyway Nan, I am now a fully-fledged OFC.

So far as extra pay goes Nan, it's the same money. There is a tremendous lot to learn but some of us were wanted immediately so we were rushed in to this test. I don't think I'll manage to add any more tomorrow so I'll say cheerio until I write again.

I really intend to increase your allowance when things become more settled. But if I can only give you sixpence, just understand that the cost of living out here is very high – 1/8 a bottle (ha ha).

8 November 1942

Here I am again. We are regaining what we lost a few months ago. I mean our hearts.

It looks as if this third 'Benghazi Handicap' may be the final one. I certainly hope so as I've had my share of the Blue. I'll just leave it all to the radio to give you the news. Desert warfare is strange. It is a war of movement, everything on wheels. There is no stopping for a fight. Armies move one way or the other and there are very few places where the nature of the country allows a stand to be made. Two of these places are Alamein and at the other end Gazala.

I had a good laugh at an article in a home newspaper by some great strategist! This writer wanted to know why we couldn't send an army off the coast then south and thereby cut Jerry off. The poor fool doesn't realise that that job would mean two armies, one to fight and the other to fetch and carry water, perhaps hundreds of miles, with the chance of it becoming tainted and the big chance of dysentery spreading like wildfire. Why don't people find another way of earning money than just by talking about things they know nothing about? Well that's off my chest dear.

Good luck.

Alex

Xxxxxxxx

8 November 1942: 'Torch' landings of British and US forces in French North Africa (Algeria)

13 November 1942: 8th Army recaptures Tobruk

18 November 1942

Well Nan, I am arranging that you receive your allowance. You see Nan, your details at home should tally with the entries in my pay book. I just want to see if all my affairs are in order (ha ha).

That was a fine parcel you sent me, Nan, and I could see that you had taken great patience in the tying and wrapping up. When I think of the time you must have spent with that brown paper I really think you must like me a wee bit. When I look in my mirror (cracked by the way) I often wonder what made that lassie wait about half an hour for me one night. Remember Nan? I believe you were angry a wee bit (ha ha). But joking apart, Nan, it was a great parcel and I really love you more than ever for it if possible. As I said, Nan, the parcel was undamaged and all the contents were in first class condition. The socks will be right handy and also the pullover which I pulled on immediately. And as for the foot powder, well dear, it is a right good idea as this foot rot trouble is something which nobody seems to be able to cure permanently in this country. The only cure I know and which certainly helps me is sea bathing. There's nothing to touch the salt water and then some foot powder after that. Of course, we can't always be at the sea-shore but if Jerry keeps going the way he is now (even faster than we came down), it may not be very long before we are all at the coast and no more desert warfare. Here's hoping.

And now we come to the subject of toothpaste (ha ha). Do you know, Nan, I am still using supplies I got when we had to come back from Mersa Matruh last time? I must have had a box of toothpaste, soap, many thousands of fags, matches and umpteen other necessities (ha ha). On our way down, we kept throwing cigarettes to the other lads who were not so fortunate. You see Nan, we found the stuff first. But the funny part of it was that when we were right down almost to El Alamein, the lads who had come to help us there threw packets of fags to us! I expect they said to themselves, 'Poor fellows! They look as if they could do with a smoke'. Little did they know (ha ha).

If I remember correctly, one of our lorries had about three tons of beer on board in tins (my lorry – ha ha), when we <u>left</u> that was. Three tons, I should say. We had a number of stops on the road and it was not three tons when we reached El Alamein!

Well Nan, to get back to the toothpaste once more, I believe I have enough to last about a year. I have a tooth less to clean now. It was left at Tobruk (ha ha).

After you've read this page, you can see what I meant when I said that the next thing to good health is a good sense of humour. As I said before, Nan, one can see humour in almost anything. Yes, even in the withdrawal to El Alamein.

If you can see a good map, you will realise why we had to come back to El Alamein and why Jerry is at present making for El Agheila. The country at these places is a bit different from the desert in between. No army can hold a front in the heart of the desert. Think of the miles and miles of flat sand and think of what it would mean to watch every mile. Perhaps our 'strategists' at home don't know that, eh?

I am enclosing a poem from the 8th Army fellows to these so-called soldiers at home. Surprising the talent we discover during the winter nights.
Yours always,
Alex
xxxxx

To The 'Grousers' at Home, from the lads of the 8th Army who can 'take it'

Hair to our shoulders, beards to our knees
Bully beef and biscuit, over-ripe cheese
Water that's salty – and slimy too,
Grit in the saucepan, and in the stew.
Miles have we travelled, months have we spent
Prowling the desert, weary and bent.
Stop here today, push on tomorrow
We've nothing to spend, damn all to borrow
Once we turned round, and said 'Thank God at last'

But we turned again, and went back twice as fast.
Arrived at a map ref, sound as a bell
Some chaps are missing, the cookhouse as well.
Tomorrow is Christmas, how happy we be,
No beer! No fags! We shan't half have a spree.
But our's is no hardship, compared with the blokes
Camping in Blighty away from their folks.
Far from a pub – at least thirteen miles
Why even J.B. Priestley complained of their trials.

So tomorrow we'll pray, for the boys back at home,
Away from their girls, and all alone.
That's solved our great problem, we know what to do.
Spend all our Christmases, weeping for you.

27 November 1942

My dear Nan,

Mail has now become very scarce, and all the chaps are grumbling, which is about the only privilege a soldier has. I have had an airgraph and one post-card during the last <u>four</u> weeks. Both from yourself. I am sending very few air graphs now, as we are only allowed to send one each week. Still, I know that you always tell all the folks at 85 and at Hamilton any news that I may send in my letters to you, apart of course from certain little passages which I write and which are only meant for you dear (ha ha). It would never do if the people at home thought I was becoming awful sentimental. As if I was – and me ever so tough (ha ha).

Of course, I'm only quoting the newspapers, when they talk about the great 8th Army. I wonder if these bells will ring when we come home, or will it be the MEF again? 'Men England Forgot'. Again, I wonder.

Well Nan, this is all for today. I may be able to write tomorrow as I have just heard from a man, who knows a man, who saw a man, who told him that a man he knows saw a man he knows carrying what seemed to him to be a bag of mail into our HQ (ha ha). Well Nan, cheerio and I hope that man's guess was correct!

2 December 1942

Well dear, I forgot to tell you about my pet (a cat). Yes, Nan, a kitten that I picked up and believe it or not it follows me about like a dog. Even at night I just whistle (that is when things are quiet) and quite soon I can feel her rubbing against my legs (ha ha).

Well Nan that is all. I'll say goodnight and God bless you all.
Yours always,
Alex

PS I have just received another parcel from yourself.
Thanks dear. I haven't opened it yet.

14 December 1942

My dear Nan,
Nan, if you haven't had the story of my many months in the desert in my own great style (yeah!?) by the time this letter arrives I'll do the novel all over again. All right dear?

The weather is much cooler now and we get quite a bit of rain at times. The flies are a bit scarcer and the Jerry news is that Rommel is 'advancing??' towards Tripoli from El Agheila. I thought that was pretty good don't you? So with all these blessings what more can a man ask for?

Oh! I almost forgot to tell you that I've had a grand mail, Xmas cards and my Xmas parcel. I am pleased to know that the parcel for the 'Three Graces' has arrived. Were the brooches all right Nan? And did the ladies like them?

Once again dear let me thank you for your kind thoughts and for such a fine parcel. I expect that Mother supplied the socks with the different coloured toe which she hoped I wouldn't mind. For myself, I don't see any difference in the wearing of socks even if they had all the colours of the rainbow, so why should I mind?

Lastly I must thank you for your very kind thoughts. You know Nan, at times I do think that you do like me a wee bit! When I come home I'll make up for all these months you have been waiting. By the time you receive this letter I suppose we will have passed our second anniversary dear wife. I can only say that I love you and hope that we won't be apart when our next 'day' comes along.

Just do your best to be patient and keep the Old Chin high up.

17 December 1942

I have had your cable Nan. I had to take rather a chance with my cable to you as they were all cancelled except for Xmas greetings, and I can only hope that you have got my congratulations for the 20th December. Yes dear, two years now since I had to move those twin beds and tell the old ladies next morning that 'we didn't hear the sirens'. Strange thing Nan is the fact that I haven't heard any sirens since that time, and between you and I Nan, I certainly don't want to hear any more.

At this time of the year all my thoughts are with you. We had a short time together dear but I would not have done without it. Having you for my wife has made a big difference to me out here. Candidly Nan, it was only the thought of yourself and home which bucked me up during those rather hectic weeks last summer, and they were at times a wee bit hectic. Still that was last summer, and as you know Nan, a lot of things have happened since last summer. Happened for the best too.

I am so pleased to read that you enjoyed the story of the 'Gateway to the East' in Cairo and the other adventure in Palestine. I thought the story of Cairo would interest you and although it may seem funny to you as regards the offer of the sister it is an actual fact. The women out here are treated just like that though these touts must have an awful lot of 'sisters'. Sad to say Nan, that the cheapest thing in Egypt is a woman.

Let's hope what has happened out here has shortened this war by a long time. I know it isn't for me to talk about things like this but there is no doubt that we made a great recovery at Alamein for a so-called defeated army and at the same time proved that Jerry's crack Afrika Corps can be beaten by men from our country when given proper equipment. Sort of disproves the invincibility of the German military machine, doesn't it? We didn't have any special training at home, but there's nothing like the real thing, although too much desert tells its own story. The whole thing is that the type of country itself always wins. People laughed when the Eyeties were giving themselves up after Jerry left them in the desert, but what else could they do? They had no water and you know what that means, don't you Nan?

And with that remark I'll say good night. My kitten has just come in and has settled down on my lap for a sleep. It doesn't seem too sure of this pen though and is trying to investigate (damn it!).

Well dear wife, I'll say goodnight again and cheerio till the next time.

19 December 1942   *Wedding anniversary plans*

Well dear, I will tell you what will happen tomorrow Sunday 20 December, our second anniversary.

In my tent, I have a 'side-board' otherwise a box standing up on end. The 'shelves' which are just pieces of wood stuck in, usually contain items such as soap, razor, toothpaste etc. On the top I have my fags, matches, a few odds and ends, this writing pad and my ash tray (a tin lid). All this, by the way, stands beside my bed, which at present is a tabletop on some linoleum. An exceptionally good bed and the envy of some others. You see, having no legs it doesn't take up much room on a lorry, so can therefore be classed as highly 'mobile'. The reason I tell you this Nan, is so you can imagine my present home. Candidly, this place is all right, and taking things on the whole, I could be a lot worse off, and have been.

But now for tomorrow, (if all's well) I intend to clear off the top of my 'side-board' and cover it with a towel I have washed for the purpose. On this I will place a stand (borrowed) and on that stand will be our wedding photo and provided there is no interruption it shall stand there for the twenty-four hours. During the day perhaps about 2 o'clock which is midday at home I shall have a 'wee fire'. Call it sentiment if you wish Nan, but there you are, I always was inclined that way.

It is my earnest wish that this is the last time it will be necessary for me to write and tell you the story of how I spent our wedding anniversary.

Well dear wife, it is getting late and cold and these two facts mean that this poor man should be starting to make his bed for the night.

The kitten has come in for the same reason and some times I believe in the story of animal instinct about bed-time. So dear wife I'll say good night, cheerio for the present and may I also add my best wishes for the New Year of 1943 to you and to all my people at home and elsewhere. Good night again dear wife.

Yours always,

Alex

Xxxxxxxxxxxx

27 *December* 1942   *The story of Alex's Christmas*

My dear Nan,

Here I am for another little chat to you and I may as well begin with the story of how I spent my Xmas. The general impression is that of plenty of beer and drunk men. Almost everyone has been under the influence now for about four days, but things are becoming quite normal now, and it looks as if it is finished for another twelve months.

We had a concert the last two nights and it was a real good show. We had a proper stage too, with curtains and scenery. The curtain was made with blankets and the scenery from pieces of old tents. The paintings were really clever and were done by one of the lads who had studied drawing and painting in 'civvy street'. The 'ladies' dresses were also well done from pieces of dear knows what and were made by another lad who was a dress designer back home. We had real electric lighting rigged up and also managed to find a piano.

The show was such a success the first night that it was repeated the next night in the presence of all the 'brass hats' from round about. We had excellent talent which included good singers, two good pianists and two good violinists. Then we had our comedian who was just his natural self and of course our actors for dramas.

As I said, Nan, it was a grand show for just a crowd of gunners and it satisfied everybody so much that there is some talk of the show going to some of the hospitals in the area. The old '276' battery again. It was a great effort for a first time and it meant a lot of hard work.

The way things are going now, I don't think this mob will go 'desert ratting' again, but rather become a sort of garrison idea in some coast town. That will mean the coming back of shining brasses etc. Dear me. What a thought.

Here I am back to add a bit more chat and give you an idea of life in this town which we can visit. They have cinemas, cafes and all the usual touts of an eastern city. A Cabaret has opened up and this is just the usual cafe with a larger bar than usual and the presence of women. Sort of 'hostess' idea. These women try and solicit drinks from the soldier, and for every one they get, the 'Boss' gives the girl a small 'chit' and for every 'chit' they get so many piastres. The drink which the man pays for is phoney and just coloured water. A modern version of the old 'Honky Tonk'.

This place has been doing good business, but things became a bit more lively during the last few days. The stuff which is sold over the bar is known as 'gut rot' such as 'Scotch Whisky' made in Egypt. Oh! I forgot to mention that some of the girls do a dancing turn on a stage. Well Nan, as I said, things became quite hectic recently, between chaps dancing up on the bar and helping themselves to just a few bottles of the 'gut rot', throwing a few bottles about (empty) and perhaps a few chairs up among the band. Just a little boyish fun that's all (ha ha).

I have just heard the outcome of their 'cheery disposition'. A barbed wire fence has been fixed up round the stage. Can you picture it Nan?

As I say, a wire fence with iron supports round the band at the 'Albert Ballroom' in Glasgow?

28 December 1942

I shall have another look at some of your own letters before I have a wee 'fire' on New Year's Day. By the way, dear, I had a 'fire' on Xmas Day, round about 11 o'clock in the morning. It was 2 o'clock here and we are a few hours ahead of your time back home. I intend to do the same thing on New Year's Day. I shall tell you how my evening was spent in my next letter.

Before I go any further perhaps I should explain the method some of the chaps use to get 'happy' – otherwise drunk. Out here, good stuff can be had, and supplies of all types of wines etc. are plentiful. These wines are the genuine article but are only meant to be sipped. But when the lads go into these wine shops they don't order glasses. Oh no! It's bottles or perhaps they just hold pint mugs under the barrels. Some of the stuff is liqueur and drunk in very small glasses at home. It doesn't make any difference, it all goes down here by the bottle. To give you an idea of prices, Nan, a large bottle of Muscatel only costs 3/-.

Perhaps you are wondering why I mention this to you, and no doubt you think that all this drinking is wrong. But, Nan, look at it this way. All of us out here have been having hard fighting under very trying conditions, and there have been nothing but setbacks to show for it. Now that things have gone a bit better, the thing is to celebrate, and the usual form of celebration, practically the only one, is to drink enough so that one forgets there was ever such a word as thirst. Put it down to another aspect of war.

Well Nan, this must be all for today and if what I have been talking about seems a queer subject for me I want you to understand one of the other sides of life out here. So dear wife, I'll say goodnight.

29 December 1942

Well today I will try and talk about ourselves.

I notice in all your letters that you mention the fact of these army broadcasts from Cairo, and of course wanting to know when I am going to do a 'turn'. As I said before dear, I don't think that yours truly will ever receive the chance.

I have enclosed a snapshot which you gave me and was taken by Fred in Maxwell Park quite a while ago. The date on the back as you will have noticed is your birthday. You see Nan this was the snap which had pride of place in my wallet, and as I was always forgetting the date I marked it down on the back of this snap. Well dear, one of my mates is rather good at colouring pictures, and he asked me if he could colour this snap, as it had a good background for colour. I thought he made a fine job of it, and I am sure you will be pleased to have it again. He has made a big difference hasn't he? Especially the flowers. I hope you like it dear.

Well Nan, this is about all I have for you at present apart from the remark in your latest letter. The remark was about the handing down of my letters and the way you feel about it.

Never mind, dear wife, that day will come and perhaps quite soon now, and I will do my best to make you happy. Just wait until I come home again. Not at all dear, it'll be a pleasure (ha ha). But remember what I said before about my being a very stern parent? (Ha ha.) So dear, just be patient and hope for the best.

Don't read this part to Mother, Nan, just to Margaret so that it makes her jealous (ha ha).

Until I write again dear wife, I'll say cheerio.

Yours always,

Alex

xxxxxxxxxx

≈1943≈

Back to the desert – the 'angry' letter – rumours of home leave – end of land fighting, North Africa – not coming home – trip to Tunis and Carthage – story of westward attack, Egypt to Tunisia – August, Central Mediterranean Forces (Sicily) – stage debut – October in Italy – turkey meal – bandaged hands – wedding anniversary – Xmas day boss, Captain Macintyre!

5 January 1943

My dear Nan,

At present mail is just coming in what you might call 'wee dribbles'. I see that you have received my letter 74. If you hadn't, I would do the 'novel' all over again.

I thought it would be interesting and to judge by your remarks it seems to have turned out that way.

But Nan, what were you so surprised about? You knew I was in the Desert didn't you? So why be so surprised at a bit of excitement? What do you think the desert was at that time? Just playing at boy scouts? The fact remains Nan that we were lucky indeed to come back with so few casualties. Few compared with other batteries of the same regiment. The fact remains that, although overshadowed by the magnitude of the Russian Front, the Desert War was not a Sunday school picnic.

I think that what surprised you most was that I had never mentioned that subject in my letters before, but always dealt with any subject <u>apart</u> from that one, so coming as it did all at once it must have come as a bit of a shock. Well dear wife, we were told that we could tell our story and everyone took advantage of the opportunity. I hope it didn't upset you Nan, as I don't want you to feel that way. There's just as much danger at home for you, as there is out here for me. So why worry Nan, just keep your faith and all will come right in the end.

Well Nan things are changing a bit now with the sign of 'Officers Only' disappearing from hotels, clubs etc. We can go almost anywhere now, which means that one can find all ranks of army, navy, RAF all together in the same place and drinking the same 'gut rot'.

I was in town last night and we went to a cinema in the afternoon. I saw the film called *How Green Was My Valley*, which by the way was a very good film, but rather heavy I thought. Still Nan, I enjoyed it very much indeed. We came out at 6 p.m. and the first thing we did was to book seats for another cinema! Then we went to a club which we can now visit and is really a beautiful building. I understand it was formerly the Italian consulate so you can imagine the floors and staircases can't you?

I haven't much time left but I want to describe my feed before I finish for today and here goes Nan and hold your breath (ha ha)! I ordered Dinner and this is what arrived. Soup, prawn mayonnaise (with tomato, beetroot, lettuce and limes), roast pork chops with chips and cauliflower, fruit (orange and banana) and lastly coffee. This was all served in a fine building with perfect service. I know you will want to know what it cost (being a woman) so to please you, it only cost 3/– !

Well dear wife this is all for today so I'll say cheerio until I write again.

6 January 1943

I'm afraid that the news I have for you today is not very good. It has to do with the last two parcels I sent from here. We have just had word that parcels posted between certain dates have been lost through enemy action. I have a funny feeling that will include the parcels meant for you.
Well dear wife this must be all meantime.
Cheerio, good luck and God bless you all.
Yours always,
Alex
Xxxxxxxxxxxxx

16 January 1943

My dear Nan,
I have a feeling, just a feeling mind you, that we have some more desert 'rat-ting' to do yet.

And now for some gossip about your latest letters numbers 75 and 77. Well dear, I'll start with 75 which by the way came after 77. This letter contained a snap of yourself and was taken at Troon. Allow me as a husband to say that you look very nice indeed, very smart if I may say so (being a husband of course).

The next part of your letter says that this is my third time in this campaign out here, well Nan it looks like a fourth time now, but don't you worry, everything is going to be alright.

I mentioned in my last letter Nan about the lovely pairs of socks you have sent me. It seems rather queer that I should have told you <u>not</u> to send any socks, but Nan I know you will understand when I say that I am doing what I think best. You see dear, this 'rot' I have had on my feet seems to be a trouble that nobody seems to have a permanent cure for out in this country with its heat and sand. Well Nan, I have come to the conclusion that this trouble is a germ which gets into the socks and no matter how often these are washed it never kills these germs. It was because of this idea of mine that I thought of doing <u>without socks.</u> I now find that by doing this and by washing my feet, and even at times washing the inside of the boots, I am quite comfortable and that my feet are very hard and dry. By the way Nan, I did have quite a few blisters at first. The heavy boots seemed to be against all the sore parts (ha ha). I know that I am making your job much harder as far as parcels go, but then dear I must be fair, mustn't I?

By the way I have lost my wee kitten. I had to leave it behind but in good hands. Goodnight again dear wife.

19 January 1943   *Back to the desert*

Yes! Dear [it] looks like more desert ratting. But do you know dear in a way I am pleased because that means there is a chance that I have seen the last of Egypt and I am not sorry. The whites in this country are the shopkeepers and they are unfriendly towards us and won't mix with soldiers. How they rob us. If I ever hear anyone boasting about this land of Egypt I'll know they haven't been in the rotten country any time. And so Nan, now that I have given vent to my feelings I'll talk about something decent, 'ourselves'.

Well Nan, you start off by mentioning the Map and of how you have followed us in your small school map. The way things are going you would be better off with a larger map and you'll see that we are getting nearer home now than we've been. Home is a lovely word dear and I often think of 85 which I consider my home. They say that a man's home is where his heart lies and well Nan dear you are 85 to me. (Tut tut becoming sentimental – the old fool.)

Now for the airgraphs from December 1942. The first one will go in the box beside all the other 'specials', which deal with December 20. These special letters are the ones which do not go in to my wee fires. You next mention twin beds and you ask me if I remember and also understand. Of course I do and I am determined to write to my MP to have such a cruel practise abolished. All right for old maids but a threat to the nervous system of us folks of flesh and blood. I take a very poor view of the whole practise which is just another form of the snobbery of the bourgeois (is that word spelt correctly?). In any case I am sure you understand (ha ha).

Yes dear, as you say our wedding group seems to have been well split up, but then Margaret is nearer home now. The last word I had from Ewan said that he expects to be back in the early summer and for myself I'm gradually coming nearer.

And this coming nearer reminds me of something. You know Nan, that when an army retreats fast as Jerry has done out here, quite a lot of stuff is left behind. Well we've come across lots of stores, etc. and although I can't give any details I can give you a warning which you must pay heed to and that is 'take great care of your gas mask'.

And now your letter goes on to the gathering of your Christmas gifts and after reading of the half dozen eggs etc., I say God bless you Nan for your efforts to make people happy.

Here I am with my new pad which by the way I don't think a great deal of. I also have an extra bottle of ink just in case, as being an old timer I know just the little extras I may need as time goes on. Before I go any further, I must warn you to not worry if my mail becomes scarce. Frankly, I'll tell you now, I don't expect to write any more letters for a week or a fortnight.

But I'll continue with my gossip and on to the subject of what you call good parodies. I know quite a few myself. The most 'choice' being one called Eskimo Nell. However, I have an idea that it will be just that wee bit too choice for Margaret and her friends. Of course I don't know too much about women (ha ha).

Yes dear, our anniversary and being two years married.

Like yourself, Nan, at times it seems to me to have passed very slowly and yet when I think of when I held your hand at 85, it seems only a few days ago. Certainly not anything like over 2 years ago. I hope dear wife that we are together for our next celebration. Things are looking more rosy now than they have been for a long time.

God bless you all.

Yours always,

Alex

Xxxxxxxxxxxx

23 January 1943: Allied troops take Tripoli – the last remaining Italian-held city in North Africa

11 February 1943

My dear Nan,

This is my first letter for about a month now but I have had absolutely no chance to write even a few lines. I have been without any letter myself during the past month and it was only two days ago that your mail caught up. So it looks as if things are becoming more settled again.

I wish I could say the same about the weather, which is a vast change from what I have been used to in Egypt. Instead of heat and sand it is now very cold and also very wet. This part of Africa really is a lovely country and reminds me very much of some parts of Scotland. It seems very fertile and the inhabitants have worked very hard indeed. The civilians have stayed put and on the whole are quite friendly. But of course, they have no other choice have they? Jerry seems to be moving very fast at present and it is not at all fair the way we also have to move to keep up with him (ha ha).

And now that I had that little talk on current affairs, I'll have a talk about ourselves. I'll deal with myself first, forgetting all about manners. I am well at present and much more cheerful, now that the rain has stopped for a few hours. It's funny, but when we were in the desert, we wished ourselves out of it and now that we <u>are</u>, we say 'Well at least it was dry'. We are a peculiar race, aren't we now?

Cigarettes are very scarce up here at present and I was a non-smoker for a day or two, until I was presented with a tin of baccy and so everything in the garden was lovely again!

I try to send you a few lines at every opportunity. But I can't just sit down and write a letter when I feel like it. Sometimes I can't find a place to sit (ha ha).

It seemed to me as if you were worrying about the lack of news from your wee man. And after all I've told you. You know I really think I am spoiling you by sending you so many letters (ha ha).

Well Nan, I'm afraid I must leave you for the present and do some work again.

12 February 1943

Well Nan, I'll do my best to write until I am forced to stop. The weather today was rather wet and breezy. The truth is that it could be termed as 'vile'. Everything is wet, including myself and the writing pad. The only bright spot is the fact that we are chasing Jerry and that the campaign out here looks like being finished pretty soon.

Remember in my last letters how I told you that I had <u>stopped</u> wearing socks? Well dear, <u>I have changed my mind again</u> (ha ha), and so the socks are being used! As you know I am now out of the desert and as the climate here is similar to home, my feet are cold. Still, not even the weather can dampen the old 8th Army (ha ha).

Nan, I'm very sorry about the loss of these 2 parcels, including your birth-day parcel. There's always one consolation however, and that is that letter of mine which gave you the whole story of my visit to Jerusalem. The one you spoke about handing down? Of course, I must be home first? (Ha ha.)

None of your gossipy letters have arrived for a long time now. Still I am quite a good second to you for a gossipy letter, as you have said yourself at times. And if that is the case, you must take all the credit yourself. Remember when you told me that I always wrote as if I was in a bad temper? Of course, I have had a terrible lot of practise since. With writing so much I'll have to learn to talk to you again when I reach home once more. I'm becoming a

bit tired of this letter-writing business dear, 'I wanna go home'. Don't want to be 'aloooone' though. Oh dear no.
Yours always,
Alex xxxxxxxxxxx

PS It's still raining.

10 March 1943   *The 'angry' letter*

My dear Nan,
Well here I am again for a little talk to you and I should manage to say a lot before bedtime. Today is dull and a trifle cold. Although a wind is blowing there is very little sand, but yesterday, especially the afternoon, was vile. One of these confounded dust storms had an outing and made things very unpleasant. While I am on the subject of weather Nan, I should add that we had rain in the night before, so don't say that we have no variety in weather. Yes, we do get plenty of variety apart from food which is the one and only Bully with biscuits. However, we do get bread now and that makes a difference. Still when you think of the speed at which we moved up here, it's a wonder that we are able to have any supplies at all. In my opinion it is the finest piece of organising I've ever seen out here. Even the Naafi have managed to give us fags, paper, blades etc.

And here's something else for you. During the past week I have had a warm shower and been to a 'Cinema' show! The shower, or rather showers, was a large tent with fourteen 'public' showers, erected near a well. The water is drawn from the well by a pump and goes through a small geyser before it reaches the actual shower taps. All they do is start up the pumping motor and then they have the fourteen warm showers. It only takes a few minutes to pack up and go elsewhere. By the way Nan, it's one of the many things that the Eyeties left behind, which rather surprised me because the Eyeties I've seen looked as if they never had a wash all their days.

And now for the 'Cinema'. Imagine a lorry standing in the sand with a white sheet draped over one side. That's the screen. Ringed round this screen we have the lorries which have fetched the 'audience'. If you are lucky you have a balcony seat (on a lorry) or you just sit on the ground. The show starts when the sun goes down and believe it or not the films are talkies 'of a kind'. How it is managed I don't know, but there you are Nan, a modern cinema show in the desert. The programme by the way was a Popeye cartoon and a film called *Confirm or Deny*. Needless to say, dear, we all enjoyed it immensely. Like the showers, this show can be packed up in a few minutes also, and be many miles away the next night.

Mail isn't too plentiful but I did have word from you last night and I have it before me as I write. You tell me that you have got over the dose of the flu and that you are yourself again. Whatever you do dear take good care of yourself and don't be going without anything you may need in the shape of warm clothes etc. I forgot about the coupons so perhaps I'd better add 'when you can get them'.

I know you worry because I can read 'between the lines' sometimes and you really shouldn't Nan. How do you expect to keep nice and healthy if you worry about an old fool like me? It won't be long before this do is finished out here and it should help to make the whole war finish much sooner. So why worry?

What a surprise I've just had. A chap has just come up with a handful of mail for me. Just a minute and I'll see what he has brought. Well dear, I have 2 airgraphs, 2 letter cards and 2 long letters all from yourself and an airgraph from someone called Mygrfhh. It looks Chinese at first glance but after a close study it really stands for Miss Kerr (aren't I clever?).

Well Nan, I have just glanced through all your letters. For the first time in my life I am angry with you because you have disappointed me. All through these letters there is a background of fear, of anxiety, of lack of faith. You know Nan, I quite believe that the reason you have been unwell recently is just through foolish worrying about me. I have told you repeatedly that you must try and stop worrying. I know you love me dear and I love you but I never worry about you. I have never lost my faith but I'm afraid that you have. Remember when you were ill and you needed me? Wasn't I at Glasgow when if things had been correct I should have been somewhere on the High Sea? Must I remind you of Tobruk? I could relate lots of stories similar to these if I wanted to, but I don't want to throw bricks at you when you are unable to throw them back. Do what I do Nan. Occupy your mind with other things and don't just continually brood on past memories.

I look upon this war and this parting as just another chapter of my life. A chapter which is coming towards its finish. Please dear wife, please, if only for my sake, try to recapture your old spirit and your faith.

Well Nan it's becoming dark now so I must finish for today. I will add some more tomorrow but not on the same subject as I honestly think I have said enough. Enough to let you understand just how I feel and perhaps after all excuse me for my first show of anger. I will say good night now dear and God bless you.

same night

I have managed a light Nan so I will continue where I left off. No, I won't. I'll start afresh and just say that I have expressed my feelings.

Your letter card tells me of the fine time you had on your night out, about your tea at the Cadora and the show at the Theatre Royal. It makes me very happy when I know that you are at least getting some enjoyment back home.

Then you tell me that you have had a bonus from McDonald's and of course being my wife you have sent me a few pennies as you call them so that I may share in your happiness. It's these actions of yours that make me love you so much. (Even though I do get angry at times.) I smiled at the part in your letter about the bed sheets. By the way, what are 'bed sheets'?

Well dear wife I must finish now as my lamp – a bit of string stuck in an empty tin – isn't so good after all. Good night Nan and good luck.

No Nan not finished yet. I've done a very intricate job on the lamp which has improved it – shoved in a bit more string (ha ha).

If it stays how it is I should be able to finish this letter tonight. The lamp's getting bad again. I'll try another bit of string. A wee bit better, still I've almost finished this page haven't I? This time dear wife, it really is good night so cheerio and good luck.

11 March 1943

Here I am dear to answer your latest mail.

You say that your last word from me was a letter dated January 2 and that you have had no word from me for a month.

You see Nan, we travelled right across Africa without any stops and of course during that time I couldn't do any writing and again there is a difference of almost 2,000 miles between where one letter was written and the next one. We cannot cover that distance in just a few days can we?

Well Nan, slowly but surely I'm wading through all this mail of yours. The first was written the night that you had your outing with the other girls in McDonald's and was written before you went to bed. You certainly speak as if you had a most enjoyable time and I am pleased to know that you were happy, although it must have been awful noisy with twenty girls! And I don't expect that my wife would just sit quiet and listen either (ha ha)!

I was a bit surprised at the fire-watching news but of course as there are a squad of girls it will make things much easier and more pleasant. I agree with you Nan when you say that you are happy and contented working with all these fine girls. I hope I can meet them all some day.

Before I finish Nan, try and understand my show of anger yesterday and forgive me. Cheerio Nan and good luck.

Yours always,

Alex

xxxxxxxxx

11 March 1943

My dear Nan,

I will start by replying to your first letter of 1943. It tells me of how happy you were at Xmas time. I can just imagine the scene when you walked up to collect your prizes. I hope that whoever had the beer enjoyed it and drank my health (ha ha). I am looking forward to my birthday parcel, which should be arriving soon. Thanks a lot Nan.

I often wish I was stationed at home and then I don't know either because out here we have no spit and polish and are left alone to do our job. I don't think I'd like being at home now. Too much parade ground stuff. We do have parades now and then but the idea is just to get us all together to tell us something, such as 'We are now able to let each man have a hundred cigarettes' or 'a bar of soap' (ha ha).

Your letter goes on to describe how you spent the New Year and you ask me how I spent mine. Well Nan, it's a sad story. Where we were at that time there was plenty of drink to be had and I honestly think that there wasn't a sober man from Xmas until the New Year. For my own celebrations I had managed a bottle of the real stuff (Johnny Walker) and I still had the tin of shortbread which you sent me. So the cake was eaten and the toasts were drunk. Of course someone else had some more bottles of other stuff and between you and I, Nan, nobody bothered about much for the rest of that day. And so I passed my second New Year out here.

At New Year I think a lot of Aunt Nellie's steak pie and when I am busy at the 'Bully' I shut my eyes and imagine I'm eating that pie. Still when the sand gets between my teeth it spoils the effect (ha ha).

Honestly dear I laughed out loud at your story of the tin whistles and of course I had to start again when I read the part about Margaret's curlers. It was a great description Nan and I thoroughly enjoyed reading it.

12 March 1943

I am taking advantage of this present quiet time to write every day. Once the fun starts again I don't expect to have very much spare time.

Well Nan today I will answer your letter 84 which starts by telling me that it is a very cold day and that you are seated by the fire with your boots on so it seems to me that 85 is back to normal after all the excitement of the New Year.

No Nan, we don't get a leave every six months. It all depends where we are and also how things are going at the time. If you remember the leave I had in Palestine was my first for almost two years. We won't get any more at present because frankly there is no place to go to. It would mean a trip of over 1,000 miles and when you realise that it would be done in the back of lorries it's really out of the question. In any case this 'do' will be finished up here soon and no one knows what may happen after that.

Your letter goes on to describe once more the fine cheery time you had at Hamilton, all the presents you received and of how you all got round the organ and sang your favourite songs. You have described your visit so well in both these letters that I just need to close my eyes and I can picture the whole scene.

Well Nan, I am sitting on a part of equipment writing this letter in the shade of course. Although the heat hasn't arrived yet the sun is quite warm and has a bit of a glare even at this time of year. The surprising part is that I have on the same clothes as men wear at home, and of course as you already know the nights are real cold. I still need my four blankets and overcoat on my bed at night. There is always a very heavy dew and everything is cold and wet in the morning. But still once we get down our hole and pull the tent flap over we are 'as snug as a bug in a rug'. The dew doesn't penetrate down so a hole in the sand is ideal for a lot of other reasons too. The worst thing we have to put up with are the dust storms which we can do nothing about. Still, like every other climate condition out here they have their season and it is almost finished now. Another month or so and we will be back to shorts again and afternoon siestas.

Well dear wife time to say cheerio and do a spot of work for a change (ha ha).

26 March 1943

I am interested in the story of the dream and I am sure you must have been disappointed when you realised I was not actually kissing you. Of course, I am a bit disappointed myself (ha ha). I'll put the small paper you enclosed beside my other small items, which by the way are inside the small purse you gave me a long time ago. It will go with the small pieces of cloth you sent me and of course the threepenny piece which you wore during our honeymoon (sentimental old fool).

So the poetry has reached 85 after all? I hope you liked it and that Fred managed to get the other one which I enclosed for him in one of your letters. I hope you didn't see it first (ha ha).

Cheerio meantime.

27 March 1943

You mention the different country out here Nan in your letter but apart from stretches of fertile land here and there the whole of North Africa is one big desert and North Africa is an awful big place. However the war out here won't last much longer now as Jerry is almost done. Some of these Jerry prisoners are just boys about 16 or 17 years of age and I am sure that they form a large part of the German Army now.

The water is a bit more plentiful now and we can have a wash nearly every day. But it is not very good being rather salty, but there you are, it's water just the same.

So you intend to keep your savings a secret from your lawful husband, Mrs Macintyre eh? (Ha ha.) You just won't tell me how much 'filthy lucre' you have managed to save. Still, I'll let you keep your secret and you can have all the satisfaction when you surprise me with your savings. It's always an excuse for another squeeze and kiss isn't it? (Ha ha.)

So your customers are now giving you eggs and telling you to keep the change? I can see you running this business before long. I can always come and ask for a job can't I? (Ha ha.)

Yours always,

Alex

Xxxxxxxxxxxxx

4 April 1943   Rumours of home leave

We are hearing a lot of rumours of going home for a spell and although it is quite possible that some of the older Units of the 8th may go home I very much doubt it myself. By the way Nan, you can include me in the old members of the 'Eighth' for we have been in the original Army from the start. For myself, I can't see our Army being broken up after this 'do' out here is finished. Why should they disband a successful Army? We are the only mob by the way which is doing any actual fighting out here. And they said at first it would be a race between the Army on the other side and <u>us</u> for Tripoli. What a race! Don't be surprised if we reach Tunis first, just for spite!

Anyway Nan we will just wait and see what happens and don't build up false hopes on any rumours you may here at home about the 8th Army. Even if we were coming home, nobody would know anything about it until we arrived in the country and I don't suppose we ourselves would know until on board a ship.

On the subject of our letters, I hope that they can continue to be delivered in this fast way. Of course it would be even better if we could talk to each other wouldn't it? Never mind Nan, we may have that pleasure soon again. Now that I am in a sentimental mood, I should mention that by the time you receive this letter we will have passed another of our anniversaries. May I now wish you all the best dear and my congratulations (on picking me out – ha ha). The only consolation I can give you dear is that every date and every day is one day nearer the end. The war won't last for ever. Speaking of our anniversary, you will be sorry to hear that my watch has been damaged and there isn't much chance of it being repaired until I reach a town of some sort. The trouble is I have repaired the damage to one wheel and I can go no further until I reach a town. The watch has seen a lot of service. It carries a lot of scars, scratches etc, but once I get to where I can purchase that one wee wheel the watch is again going to see some service.

Now for the weather. The old battledress is back on again and I still feel cold. Of course it won't last long and in a few days the weather should become warm again. Perhaps too warm.

And now before I finish for today I have to talk to you about that awful subject of money. Did you get my letters telling you that I had sent you £5 through the Army? Well dear, I am going to continue to send you a £5 now and then. My idea is to save say £10 in case I get leave and keep sending you anything I may have over that amount. But here's the snag (ha ha). I will send you this money to bank for both of us and I'll leave you to decide your own method. Whether you continue to add to that Savings book, or your own, or for that matter a new book altogether. What do you think of the idea Nan? Write and tell me will you?

Of course, if by any chance there happens to be a longer gap than usual you will understand that I will be at some place where I can spend some money and I know that you won't grudge me my little piece of enjoyment when that time comes!

All right Nan?

5 April 1943

We have just had a new issue of summer kit. You know, shorts etc. so what's all about these home rumours now eh? (Smells a bit.)

Well Nan, this last letter from you was one of those kind which I hope I never receive again. All full of worry just because you didn't get any word from me for a few weeks. In one of my other letters I said all I want to say on the subject. I only hope that my little show of anger served its purpose. I know you love me Nan and I love you but I don't want to be a source of worry to you. We didn't marry just to worry about each other, did we? (Silly Lassie ha ha.)

Nan, give my regards to everyone at home. I must say cheerio now, so good luck and God bless you all.

Yours always,

Alex

Xxxxxxxxxxxxxxxx

7 April 1943

My dear Nan,

We have handed in our warm clothing and are once more into the thin summer clothes. The rigout is a little different from last year with regard to the shirts. These new ones are similar to the ordinary open-fronted shirt I used to wear at home. The idea is that the shirt can be worn inside the trousers or shorts as an ordinary shirt or can be kept outside and worn as a kind of jacket, having the pockets, epaulettes etc. the same as last year. I'm not much use at describing dress am I? You will just have to try very hard and imagine what I look like. Between you and I Nan, I did look !-?!-!! <u>awful</u> at first – the fact is we all did, but by use of scissors and a needle matters have become much improved. As you know Nan, there are only two sizes in the Army clothing. (Too wee and too big.) So much for our new rigout.

Now dear I am going to be rather blunt but I know you will understand. The fact is <u>Nan I want you to stop sending me any more parcels</u>. I have so much kit now that if I get any more I just won't be able to carry it all. I have everything I need at present when you think of toothpaste, socks etc. And there really is no sense in hoarding it all. I know how you will feel reading this but I honestly think it is for the best.

Tell you what Nan, I'll give you a concession (ha ha). I'll look forward to a <u>small</u> parcel (very small mind you) at the New Year if I'm still abroad.

And this dear must be all for today.

Cheerio.

8 April 1943

You do understand what I wrote about yesterday don't you Nan? I thought of telling you this a while ago but as you seemed to have so much pleasure in the sending of the parcels I just didn't have the heart. As we move so fast, it is becoming awkward to have too much stuff. I promise to ask you to send me anything which I may want, or rather need, and which I can't get out here. OK?

Remember I told you that I had managed to borrow a book from a certain chap who was going in for a commission? Well Nan, that chap has gone now and taken his book with him. I tried all my powers of persuasion etc. but after using every argument he still couldn't see his way to part with it. I even went so far as to offer him more than the original price, but no! Alas, I was beaten (ha ha). Well dear there seems to be no chance of getting the book out here and I am asking if you could possibly get it for me at home. The name of the book is *The Outline of Wireless* by R. Stranger.

I'm pleased to read that to use your own words 'the mail these last few weeks has been marvellous'. I did do a lot of writing at that time as I was by myself for a few days. I was looking after a piece of our equipment which had been damaged and there was nothing I could do until the repair mob caught up. So all I did was to read a lot and write a lot too, hence your good mail.

I'm both sorry and yet glad to know that I was wrong in thinking the way I did about your worrying about me. I'm sorry I was boorish and glad I was wrong. Just put it down to the fact that I honestly did think that you were worrying too much and of course I became a wee bit upset myself. Will you try and forget it dear?

Here's something else Nan. My letters will become scarcer again soon. So don't worry.

9 April 1943

I'll mention my present surroundings. This morning it is very blowy and very cold. Quite a change in fact. But to make matters worse we have only got summer togs, all the very thin linen stuff. So here we are sitting in our little hole in the sand with overcoats. We will probably be sweating tomorrow. Although the sand is blowing rather badly we are fortunate in the fact that where we are there is quite a bit of what is called 'camel thorn'. This stuff grows about two feet high in clusters which are about two or three feet apart. You may wonder why I mention this fact Nan but this stuff makes a great difference to our comfort. You see dear this 'thorn' holds the sand and although all around us the sand is flying around it just doesn't get the same chance to rise in our particular spot. Understand?

Of course, this isn't a real sandstorm. Oh No! A real one, when it gets going, blots out the sun and turns daylight into a sort of greyish dusk. Remember I told you about them last year?

Now for today's gossip which is real good. Late last night I heard someone yelling for me. I thought at first it was the Officer (it usually is – ha ha) but it was one of my mates with a fistful of mail!

12 April 1943

Well Nan I'm sorry I had to finish so abruptly three days ago. You're right. We moved again, and for the second time since I left home, I have come across real friendly people. The first time of course was in South Africa.

This time we moved <u>in</u> the same day as Jerry moved <u>out</u> and we really had a great welcome from the civilians.

As for the town itself, it has been rather badly damaged, but according to what I can see of it and the buildings, it must have been a lovely city before the war. Here I have seen some of the finest buildings since I started my 'tour' of the East.

I am glad to hear that you are well now and having quite a time with the 'big bottle'. That's right dear, you take good care of yourself. I want a healthy family (ha ha).

Don't read that part out (ha ha).

I was interested in the remark of Ewan's about wishing he could see rain. I often wished that myself but not now. I hope it doesn't rain any more for when it rains up here it certainly believes in a thorough job of it. However the rainy season is past now for a few months. I know that this seems queer to you Nan but out here you know exact to the date when the rains will start and when the season finishes and it means that when I say we will not have any rain for months, I don't guess, I <u>know</u>. A lot different from old Glasgow isn't it?

I am looking forward to the arrival of Margaret's photo in her khaki and I am sure she will look well.

Nan, this big difference in the time of our letters gives me a feeling of being very near to you. Of course I am a lot nearer you anyway but apart from that I just get this grand feeling. Well I must stop now and go for lunch, probably the inevitable 'bully and biscuits'.

I was wrong Nan about lunch. Supplies must have come this morning for we had cheese, jam and even bread.

Now back to my gossip.

Dear me, it looks as if I'll never manage to post this letter as it looks as if we may be on the move again.

We got water today which we can drink, and it tastes good too. Hasn't got that salty flavour, which we have had for a while now. Two years and three months now Nan? Soon be three years eh?

Well dear, you finish by asking if I am near a town and if I get much time off? I'm afraid you do not understand. You see Nan, what do you expect a town to be like that has been occupied by Jerry and also had a blasting from us? And where would we go in any case? We can't just walk into a restaurant and have a feed, because where will the food come from?

Cheerio dear.

Yours always,

Alex

Xxxxxx

15 April 1943

My dear Nan,

Well Nan I am pleased to read that you have got over your bad cold and are now almost back to normal. You mention the matter of yourself and the Big Bottle, but that's nothing, you should see what I can do to a big bottle! No, not the same stuff I'm afraid (ha ha). Joking apart, I'm glad that you're taking care of yourself. Of course what you miss most of all is me keeping you warm at night (ha ha).

Before I go any further Nan, I would like to say a few words on all this talk about the 8th Army and the 51st Division. Certainly the 51st Division has done well since coming out here, but no more so than all the other lads who have been running up and down the desert for over two years. It was only after we held Jerry at Alamein that we at last got the equipment and you can see for yourself what has happened since. Up till that time we just did our best with what we had and it is no use trying to stop a Panzer Division without the proper weapons. I always said that if we were given stuff equal to Jerry we could make him run and the last few months have proved that statement. The so-called German superman is a myth and he can squeal and run just as well as the Eyeties. And that's that off my chest.

And now for what you actually say in the letter which was written in your usual cheery style. After telling me of how good you feel you give me the reason for it. Three green envelope letters and airgraphs in the one week! Dear me! I must be writing too much or perhaps it was a time when Jerry stopped running for a few days and gave me a chance to sit down and write.

I'll tell you exactly how I do my writing. I sit down on the edge of my 'bed' (the ground by the way) with my feet down in the hole or small trench dug down the centre of our 'room' (another larger hole in the ground). Then I get out my writing materials and my 'desk' (a small board the same size or nearly the size of my pad). This board by the way I got from the ship I came out on, and carries a notice about the scarcity of water, and of how great care must be taken etc. (ha ha). I cut the board to fit down the inside of my Pack so it serves the double purpose of a writing desk and a Pack stiffener. To go further with this story of my writing, I sit down and place the desk across my knees and 'away I go' (ha ha). So much for my method of writing.

By the way Nan, I tried to write a letter in Cairo on a proper writing table, but I had to give up after a short time, go into my room, take the 'desk' out of my Pack, sit down on the edge of the bed, and continue in my old way!

Here is a piece of news for you Nan. No doubt you will have heard on the radio of how there was a Parade for Monty in one of the towns up here, complete with Highland Division and pipes and drums. Mention was also made of a Heavy A/A Battery standing by during this Parade. Well dear that A/A Battery was us. I had a good view of the whole proceedings and believe me it was quite a pleasant change to see and hear a crowd of civilians waving and cheering and throwing a few flowers.

Well Nan, I've just come back from lunch which was fish, cheese and jam with of course the ever-popular tea and now I am going back to your letter.

So you saw the film *Desert Victory*? None of us here of course have seen that film, but in any case we don't need to be reminded of desert, bully and biscuits. Oh no! What we want is something to help us forget these times. I've had two years of this country and between you and I, it's long enough for one lifetime.

My, my how the next part of your letter has shaken me. Ewan is a pilot officer and poor me still digging along in the desert and still a poor gunner. And to think I was the man who looked upon Ewan as the young one and I may have to call him 'Sir' some day. I've blackened the family name of 'Macintyre'. Woe is me! Tra-la-la-tra-la-la! (The sun is warm but I do wear a hat. Ha ha.)

Being serious, I am real pleased to read of Ewan's success and I certainly wish him all the best for the future.

Eight pages Nan! Dear me, when I think of the days when it was an effort for me to write two pages and even they were written under a strain. No wonder you told me that I seemed as if I was in a bad temper. No doubt I probably was (ha ha). I never could write letters because I just didn't like the job. And now dear me! And without any sentimentality (big word) eh?

Of course, I could say it was brought about by my meeting you, but then that would be sentiment wouldn't it (ha ha).

Well dear wife I really must finish this time.

Yours always,

Alex

xxxxxxxxxxxxx

28 April 1943

My dear Nan,

Today I want to say a bit more about the parcel I have sent <u>you</u>, as I am sure you will be full of ideas, thoughts etc.

You see dear, we will be losing our kit bag and will only be left with our 'Packs'. As you know Nan, the Pack can't possibly hold our issue and our personal goods too, and we have no choice but to try and make room for the issue. Another thing, Nan, is that apart from any kit actually destroyed in action, we have to pay for any shortage. There are lots of 'tricks' with kit of course but the trouble is that although we are 'old soldiers' the officers are also well experienced too (ha ha).

The largest article in the parcel is the pullover which believe me I am rather sorry to send home but Nan it is very bulky and so you see I had no choice. It has been well travelled but it has never been worn. I know you spent a lot of time and had a lot of work with the pullover dear and I certainly appreciated it. I could easily have given it away or sold it but you see I am a very jealous husband and didn't like the idea of some other man wearing what you had made for me (ha ha).

The other articles in the parcel are a torch which if you remember I borrowed from yourself one night at 85. Remember Nan? I've always carried it about just for what you may call sentimental reasons. The handkerchiefs are still wrapped in the same piece of Xmas paper they were in when I left home. Remember Mother wanted to give me a new piece of paper and I wouldn't hear of it? Sloppy me (ha ha).

The first gossip, naturally, is the arrival of my birthday parcel! All the contents were intact and undamaged. The first thing which we made use of was a packet of fags. After the smokes, the biscuits were gobbled up along with the sweets. All in very short time too. The rest of the parcel will be right handy. The scarf, toothpaste and brush, OXO cubes and reading matter. I certainly thank you very much dear and I am only sorry that I am not in the position to show my appreciation more fully.

By the way Nan, I think the snap of Margaret and yourself is very good. Especially my wee sister's legs! (Ha ha.) Honestly though, you both look real well and happy.

I am glad you have got over your cold and that the bottle has helped a lot. The right bottle right now would certainly help me! We have plenty of water at present and that makes all the difference. Although mind you Iced Beer would be much better!

Nan, I'm not trying to build up hopes for you but out here Jerry is finished at last and no one knows where we may be before the year is out.

You mention my 'human being' suits being pressed and aired. All ready for me eh? I'm afraid that they will need a lot of tailoring, especially round the middle (ha ha). Must be that middle age I hear so much about! Of course, being away from all the nightlife such as dancing, cinemas etc. you can understand. Then again away from the wiles of my wife too. Bound to have a marked effect isn't it? (Ha ha.)

So my 'wee sister' is 22 years old? How old does that make me I wonder? Nan, you've shaken me again.

I will look forward to the arrival of the book I asked for and will manage to carry it some way, never fear. If I managed to carry the contents of your parcels all over the desert I can surely find some way of packing my book away.

Yes dear, another anniversary gone and our only consolation is that another day has passed and we are a day nearer the end. I remembered the date and mentioned it in a letter. I think it was by way of congratulating you on your good judgement in choosing me out of so many, Lucky Lassie. Never mind dear, it must all end some day although I hope it is soon. Getting a bit tired of it now 'don't yer know'.

So you go out to visit Ewan in the company of Bill Rankin eh? Woman – thy secret passion no doubt! I shall be avenged forsooth come what may (ha ha). Don't tell me that Bill is going to be another RAF Officer? I can't stand it! And I am but a poor lowly gunner (tears etc.).

Well Nan, I've just opened your letter number 97 and it is a real fine cheery letter and you seem to be in the mood I love, cheery and very happy about everything. None of that depressing mood which showed in some of the other letters and all because you didn't have a lot of written pages from me.

That reminds me. Do you know that you are at present witnessing an event of far-reaching possibilities? Macintyre has at last reached page 12 in the one letter! I won't be able to add any more because of weight!
Yours always,
Alex
Xxxxxxxxxxxxxxxx

30 April 1943

My dear Nan,

When you receive the snaps Nan, you may be surprised that I have not included snaps of Cairo or of Palestine. Well Nan, you see collecting snaps was not one of my hobbies, except snaps of actual desert scenes which are much more difficult to get. Oh No! As usual I wanted something different. It was only after I had collected some original snaps of the desert that I realised a few views of towns would also be of interest. All I could get at that time were views of Port Said and of Alexandria, in my opinion the finest of the Egyptian towns.

I don't believe I've mentioned Port Said. The native quarter of Port Said is vile. So much so that apart from a few streets the whole of Port Said is placed out of bounds to troops. There have been two outbreaks of bubonic plague there since I arrived in the country, and I was in the town during the second one. Confined to camp of course. Port Said is full of exclusive smells and filthy postcards. I think I'll write a book on my travels when this war is over eh? (Ha ha.)

Well dear this is all I can manage today.

1 May 1943

I've had a shower and a visit to the Naafi which is now in the area. With being able to do these things again I feel like a 'base wallah'. Probably, I'll be polishing my boots next (ha ha). The showers were very good and they were left behind by the Eyeties. The Naafi had quite a variety of articles, including tinned food, chocolate, soap and cigarettes. I wasn't interested in anything apart from fags and chocolate.

You say of how you are looking forward to my telegram saying that I am coming home. I'm afraid, Nan, it looks as if it will be an awful long time yet before that message arrives at 85. I know I'm right dear, but I hope I'm wrong (ha ha).

You go on to talk about your New Year and the fine time you had with the pork chops. Nan, that place where I had the rather hectic time at New Year was Port Said. Whenever I think of that place my head feels sore again. It was a wild week while it lasted between such things as wrecking cabarets, taking command of the ferry boat and going for a cruise, drinking everything but water to mention just a few of our escapades in that town. Remind me to tell you the full story some day, or perhaps you'd better not know about it eh? (Ha ha.)

I'm sorry to read about Margaret's rotten time with boils and I hope that by now she is much better and back to her own cheeky! – I beg your pardon – cheery self. I hope Ewan hasn't got the boils now after his wee while with Margaret in the parlour!

I agree with Ewan when he says that although travelling abroad is a great experience and long to be remembered, the greatest thrill would be returning home once more. Dump me on any part of that small island and I would do the rest with the greatest of pleasure believe me!

2 May 1943

I have had another letter from you and it contains a postal order for 10/- and your Glasgow theatre ticket. I am certainly surprised at the size of the postal order. You know dear it seems funny when you think of it. You send me postal orders just in case I'm short and instead of being short I send you money as a present. Still Nan, it isn't the money that counts, is it? But the principle behind it.

In your letter, you remark about the long time I have been overseas. At times it seems only a few days since I was with you at 85 and yet at other times it all seems a part of some other life, or a dream. It can't last for ever Nan, can it?

3 May 1943

The news is that I had a game of football last night which started at 6 p.m. in the cool of the evening you know. We had rigged up proper goals with timber and camouflage nets and we even had boots, and jerseys too. Nae bother! The O/FCs played the drivers and the game ended in a draw, 2-2. Of course being an ex-driver myself some of the spectators had the opinion that I was a 'fifth columnist' (ha ha). Still they changed their minds when I scored a goal for the O/FCs (ha ha). It was a good laugh although we are all feeling very stiff this morning. None of us had played for about two years and it was a case of 'bellows to mend' in no time.

You go on to tell me of how you had a grand feed at your night out with the girls from McDonald's. Tell them that I wish them well for the future. They may not think so, but I almost believe I know them all. Of course, I was always a great ladies man. Look how my personality overpowered you – that was when I was young wasn't it? (Ha ha.) And how I can imagine that feed of sherry, chicken, trifle, cream and coffee!

Of course, you haven't the very high food value of the dinner WE have every day. Mangled bully, spuds and rice.

Apart from all these attempts to be funny, Nan, I am very pleased that you had such a nice time and that you enjoyed yourself.

Do you remember when the newspapers spoke about the 51st Division, said that was the first time the skirl of bagpipes had been heard in the desert? Well, that's wrong, because they were heard here in the 276 long before the 51st even came out here! You see Nan, one of our officers (nickname Plodder) has had a set of pipes since we came out here. He usually starts to play just after dark and as he isn't a Scotsman he delivers some weird and wonderful tunes. Needless to say he goes about a quarter of a mile away from camp and I suppose you can guess why (ha ha). The usual remark is 'My God! Plodder's started now!'

Yours always,

Alex

Xxxxxxxxxxxxxxxxxxx

16 May 1943   *End of land fighting in North Africa*

My dear Nan,

The land fighting is finished out here.

Do you remember I told you a while ago that the 8th Army would probably take Tunis as well as Tripoli just for spite? Well Nan was I right? Certainly it was said at first that the 1st Army took Tunis, but afterwards it was admitted that the first troops to enter Tunis were the Desert Rats of the 8th.

You see Nan, what happened was that Jerry was bluffed. We prepared for the attack from our side while all the time most of our stuff was slowly moving over to the 1st Army side, and just leaving enough to kid him on. As you know Nan, the attack came from the 1st Army, but it was helped by almost half the 8th. And so Jerry was beaten out here as he will be beaten elsewhere by men who for the first time had the proper equipment. The whole story of the success out here is that for the first time in this war the British soldier was properly equipped and that was only caused by the withdrawal to El Alamein. I've always said that given the stuff we could beat Jerry but not until we were given the leaders who could use it the proper way. Churchill gave us Monty and sacked the rest. He also realised how things were out here.

Well, dear wife, that's that and now all interest is in where we may be going next. There are, of course, lots of rumours, some of them being really ingenious, but of course absolutely without any foundation in fact. It's just a case of wait and see.

Well dear, you start your chinwag by saying that Ewan has just gone back to Harrogate after three weeks' leave. Lucky fellow! However, my turn may come soon, and I would like to see them saying seven days' leave to us! However, it won't happen because they know that nobody would turn up after seven days (ha ha).

I very much doubt if I will see him soon. There is a lot to be done yet and I don't see them breaking up a successful army and sending men who may be termed as veterans home. It doesn't make sense to me, Nan. My own opinion is that although we may go away from this part of the world, I can't see us arriving home. I know that over two years may not be termed 'soon' in the ordinary way, but this is war dear, and things do change. Even the meaning of words (ha ha).

You talk of the things we will both need when I come home but that should be a very easy job, because if I am able to save money the way I'm doing now we'll be rolling in wealth by that time (ha ha). Anyway dear, you can keep my bank book for a nest egg as you call it, and we will have a real good holiday when that time comes.

18 May 1943

Well Nan, here I am again. Of course, I could tell you just what happened yesterday couldn't I? And that story would help to fill up this page. Then again, I could start to make my writing much larger, and that would fill up more space (ha ha).

Yesterday was in the nature of what could be called a holiday. We had some Naafi supplies first of all which we were told were a present from the 1st Army. I don't mean a free gift you know. We were able to buy fags, soap and chocolate and 1 bottle of beer per man too. My goodness, living like lords (ha ha).

Later on in the evening we had a cinema show but the film was rotten. It was called *Time out for Rhythm* with Rudy Vallee. I was only sorry that I didn't have my beer as I could have drowned my sorrows!

The best show I've had out here was the film I saw with the Yanks. Although it was only a tent, the projector was marvellous and the talking as good as any I've heard anywhere including home. The show was shown at a Yank drome and we were all so interested in the film that nobody took any interest in the Jerry planes who were dropping flares all around trying to locate the drome (ha ha). He didn't find the drome and we didn't fire at him to make him any wiser (ha ha).

We also had a Naafi show called *Hello Happiness*. Well Nan, you know my opinion of Naafi so-called entertainments. Usually cast-offs from home with a few poor songs and a lot of rotten stories. Well, this show had 3 men and 3 girls and quite a lot of us weren't too keen about going at all. However, as it turned out it was a good and clean show which as you can guess was a surprise to most of us.

There is talk of us even trying to arrange a dance in town, but I don't think very much of the local talent. I've been in a good many countries and seen many types of girls, but I honestly think that our girls at home have them all beaten. There is a freshness about the girls at home which is lacking out here. Certainly, the French women out here both in Egypt and Tunisia are very smartly dressed and do leave a wave of perfume when they (what is the word?) oh yes, <u>glide past</u>, but I wonder how they would look if they washed their faces? And furthermore I don't believe that soap and water would remove all the paint. Yes Nan, our own women at home seem clean beside these other smart races. Of course I'll never state my real feelings when some day I'm dancing with Yvonne or whatever the common name [is] out here; of course! Marie, that's it!

However, apart from that teasing Nan, we are all pleased that the war is over out here, although we would all like to know where we are going next. There is no need for me to tell you where we <u>hope</u> we are going but the fact is that we are sure we are going somewhere else, but where that some-where else may be we have yet to find out (ha ha).

Well dear, I know it is a letter of nonsense but then that's me all over!

Yours always,

Alex

Xxxxxxxxxxxxx

20 May 1943   *Not coming home*

My dear Nan,

Well, dear, I can tell you that we will <u>not</u> be coming home for what looks like being a very long time. Looks as if we have another job in front of us yet.

There is nothing I can do about it Nan, but to repeat that I am very sorry to crush your dreams. Who knows that this next campaign may not last so very long after all

It would be as well to warn you again that my letters to you will probably cease for a while. So don't worry dear or I may have to write you another angry letter again (ha ha).

Now for my gossip. Yesterday was an awful day and we had the job of baling out the tent during the early morning. As you can guess I feel the cold much more after two years of Egypt and the desert. Do you know, Nan, I had less clothes on at Xmas time than I am forced to wear now. We are of course still dressed in summer shorts etc. and the sooner we have the ordinary battledress back the happier I'll be.

This country has its good points too. We get a good ration of water and of course we never feel very thirsty. Speaking of water Nan, it's surprising what a gallon a day can do. I can keep myself clean, wash my clothes, have an occasional 'barf' (in bits) and have one or two fly cups of tea (ha ha). I had to make do with a bottle-full for the best part of two years in the desert when we were warm and very thirsty. Still desert warfare is now only a memory and not too bad at that. The desert is a very healthy place and has none of the diseases which are found elsewhere out here. Of course there are plenty of crawlies with poisonous bites etc. but nothing lasting like malaria. All of us are wondering where we will be fighting next. Still being human we will probably grumble and no doubt say that 'We were better off in the desert'. We wouldn't be human if we didn't.

So you don't think I have altered very much Nan after 2 years eh? And that I still have the smile you love? Dear me if I lose any more teeth I won't be able to smile at all. Do you know Nan, I've lost two teeth since I left home. Imagine two whole teeth eh? (Ha ha.) The first one in Tobruk and the other somewhere in Tunisia. Perhaps I'll leave some more elsewhere yet before I'm home again.

Never mind dear, I'll smile for you even if I have to show the gums (ha ha).

21 May 1943

The supply of green envelopes is very poor and has been for a long time now. We <u>should</u> get one each week but we haven't been getting that. I have reached the last but one and we may not receive more. I have become so used to these <u>private</u> letters that I don't know how I will manage if the supply of the green envelopes stops.

Dear me you have no idea of the worries I have (ha ha).

But enough of that for the present. In your letter card of 10 May you tell me of the incident of being awakened by the news of the fall of Tunis and Bizerta. I know you will be pleased now that the actual land fighting is over here, but this, Nan, is only the beginning and there is a long road to go yet and a long time before I am on my way home. I miss you very much dear wife and love you so. Dear me soppy again.

I'm pleased to know that yourself and the folks at Hamilton understand why I am not able to write them so very often. Another thing dear, and this is a sort of confession, if I did start to write a long letter to Mother, I wouldn't know where to begin.

If you cast your mind back to my first letters to you, and of how you said I was a very bad letter writer, always seeming to be in a bad temper, I am sure you can quite believe what I am saying. My letters up till you 'hen-pecked' me, were very short and to the point. But of course, I've changed now, but it's just when I write to you, because when I decide to write to someone else, it's usually a case of a few words and then a long time chewing the end of my pen (ha ha). I am quite content when I know that you do keep some of the 'juicy' parts to yourself. I don't want everybody to know that you want me to be a father and a very stern one at that (ha ha).

I'm afraid, dear wife, this finishes our talk for today as I have a few odd jobs to do before the end of the day. I'll try to give you at least 12 pages now before I use my precious envelopes. You never knew my capabilities until you taught me how to write letters. So you have yourself to blame for my long-winded affairs (ha ha). Until I write again dear wife, cheerio.

23 May 1943

I had a real bad night last night with mosquitoes. Of course, we have mosquito nets in our small tents but I wasn't sleeping in my tent last night so believe me Nan I was almost eaten alive and the rest of me carried away by the flies this morning. Let's hope that I had no visits from any of the malaria variety during the evening. Mosquitoes are funny things because some nights we have really very few and other nights too many of them. Last night belonged to the second kind of evenings. (You're telling me!)

Well Nan, I will start by talking about your letter 100. You have made a very special job of this letter dear which starts by going back over the past two years. What may be termed a 'review of events' (ha ha). I know Nan, just what your feelings have been and I always tried to do my best to allay any worry which you may have had. I knew my being in hospital would upset you and I had no intention of even telling you until I was told that I had been reported by the Aussies to our Red Cross as a casualty. Anyway Nan, that is all in the past and my only remaining memories of Kantara are very pleasant. I met a bunch of fine lads there, most of whom were very badly knocked up but never complained and were always up for some sort of fun.

Yes Nan, these have been two long years apart. Things are going a bit better for us now and after two years of running up and down the long stretch of sand Jerry has been licked and he will be given the same dose everywhere else. Just send the old 8th to Germany and Jerry will run as soon as he hears we have arrived (ha ha).

You have had your worries dear. Depending on how events are shaping now, you must still keep the old chin up and it may not be too long before it is all over and I am home again, resolved to have no more partings ever. During these past two years dear, the knowledge of your love and what it stands for has been a big help and I dread to think of what I would have felt like without you at times. Yes Nan, if we needed any proof of just how much we meant to each other, these years of parting have provided the answer. Just be patient dear wife and all will come right in the end.

27 May 1943

You know Nan, the folks at home thought that this fun out here was only a small affair, so perhaps they will now realise when they see the figures of captured booty that it was quite a big thing. Another thing too is that the newspaper figures of thousands of tanks, guns, planes etc. does not include what is strewn all over the desert from Alamein to Tripoli. The enemy has lost over 1,000,000 men out here and it wasn't until El Alamein that the 8th Army truly became an Army. I don't believe we were any more than a hundred thousand strong and even at that we chased Jerry back to Benghazi once and held him in the desert for two years. Old Wavell chased the Eyeties with only 30,000 men (ha ha).

And Jerry was supposed to be unbeatable?

Give my best wishes to your friends in McDonald's. However, you might please tell them that no amount of teasing of you will make me change my opinion about that second honeymoon. My mind is made up. 'I have spoke' (ha ha).

Well, so all the women get together and read the cups? I suppose they were very clever and told you about a 'Fair man across the water' eh?

You can tell Ewan that my new job is much different from any at home, being much more mobile and believe you me, much harder graft than just driving all day. Later on, we may have to do our own driving as well, dear me, I'll lose all my fat (ha ha). Anyway, I like the job because it's very interesting indeed and really a very responsible part of A/A. It is fast becoming the main thing in all A/A. Ewan may be responsible for <u>dropping</u> the stuff in the right place, but I've the job of seeing the stuff <u>goes up</u> to the right place (ha ha).

2 June 1943

Yes Nan, the 2nd of June and I haven't written since May.

I have been very busy with a lot of wee jobs and I have also been away from the camp for three days. Believe it or not I had some leave and I had one day in the town of Tunis. It took a whole day travelling to reach there and another day back home. However, it was an interesting trip.

I've had rather a bad time with my teeth for the past few days and I was unable to get to a dentist until this morning. Even at that, it was a favour I begged from the Yanks as there is no dentist of our own near us. Of course, he couldn't spend a lot of time with me, so he helped by pulling a rather nasty one out. I'm a lot easier now although the unpleasantness of the past five days has left my hand a bit shaky, as no doubt you have seen by the writing. What do you mean? Well, it's a good excuse isn't it? Still enough of my trials and tribulations, let's go back to where I was a few days ago. (I mean with the letter).

This card tells me that it is a lovely summer's day at home, Mother and Dad have gone to Knightswood, and Fred is repairing his boots. You then go on to tell me of how you spent the few pennies I sent you. Well dear wife, I hope you enjoyed the spending as much as I enjoyed the sending and my wish is that you will always have the health to help you enjoy your odds and ends. I miss you very much dear wife.

You describe your visit to Hamilton and of how you went complete with new blouse, shopping bag etc. I can almost picture your visits to Hamilton Nan, because like yourself I have a great opinion of my folks at Shawburn

Street. Did Aunt Nellie tell you of how we used to spend our holidays with her? I believe the longest back I can remember was my Grandfather giving me a bit of toffee out of a drawer. I think I was very young then.

However the memory which has never left me is of Aunt Nellie and Muir Street and the smell of flowers and whenever I think back to these days it's the memory of that clean fresh smell which comes first.
Goodnight and good luck.
Yours always,
Alex
xxxxxxxxxxxx

6 June 1943   *Trip to Tunis and Carthage*

Dear Nan,
In my last letter I promised to tell you of my trip to Tunis. However Nan, before I go on to this novel of mine I should perhaps tell you once more of the arrival of your mail and of the puzzle from Fred. Believe it or not I solved the puzzle before bedtime last night as I just couldn't let it beat me! One of the chaps has it at present beside me in my small tent and for the first time since ever I met him he is very quiet. That is of course apart from the occasional ??!! now and then (ha ha).

This story of Tunis should perhaps be interesting to everybody at home and so Nan here goes to start my novel.

Imagine yourself with me on Saturday 29 May somewhere in Tunisia. It is very early in the morning and just becoming daylight. I have shaved the previous evening so after packing up my kit and storing it in our big tent which by the way we picked up and now use as a mess tent – it is always in a mess hence the name mess tent (ha ha). The next thing is to take down our own small tent which we will require for the camp at Tunis. At last everything is ready so off for a wash and then dressed with the usual shorts etc. and of course the addition of the 8th Army sign on my shoulders. (This is a white shield with a yellow cross and on a blue background and they are made to fit over the epaulettes of our shirts.) All that remains is breakfast and then the arrival of a lorry to take us to our camp in Tunis. It is now 6 a.m. and breakfast is ready (bacon, bread and tea). I have just finished and washed up my utensils when the lorry arrives, so we bundle ourselves in complete with small kit, tent and blankets. There are 14 of us, Nan, and bundle is the word. However, as old soldiers, we soon make ourselves fairly comfortable and off we go. We are all wrapped up in our overcoats because in the first place it's still early and secondly it's an open truck. We have a long road to go, almost 150 miles, so I settle down for the journey.

Being an open truck we see all that is around, and the first thing to attract my attention is the fine broad road, passing through mile after mile of cultivated land. It is a great change of scenery for me after years of living and travelling through an unbroken desert. Here on this road I see fields of poppies, of wheat and of corn, all browning in this fine sun. And then Nan, there are trees. Yes, trees, which I haven't seen for many a day. It looks very peaceful and if it were not for the transport on the road, which by the way is almost all 1st Army, and the burnt-out enemy vehicles here and there on the roadside and among the trees, one would think the war very far away. Whenever we come across the civilian population we had shouts of good luck and plenty of hand waving. Of course, as the majority of the civilians are women and young girls, it's quite possible that the first signs of friendliness came from our lorry (ha ha). Our lorry is making very good time so after two hours we have a halt to stretch our legs etc. Mostly etc. (ha ha).

After a short discussion of what we had seen and of the truth of some of the latest rumours we moved on once more, travelling another two hours or so. This time we stopped for lunch of bread, salmon and tea. We wait about an hour and after the officer had caught up with us we pushed on again. We were very pleased to have this man in charge because he likes a good time himself and doesn't care much for the Old Bull except on parade. When he is away from camp like this he is one of the boys and he forgets all about 'Pips' and 'Yes Sirs'. A good sort.

After another hour or so of travelling we reach our rest camp about 14 miles from the town of Tunis. It is only a matter of minutes until the lorry is unloaded and our kits are off and the small tents up once more. We are told we are not allowed into Tunis today but must wait until the next morning, but that we could go to two small French villages which were just a few miles from camp.

We decide to spruce ourselves up first. Boots were polished, badges shined up and we made ourselves as smart as possible. It was 4 o'clock now so we had dinner consisting of fruit, bread and tea. A real good feed too. We weren't long until we were in the lorry once more and on our way to Hamman-Lif. We drove right down to the beach, which looked very inviting, but, however, used as we are to bathing in the nude, we had a shock. There were girls in the water and more were lying sunbathing on the sand and we were having nods and smiles from most of them. But the thing was, I wanted a swim (ha ha). However the officer had a set of bathing pants and was also wearing a nice light pair of civvy underpants, so to cut a long story short, after quite a bit of struggling, he had his pants off, I had them on, we were in the water and no girls had cause to blush. We were the only chaps to go in the water, as the presence of the ladies had shaken the others that wee bit too much. I had a good swim, came out, dried myself and after some more struggling dressed myself once more.

The next question was beer but after going everywhere in town we found that it was all finished apart from a hotel which was 'Officers Only'. As you can guess Nan, this was a blow, but our own officer goes across to this hotel and speaks for a while to the manager, and the result is that we all find ourselves having a glass of beer in a side room of this hotel, ordered and paid for by the officer!

7 June 1943

The next day I am up at 6.30 a.m. I enjoyed a good helping of porridge, sausages, bread and tea. Then I was told that we must parade for a talk by the Major in charge of the camp. Well, he told us a lot of nonsense in my opinion – that we were not to cause trouble in Tunis as the Red Caps were 1st Army and would not be very forgiving, that we were not to argue about the merits of the different armies, that the wine in town is very potent and that the percentage of VD cases was very high. As I said, Nan, a lot of nonsense because we've been out here long enough now to know what to expect in any of these towns. We had already spoken to a lot of the 1st Army and they were not looking for arguments, but were very friendly and told us that they really thought we were the best of fighters.

As for the wine, potent or not, I knew it would be swallowed just the same!

Now to return to my story. We now walk into Tunis itself and the first impression I have is a memory of my day in Paris. The fine broad boulevards and trees, pretty women and colourful dresses and the posters stuck everywhere and anywhere. The town itself shows very little damage apart from the docks. Of course, very few shops are open and most of them are wine shops which you can guess are rather well patronised. After enjoying a couple of glasses of vermouth, I walk round the town. I made eyes at a lot of girls for one purpose (ha ha). To find out where I could get stockings for you! But the answer was always the same – 'Impossible Monsieur'. That was that. I make my way back to the lorry for lunch.

Our officers had decided that Tunis itself is rather disappointing and that we should go elsewhere for the afternoon and we decide to visit Carthage. And so, travelling for about an hour we reach Carthage which again was a bit disappointing as far as ruins went but had a very fine cathedral which we were allowed to enter. The only remarks I have for this place is it is a real showy R.C. church, full of all that glitters and nothing else. We decide on a swim and go back on the lorry again and head for El Marca where we find a lovely quiet beach. There are no females around although we do see some in the houses. As before, this stopped everybody from undressing apart from the Officer. He is the only man with bathing pants. However, I was sticky and I wanted a bathe, so in I went in the nude. I kept out rather far so everybody was happy (ha ha).

But here I come to the most worrying situation I have ever been in. Six young ladies came out of one of the houses dressed in their swimming costumes and while two of them decide to sit and sunbathe next to my clothes, the others jump in for a swim. I, of course, tried to get as far away as possible, but it seemed to me that they were determined to try the water just where I was (ha ha). Well Nan, you can imagine yourself in my position and believe you me I didn't get any help from the rest of the chaps, who were sitting on the sand and enjoying themselves at my expense.

However, the officer came to my rescue by fetching my towel to me while I came in as far as I could, still trying to keep down in about 2 feet of water (ha ha). All ended happily and I managed to get dried and dressed again. We went back to camp and had a great dinner, which was steak and kidney pie, fruit and plenty of tea. Later, we strolled around the village. Things were a bit noisy as the wine flowed freely, but it was all singing and laughing. And that ends my second day and my talk to you.

9 June 1943

Well dear, next day, it is an early start. We must be away before 9 am and when you realise that all tents have to be packed up, including the cookhouse, we do require to rise very early. Now there isn't much to look forward to except the long run back to camp, but as I said Nan, we have a very good officer, who instead of going straight to camp, decides to make a circular tour of it.

It's very much like Scotland here. We head for the town of Karochan where is found the second mosque of the Muslim world – a pilgrimage to Karochan equals one to Mecca. By the way Nan, I don't know if this is the correct spelling or not, but it is pronounced Car-o-an. The most pleasing part I came across is the remarkable coolness inside the mosque itself. The inside was really wonderful. The building itself is very plain, just a stone floor covered with straw prayer mats. Mats have been removed however, and a passage cleared for us so that we do not soil these mats. The soiling isn't the dust from our boots but the fact that we are unbelievers. Nothing showy about the place and a high roof, supported by a great number of pillars, and again very cool.

Yet again we go back in our lorry and make for camp. While we stop for lunch I take a walk through a small cemetery and near a wall are new graves. Yes Nan, some lads of this war, 'ours and theirs'.

Well, Nan, that finished my novel because the day finished by going back to our camp once more, where I still am. I hope this travel talk suits you all at home and that I have managed to give some idea of what I saw and experienced. I'm sorry about the faint writing but this is the only ink which I can get at present.

10 June 1943

Now for your letter 101, which contained the small piece of cloth from your dress. I have packed this in my small purse, which is about the only personal item I have left apart from our wedding photograph, still wrapped in the original paper.

You seem to understand about the sending of the parcels. I know you enjoyed sending them and I was keen to spare your feelings.

You also mention our new kit. Well dear it now looks a lot smarter. I've cut out so much and sewed so much that it looks just like our old issue and everybody is happy. You know, Nan, that the British Tommy was the worst dressed soldier in the 8th Army. All the other fellows, Aussies, Kiwis and South Africans are much smarter and much cooler.

We are beginning to wonder when we are going to have our deserved break. We are now meeting chaps who have just come out here and they won't believe us when we say that we are now in our 3rd year. They seem to think that no man could stand that time out in this country and yet all these new chaps have come across is <u>this</u> part of North Africa, which is heaven after that desert between Benghazi and El Alamein. It's when I think of the time we are out here that I become browned off. Mind you Nan, I'm not grumbling but I do think that we have done our bit and should have at least a spell at home. There are very few chaps out here as long as us now as most of the original 8th Army were lost last year when Tobruk fell.

That's right Nan, you buy a new message bag. A real big one! Because I'll need an awful lot of food to make up for these years of bully and biscuits.

23 June 1943

My dear Nan,

I must tell you of how pleased I am at my mail which came today. I had 7 parcels of papers and also <u>my book.</u>

Yes Nan, I cannot say a big enough thank you. It will be very interesting and will keep me going for months to come. I would have sent you a cable or at least a letter card but first of all I am not allowed any more cables and secondly I have no letter card!

This is now my third summer out here. Two and a half years since I left home and you. I miss my home, Nan, but if I may be just a wee bit senti-mental, I miss you more than anything else. I love you so much dear wife. That's the sloppy part of this letter finished (ha ha).

Your card tells of one of the presents you had from a customer and that reminds me to tell you that I have never been able to buy any article for you Nan, since I left Egypt. Where I am at present clothing is very scarce and I understand that some sisters share the same one good dress! Still Nan, I'll keep trying. Perhaps now I can get some more intimate things eh? After all I am your husband (ha ha) even though it has been more in name only, but some day this spot of bother will end and I will do my best to make up for what I look upon as wasted years. Dear me, I thought I said my sloppy part was finished (ha ha).

You also mention of 'A place a long train ride from here', and if I can possibly guess where it really is. You also give me a hint, that it is a place you have never visited before. Well dear this is all very well, but believe it or not I am going to have a say in that matter and if all goes well, the place I intend to go is, I am sure, quite a long way from where you intend to drag me.

Poor me, as if I hadn't done enough travelling already. South Africa, Egypt, Palestine, Libya, Tripoli, Tunisia? Dear knows where I may land before I reach home and yet when I think I'm due a rest my wife intends to drag me on long train journeys. Have a heart Nan (ha ha). Some place where there is a nice beach and where I can splash in the water, Nan, and I'll be perfectly happy. Oh! I forgot the pub as well, because salt water does make me a bit thirsty. Of course, I may be content with lemonade, you never can tell (ha ha).

You card finishes by telling me that Mother is busy at the machine and that reminds me that tomorrow is going to be my wash day. There is of course no reason to doubt that it will be a fine day (ha ha). I have a vest to wash, shirt, trousers and a pair of socks. By the way Nan I still have plenty of socks and I always darn them before the hole gets too big. Yes Nan, Darn and Sew and Wash clothes and Cook too. In future call me Mrs will you?

By the way Nan, we have been told that we may tell our story up till the end of the actual land fighting in North Africa, so it should make quite good reading. I saw the film *Desert Victory* two days ago and it was quite good. It was interesting even to a one time Desert Rat like me (ha ha).

It's too dark now Nan so I'll say goodnight.

26 June 1943   *Story of westward attack – Egypt to Tunisia*

Well Nan, I promised you the story of the trip from Egypt to Tunisia. The story of the last adventure ended at Alamein so I will try and continue from there. I can't give all the dates but in any case it doesn't really matter does it?

Well dear after we reached Alamein last year we handed over our guns etc. to fresh men who had not seen the desert. We thought we were going back for a rest, but things were a bit too serious so although we were out of the actual line we had to go on to the defence of Port Said, which as you can guess was a fine target for Jerry with the docks, shipping etc.

We were camped just outside the Arab quarter, and we were not allowed to walk into town, but must go through the area in a lorry. Many the day we had to duck passing through on the lorry! However, we stayed there until Xmas 1942, and practically all the troops in the town had a rather good time during that whole period.

However, Nan, like all good times it came to an end and we got moving orders once more, but of all places to be sent to Cairo? It just didn't make sense. You see, Jerry was on the run in the desert and we knew that a lot of the original 8th had gone back up again.

But we soon learned the reason why. We were only in Cairo two days, before we were told that we were going back to our first love – the desert. Of course it was a case of groans and grumbles but that was as much as we could do (ha ha). And so Nan we set our faces and headed once more to our old stamping ground. But what a difference from the previous summer. This time we were <u>after</u> Jerry for a change so the remains of the old regiment was looking forward to a bit of our own back this time. We didn't see very much of <u>our</u> desert. Yes, Nan, we had spent so many months there that we looked upon it as ours (ha ha).

We kept to the coast road and I can assure you that we did travel!

Every day was the same old story of 'keep moving' and move fast. We even kept going some nights by moonlight. We passed through all the old familiar spots such as Alamein, Mersa Matruh, Bardia, Tobruk etc. and we reached where we came back from the previous year. The whole roadside was strewn with all kinds of burnt out enemy vehicles. Among them were quite a number of our own lorries, with the black cross on them which had no doubt been repaired in Tobruk. Of course, there were all kinds of materials like guns etc. and tanks, so between Alamein and Gazala there was a million or two pounds of equipment all scattered about the desert. However, Jerry was still running and we just couldn't catch him at all, so after nine days we reached Benghazi. Having moved 872 miles that was our first real halt and we welcomed the chance of a rest and a chance to dry our clothes. By the way, Nan, it rained practically the whole journey and as we had open lorries with no cover we did feel a bit miserable, but going the right way made everything not just so bad (ha ha). Well, we stayed outside the town for an afternoon and moved off again the next day, passing through Benghazi and heading towards Tripoli.

Perhaps you saw a picture of the 'Marble Arch' in the newspapers, Nan, which marks the boundary of Libya and Tripoli? Well, in two days from Benghazi we passed under that and now found ourselves in Tripolitania with Jerry still running. The country by the way round here is vastly different from the other part of Libya, being hilly with plenty of green fields and trees. But it rained so much that the whole country reminded me of some parts of Scotland.

I have a job to do now dear so I'll stop now but if all goes well I will continue tomorrow. Cheerio meantime Nan.

27 June 1943

Well Nan, to continue where I left off yesterday, but before I go on with my travels, I should like to say a few words about the Arabs both in Tripolitania and in Tunis. Compared with their counterparts in Egypt, they are very sociable and friendly and give us no trouble at all. We have had no cases of theft from our camps or any trouble like that. Of course, they do come round selling fruit etc. but if we say 'No' and tell them to go away, well, they just go and that's that. They have, of course, been under Jerry for a time and I don't think he is as easy going as us. The Army make it a serious charge to strike one of the natives, and in Egypt they know of this and take advantage. All that the people in Cairo, or for that matter in Egypt want is money, and no method by which money can be had from the soldiers is too low. Things are a lot different here, and in any of the towns we can always visit a house and be made welcome. Again a result of life under Jerry. And now that I have finished that subject, I'll go back to my travels again.

Yesterday I finished somewhere inside the Tripoli border.

Well Nan, we still kept heading towards Tripoli and by now the road was very bad with bridges destroyed and of course plenty of mines. However, all went well and we found ourselves nearing Sirte where we again stopped for a few extra hours. We had been going eleven days and had covered 1220 miles. What advance eh? The countryside is just the usual desert and we seem to have left the more fertile country behind. However as we near Misurata the country is again fertile and also well cultivated by the Italians. All this area from Sirte to Tripoli was where Mussolini sent his colonists from Italy. Remember all the fuss about the mass marriages etc. years ago? They certainly did a good job of work, but of course we realise now that this colonisation idea was to grow food for his army in later years and to do away with the necessity of sending food from Italy. But then in these days he never knew of an Army called the 8th nor of Monty!

It was no time at all until we reached the town of Tripoli itself which had just fallen to us. However we didn't wait to admire the town but kept pushing on until we reached a place called Castel Beneto where we went for the night. Jerry was still going fast and we moved again the next day another forty-odd miles west until we reached Soliman. All this time it was raining and although we were used to desert and heat and naturally equipped for same, the cold and the rain made things a wee bit unpleasant. On top of this no one had any fags, so it didn't help any I can assure you (ha ha). As for our holes in the ground well, we were washed out pretty regularly at night. We couldn't dry our blankets, but as they had been wet for about a fortnight, we didn't bother about a few more days (ha ha). We stayed for a few days and it [was] while we were at this site I wrote my first letter for almost a month.

Now you remember, Nan?

There you have the reason why my letters were very scarce for about five weeks and why I was angry with you when you started to worry about that same scarcity. Well, Nan we stayed here for nine days and I received some letters from you here. I wrote Nos. 90, 91, 92. Well dear, lunch is up so I must go and get the usual tea and cheese (ha ha).

I was right in this guess, Nan, it was tea and cheese and bread, which by the way does make rather a difference to our meals.

Still, that's by the way, where was I? Oh yes at Soliman. We stayed there for nine days with most of them wet, and one or two nights we were completely washed out and had to try and sleep somewhere else out of the mud. However, towards the end of our stay the rain stopped and although the wind was high and a bit cold, it was an improvement.

Well, we headed west again and got as far as Ben Gardane which was just like <u>our</u> <u>own</u> desert. And of course much drier. But to sort of finish the whole thing off we had to put up with sand storms. Imagine that Nan. However, the first day we were here we had a fag issue and felt a lot better although water was again a bit scarce. There were plenty of wells in this area but the water was bad and unfit for drinking. It was even bad for washing, being a bit salty and left the body very sticky. Well Nan, we stayed here for rather a while and the food was quite good. We also had bread here, the first since leaving Cairo. We were here another nine days, where I had some letters from you. I wrote 92, 93, 94.

From here we moved up the line which was the Mareth mountains. You know Nan, the so-called Mareth Line is a much more serious obstacle than Alamein. We didn't stay here long as Jerry spotted our position and started to shell us with long range guns from the top of the hills. He was firing from about 12 miles away which was just too much for our own guns, and after his first shot fell rather wide I can assure you they didn't (ha ha). He kept it up for an afternoon and also through the night, and all we could do was sit and take it, which wasn't my idea of a pleasant afternoon (ha ha). As these Jerry guns are well dug in up in the Mareth hills, it was decided to move to fresh positions, until the actual attack came. Well, it did come from Jerry, but he was held in his drive for Medenine, and of course, weakened, which was the intention of Monty. While he was in these mountains we couldn't get at him, so the intention was to draw him out, and Jerry, of all people, fell for it. The target of the Jerry attack was Medenine with its plentiful water supply. However, he didn't manage it, and it wasn't long before we were back again and this time we didn't stop, but went right through the Mareth Line on the coast road as a support to the 51st Division and to fighter landing grounds.

It was not long before we reached Gabes and as for stopping there, well we just didn't. However, we stopped outside the town for the night and believe it or not we lost our officer. Or rather he lost us (ha ha). Still we found him the next morning and all was well, so we passed right through Gabes and took up positions on the road to Sfax. It was between Gabes and

Sfax that the worst infantry fighting of the whole campaign took place. At the crossing of the Wadi Akarit. A big part was played here by the 51st division, especially the Black Watch who really made the road across the Wadi. The meaning of Wadi, Nan, is a sort of valley or gully. The Wadi Akarit had water at the bottom and our troops had to come down one side, along the bed of the Wadi which had about 2 or 3 feet of water in parts and up the other side. This, mind you, all under fire from guns at the other side. However, it was done, and we were now on the road to Sfax which apart from mines, booby traps etc. was not seriously defended. By this time we were hard on Jerry's heels so close that when we came into Sfax it was the day same day as Jerry got out.

Well dear wife I'll leave you in Sfax. (Eternally – ha ha.)

28 June 1943

And still I continue (ha ha).

Yesterday I left off at the time when we entered Sfax, so a few words of that place, as I expect that is wanted now.

As I said, Nan, Jerry just managed out of the town at ten o'clock on the morning of 10th April, and before night of the same day we had settled down ourselves in the town. We took over the defence of what was left of the docks, as it was intended to use them for our own supplies for the rest of the road to Tunis. Yes, Nan, the troops who took Tunis were some of the Eighth who had gone over to give the First a hand. For obvious reasons, of course, no-one knew that this was the case, as Jerry was expecting the main attack from the 8th Army front, and knew that the First Army was weak. But Monty sent most of the units to the 1st Army, and very few of the 8th kept the stuff going. The so-called 1st Army attacked far stronger than Jerry expected, and he was beaten. The news was given out that Tunis had fallen to the 1st Army, but the actual fact was that the first men to enter Tunis were men from Alamein – the 8th Army.

Do you know, Nan, that the 1st Army was supposed to meet us before we reached Tripoli? Imagine, <u>before</u> <u>we</u> reached Tripoli (ha ha). I told you that the 8th would take Tunis, just for spite too (ha ha). I seem to be doing a lot of boasting Nan, so I may as well give you it all at the same time, and this is real boasting too. Here it is. The 276 Battery have a whole list of honours and recommendations at GHQ, and it all records us as the finest mobile heavy A/A Battery in the Middle East. Our method of drill etc. is being taught in training schools out here, and notices are to be found in these places telling everybody to visit the 276 Battery if they are anywhere near, and observe our method. How's that, eh? (Ha ha.)

And here's something else. A statement in that film *Desert Victory* was wrong, because the part of the desert at Alamein called the Depression, which the film said could not be crossed by lorries <u>can</u> be crossed, and was crossed by one unit last summer – The 276 Battery again, (ha ha). It has not been done since, and even Jerry thought it impossible, and yet we got through. With all our equipment, including guns. We took a whole day to cover 14 miles, but we certainly got there. Well Nan, that's all that sort of talk finished.

So I'll start again at Sfax, and I must say that we did have a fine welcome from the civilians, who gave us plenty of wine etc.

The next day, the 11th, Monty came in and had a parade of the Black Watch, and it was that parade I told you about, and which you thought was held in Sousse.

We were in Sfax when the campaign finished. And that Nan is my story from Cairo to Tunis. I expect you will have my other letter, giving you the story of my leave in Tunis by now. These two letters complete the second instalment of 'Adventure and Travel' by 'Macintyre' (ha ha). I hope they prove as interesting as the others you enjoyed so much. Let me know Nan if there are any parts you don't understand and I will do my best to help you. All right? (Ha ha.)

Dear me Nan, 28 pages and I haven't finished yet. I was intending to finish sooner, but I have had another letter from yourself, 107.

I am pleased to know that the snaps arrived safely Nan, and I do hope that they have proved interesting. So, according to the snaps, I haven't changed much eh? Don't you know that all cameras tell lies? Still Nan, apart from joking, although I don't know how much I have changed in appearance, I am certainly feeling very well.

'Margaret writes to Ewan every day'? (Ha ha ha ha) such a funny way to pass the time, isn't it?

It's fine to read of how much you enjoy your visits to Hamilton. You know, Nan, I honestly believe that Mother is as happy now, even with this war, as she has ever been. I know I told you this before, Nan, but Mother's lot has never been a very happy one, due to the drinking habits of my Father. That's one reason why, although I may talk of beer etc. in these letters, it's stuff I very seldom touch. Out here I have been very thirsty at times, and I also had a bottle of beer at times, which I have thoroughly enjoyed. But as for developing the habit, no. I have seen the trouble it can cause. Yes, Nan, Mother has suffered a lot through a man's weakness for drink.

Take care of yourself dear. Keep happy, though it may be hard at times, for a happy wife is the best present you can give me. By the way, Nan, thanks very much for the snap you sent me in your letter number 103. And it was good of you to think of the other one not reaching me, and sending your own. You are looking very well, and positively stout (ha ha), although I don't like your hat (ha ha). What is it Nan, one of these utility ones I read about (ha ha)? Never mind my teasing dear, I really think you look real smart. That is of course apart from the hat (ha ha).

Give my regards to all our friends everywhere.
Cheerio Nan and God bless you.
Yours always,
Alex
Xxxxxxxxxxxxxxxxxxxx

5 July 1943

I suppose by now you will be aware of Churchill's speech with regard to the chances of us chaps coming home, so you will realise as I told you Nan, that I look like being away from home for a long time yet. It would be wrong to say that I am not a bit disappointed, as I did have a sort of wish that I would be able to have a break. However Nan, it's not to be, and all that's left now, is just to hope for the best, and that our chance does not take too long to come now.

The weather is getting us all a bit down. It is very hot and a bit different from the desert. Although hot there, it was a dry heat, but here it is what may be termed humid. I am pouring with sweat from early morning until late at night and to make matters worse we have mosquitoes when the sun goes down, so in the cool of the evening we must put on clothes and miss the chance of a nice cool breeze. What a country!

We have an ample water ration, but before long it becomes very warm, and although it helps thirst, it just doesn't cool. We even have the sea near at hand but it is very shallow for almost two miles and to enter the water is like going into a hot bath. All this talk may appear to you as a grumble Nan, but that is not my intention. It is just that I am trying to give you some idea of my present surroundings.

I have just had your letter 104 which contained a snap of yourself and Margaret at a window. You are both certainly looking well and looking at you Nan makes me wonder just when I am going to be beside you again. When I left you Nan, I had an idea that it would be a parting for three years and although I didn't let you know what I thought, I did give myself these three years. At present it looks as if I should have made it more as, of my 3 years, 2 and a half have already gone and I don't think that events will move fast enough to enable me to get my wish.

Looks like another grumble Nan doesn't it? Still never mind me, just blame the sun and the sweat.

In your letter 106 you tell me that you had just received the few snaps I sent and that you hadn't time to examine them all, but left Mother looking through them as you went off to work. I didn't expect this Nan, so I hope no one was shocked by the snap of the Sudanese woman (naked). I had some more snaps from Sudan but I didn't send them because neither the men or the women wear any clothes so the snaps containing the men in my opinion were not just quite the thing for the ladies of 85. I haven't given any offence have I Nan?

So Ewan is at 85 again? And calls to see Margaret at the unheard of hour of 10 a.m. on a Sunday morning? I thought the idea of Ewan's to visit the Art Galleries with Margaret, Fred and yourself was very patriotic (ha ha). I don't believe for one minute that he had the slightest interest in planes or anything else apart from Margaret. What else can I think when they write to each other every day? (Ha ha.)

I haven't told you that I have a ukulele out here and that I do strum a few weird and wonderful tunes at times. Of course as the strings are bits of telephone wire it doesn't sound so hot but in any case with all the voices going it really isn't heard so it makes no odds (ha ha).

7 July 1943

I have managed to become friendly with a French family out here and I spend my hours off in their company. They don't speak English and my French is really very poor but we get along quite all right. Of course there are very pretty daughters, who say that 'Alex parlez francais tres bon' but perhaps that is due more to my personality than to my ability as a linguist (ha ha). The first question Odette asked me was if I was married and although it seemed a shame to disappoint the poor lassie, I told her I was, adding, of course, the word 'unfortunately' (ha ha). Just manners, Nan, just manners (ha ha). However I had to show them my snaps and the general opinion was that 'madam est jolie, tres jolie. Mais n'avez vous pas de la famille?' Naturally I promised to do my best after the war was finished (ha ha).

Apart from all this joking, I enjoy my visits and I am sure they also enjoy mine. However they have not very much and it is not every night I have supper with them. I always bring a few fags for Papa and once or twice I have had a piece of chocolate for the youngsters.

If you don't mind Nan I will tell you something of how these people live here and a little of their customs.

As I told you before the girls marry very young, and become engaged at the age of twelve or so. Another point I noticed is that the husband is very much older and it is nothing unusual for the husband to be 39 and the wife 15. A man of say 21 is according to what I have been told 'only a baby'. Another change from home is that the whole family live in the same house. When a daughter marries she just occupies one of the rooms with her husband and the whole family just carry on as usual with the addition of the husband at the table. That itself is a vast difference from our habit at home of a young couple trying to get as far away from the old 'battleaxe' as possible (ha ha). I mean the young couples who have any sense that is (ha ha).

You know Nan when I started today's gossip I was not in the mood for writing and now when I see what I have written I was wrong. Of course when I started to talk of Odette it was different. I could speak about her all day. She is very pretty, though not what could be called young, being the age of 17 (ha ha). Again I would add that her flame is a very nice young man being the same age as myself but that would spoil the whole effect of my teasing!

To write some sense for a change I would much rather be home with my own people, and dear wife, with you. Although the folks out here have had a bit of war, mostly from the air, they have not had anything compared to the folks at home, and while the folks at home may have a lot more to stand up to yet, the war is finished for the civilians out here. They really are better off than you people at home and are receiving quite a good ration of food which naturally is supplied by us. As for clothes, well everybody I have seen seems to be well dressed, the men with suits of all kinds including white flannel and the girls with very pretty dresses. Again as the girls wear very little apart from a dress they haven't the same difficulty as you girls at home to look smart. Shoes are very scarce but as sandals are worn by everybody it isn't a great loss. The sandals by the way are wooden and fixed on by brightly coloured bands of cloth. This is not a wartime measure as these sandals have always been worn out here.

Sorry Nan but I must finish now. Cheerio dear.

9 July 1943

We had a concert last night by some Americans and it was real good. Of course a party which contained four pretty girls would be a good show to us (ha ha). There was singing, very good dancing of the acrobatic sort and the usual Yank comedy – very slick. They were a bit late in arriving so we put on an impromptu show ourselves until the official party arrived. Where we are now we are about the only unit of the 8th Army left here. We were first in and it looks like we will be last out. The reason I tell you this is because a joke was passed last night when the hall was packed with mainly 1st Army men and only a few of us 8th Army scattered about and strange as it was it didn't cause any trouble!

Here is the joke Nan.

An officer of the 1st Army told his men that he would give them 5-/- for every German prisoner they brought in.

Two or three days later a chap came in with 10,000 of them. The officer was astonished and asked the soldier where he found them. Well, the chap said it was 'easy'.

'I just went over to the 8th Army and bought them at 1-/- for a thousand!'

And that Nan, is my talk for today.

Yours always,

Alex

Xxxxxxxxxxxxxxx

10 – 11 July 1943: Allies invade Sicily

25 July 1943: Italian dictator Mussolini forced to resign

25 July 1943

My dear Nan,

I have just received your letter 107. To be honest, if I hadn't received your letter I don't suppose I would have started to write at all. But now, of course, being a woman you are naturally curious to know why.

Well dear, this is due to a variety of reasons. First of all there is absolutely nothing to write home about. Things are very quiet and it does not agree with me. Secondly, mail from home is real scarce right now. The last reason, and believe it or not, a good reason, is that I am blessed with a very bad pen and very poor ink. Don't you see Nan that if the pen will not flow easily it cramps my style very, very much (ha ha).

Still it takes a good deal to get me down now after two and a half years out here, so I'll just say 'never mind' and do my best to write.

However to get back to my first reason, I could fill a host of pages with all that loving husband stuff, but even that subject sort of bores one through time. Or does it? (Ha ha.) And also I do give you so much of that kind of letter as it is that I am sure you must be tired of it. (Or do I?) That's right Nan, you are supposed to laugh again. What? You haven't laughed once yet? Dear me! I must be out of practise.

As for my second reason Nan well the long letters are much more interesting and we can both say a lot more to each other in them.

As for my last reason. Well, what else can you expect from a mixture of wog, Eyetie and French inks? Nothing of any good ever came from these countries, so a combination of the three can't be of any use. Just logic, Nan, just logic. To finish up with my international writing I have a pen (England) and a nib (America). The pen, Nan, is the one you sent me last year and it would still be very good if the other parts were up to the same standard.

And now Nan, that I have managed to write almost two pages about nothing at all I should manage a lot more when I do start writing in earnest!

You start your letter by remarking how long it has been since I left you. Do you know Nan, I will be three years in the Army next month. 'An old sodger.' It has been a long time Nan. At times I feel a bit fed up myself but then I say if I can manage the best part of three years without a real grumble then I can surely manage the rest which should not be too long now. Again dear it seems a long time yet and frankly I am fast getting to a stage of just living for every day as it comes. I haven't just reached that stage yet and between you and I Nan, I don't want to really. It isn't a very good way of living Nan, but I am just that wee bit browned off.

Sorry Nan I must finish now.

26 July 1943

The reason I had to finish so abruptly last night was that I had a lot of the 'Old Bull' to do. I should say some <u>more</u> to do as we have been having it now for the past three days. Visits by Majors, Colonels, Brigadiers and even a damn General. I don't know why they choose our Battery for this stuff. To me it 'smells a bit'. Especially as they are all 1st Army brass hats. But in any case their visits will <u>not</u> stop me from writing my letters!

I expect that by now you will have heard of the Musso business. Poor fellow, just couldn't take it. I am not surprised by the news because events have been moving that way for a while now. The fall of Tripoli was the end of Musso. Even in Sicily, it is the Jerrys who are making any resistance and between you and I that was why the 8th Army was sent to that coast of the island. It's rather obvious Nan, isn't it? I can assure you that it really is a fact that some of the 8th in Sicily are men who fought in the desert and all the way from Alamein and we may be over in that part of the world ourselves some day, although there are no signs of it yet.

You tell me on your letter of the great mail you have had – 'A Red Letter Week' you call it. You then go on to say of how neatly number 116 was written and that you tie up all my letters. Interesting, eh? Do you by any chance use pink ribbon? Or is it blue?

Alright! I know I burn them on a Sunday but then that's different. Oh what's the use! We are both full of the same ideas (ha ha). If I'm out here much longer Nan you will need a rope to tie up all my letters. A nice strong and long rope.

It was interesting to read that the papers back home were full of news that we were coming back when we knew for a fact that it was a lot of nonsense. I can assure you that the only men who have gone home have travelled in hospital ships with of course the addition of some chaps going home on compassionate grounds.

You'll see I have new ink. The battery have managed to get a large bottle and we are all able to have a small bottle filled from it.

We are getting plenty of the usual dope. Malaria tablets every day and now typhus inoculations. I'm a proper sticking bag now. A form of pin cushion that's me. What a life!

Added to all this, there are rumours that we will become garrison troops. It breaks my heart to think of it (ha ha). I certainly hope that it never comes off. We have been so well used to moving about that the idea of perhaps being stuck in the same place for many months is too much.

So Margaret has been chosen for a guard of honour? Who is the special visitor? Another useless old fogey like the majority of our so-called leaders who should have been kicked out years ago. It's a good job for us that we have one or two good leaders. As for the rest, well, we call them 'Temporary Gentlemen' and a more useless lot of officers I never did see. With a few exceptions, their whole aim in the Army is a good time and so long as they can manage that they are content. As for their men, well they can look after themselves. Last year in the desert when the ration of water was a bottle a day for all purposes, the men got that ration, and felt thirsty all the time while certain officers at the same time could have a shower. That's only one of the many incidents of the ignorance of those 'Temporary Gentlemen'. What a 'shower'.

Now I must stop for a news flash. Remember I told you of all these brass hats visiting our site? Well Nan, they have just reported that <u>we</u> are the best trained Battery in the Middle East. And yet there are rumours of us going garrison. What a comedown for a crack mobile battery (ha ha).

No Nan, I'm afraid that I can't think of the place you have decided upon for our second honeymoon. Still, why worry – any old place will do me (ha ha).
Yours always,
Alex
Xxxxxxxxxxxxx

31 July 1943

My dear Nan,
I have just finished the story of your time at Ardifur. Now dear don't be thinking of me so much to the extent of spoiling your own spell at Dunoon with Fred and Peg. I know that you miss my company but there is very little you or I can do about it. I know how you are feeling dear because I'm sure I miss you every bit as much. But there you are Nan, why worry?

So the wee boats are still doing well at Dunoon eh? We did have a pleasant time with them Nan, didn't we, and it certainly doesn't seem like three years ago. My, my how time flies? (Ha ha.)

By the way Nan, in my last letter number 129 will you tell me if there has been any cut out? You see I started by telling you of how we were again being pestered by brass hats who were doing nothing for us but causing a lot of discontent among the men. The sooner we go onto the line again the happier we will be. We will not have any of these decrepit old B...... fussing around us then. They will be, as usual, many, many miles behind us and well out of the way.

I did mention this in my card so I was wondering if it had been cut out. You see the officer sends for you and usually starts by saying 'Now look here this isn't done you know' etc. etc.

He has been very busy recently too (ha ha).

2 August 1943

Yesterday I had the chance of a swim in the afternoon. Only a small group went because it was a basin of dock and as the water is very deep, between 30 and 40 feet, only men looked upon as experts were allowed to go in. Well Nan, it was my first go at real deep water but I managed alright. I started by swimming across the corner of the dock to a rope and then after a little while I was swimming right across the full width and also back again. 'Nae bother at a'' (ha ha). The reason I have told you this Nan, is because it is quite a thrill conquering deep water for the first time believe me, I mean real deep stuff.

You know dear, you certainly flatter me, always telling me of how neat my letters are and now you have started to line off your paper first with pencil before you start to write! I don't know why you do this Nan because although I do spend perhaps a little time with my letters it's just because I have more time than you and I find that it's really a good way to pass what would otherwise be very weary hours. Another thing dear, is the fact that writing is a part of one's nature and I don't see why you should try and change it. You say that your writing is always a scrawl but Nan I like your scrawl as it's just part of you. So don't try and be all neat, just be yourself. Your way of writing is as much a part of you as your very quick and smart walk and I like your walk (ha ha).

But perhaps you will be saying that I'm flattering you now? So just in case you are thinking of such a terrible thing, I'll go back once more to your letter.

Now I am at the part when you talk about sets of pink and of blue. Dear me, putting ideas in my head (ha ha). Not content with doing all that damage, you go on to tell me of blue nighties and pink pyjamas. Look Nan, my hand is shaking already. How do you expect me to concentrate on my letter after that shock? Perhaps it would be better if I said cheerio for today?

Well dear, I have just had a smoke and I feel a lot better now so I'll just carry on. But don't do it again (ha ha). You finish off this subject by wishing that before long you are packing my pyjamas with yours. It will be a change to wear them again if only for a little while! Never mind my teasing dear, I am looking forward to these days every bit as much as you are, and I'm in every way just as sentimental as you are, although being a man, I try to act big and pretend that I am not but very hard instead (ha ha).

You finish your first day's talk by saying that the tea is ready and that reminds me of a bit of gossip for you. A Naafi has opened where we are now and all they sell is tea and buns. But when you realise that this is our first chance of tea and a bun for over six months, well it is a right good thing. The charge is 1 franc for tea and 1 franc for buns. A big difference from the drinks of lemon water we used to buy from the civvies at 5 francs a glass.

1) Alex and Nan, Clyde coast, Summer 1940.

2) Alex and Nan's wedding day, 20 December 1940.

3) Alex in Durban, South Africa, April 1941.

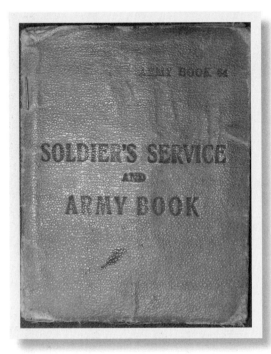

4) Alex's Soldier's Service and Army issue book.

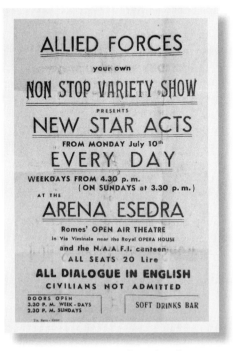

5) An advert for an Allied forces' Variety show.

6) 'Oh what hairy knees. The old smile.' Alex with the Middle East Forces (MEF), August 1941.

7) 'Is it true what they say about the Middle east Forces?' Alex, August 1941.

8) 'If only I could have a nice pillion lady.' Alex, April 1942.

9) Alex, May 1942.

10) Alex's diaries.

11) Nan in Dunoon, 1942.

12) 'Just a bunch of nice quiet boys somewhere in the Western Desert.' Alex, April 1942.

13) Nan at '85' in Glasgow, April 1942.

14) Alex: a picture with a story.

15) 'Another view of the romantic desert. Just a little sandstorm! Two of our officers.'

16) The 276 Battery at work.

17) In the desert: 'Near misses at MERSA MATRUH. Jerry had hit our petrol dump.'

18) 'At the top of Hell-fire Pass (Halfaya Pass). Note the tea can hanging nice and handy on the side of the lorry.

19) Above: A selection of Alex's letters to Nan.

20) Right: Nan and her sister Margaret in front of '85' in 1943.

21) 'Don't I look stern?' Alex, January 1944.

22) Nan's telegram from Alex informing her of his discharge from hospital.

23) 'A leg show.' A photograph of Nan and Margaret received by Alex in December 1944.

24) Alex in Rome, July 1944.

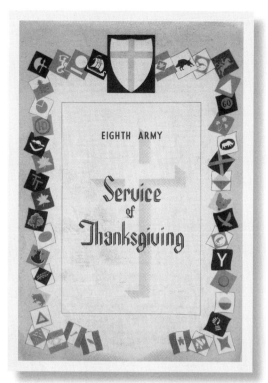

25) This leaflet was among the suitcase memorabilia.

26) Memories: a small tin in the suitcase had train and cinema tickets from Cairo and a tiny note sent by Nan.

27) Alex in Florence, February 1945.

28) Alex in Venice, May/June 1945.

29) Reunion: Alex and Nan in
July/August 1945.

30) The Macintyre family, summer 1955.

31) Alex (Dad) and me, winter 1958.
At forty-eight years old he already
has heart problems.

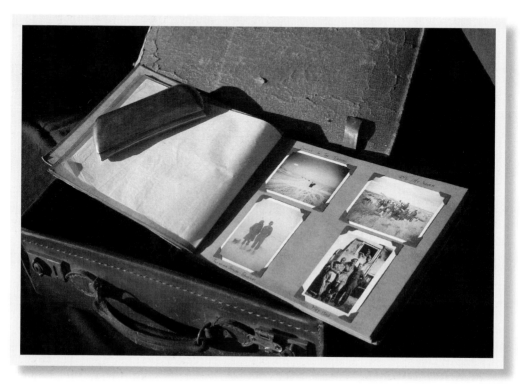

32) The suitcase with the original photograph album and Alex's reading glasses.

So on my night out I just go down to the Naafi and guzzle cup after cup. The cups by the way have no handles and we are told that they are the kind which are now made at home. Sort of 'Utility'. Anyway they are no good because by the time we carry the hot tea from the counter to the chair half of it has landed on the floor, either with or without the cup. Still at present, there are plenty of cups, so why should we worry.

And now for your letter again, which by the way you haven't added to from the previous day. Terrible I calls it (ha ha).

You mention the weather and of how warm it is and of how you are all complaining of the heat. I suppose that if I was with you I would say it was cold. As for my standing the heat out here, well Nan, one gets used to anything. Even now as I write this my body is glistening in its usual way. Hasn't started running down my legs yet, but as we are nearing the heat of the afternoon it won't be long now. Still, I don't worry because I'm quite satisfied to sweat. I would worry a lot more if I didn't.

Don't you worry about the mail bag coming here and with none for yours truly Nan. That doesn't happen very often I can assure you. As for my writing to <u>you</u> well its common talk here of how Mac' writes every day when he gets the chance. But what bothers them is what I find to write about (ha ha). They don't know but the answer is 'Them'. (Ha ha.)

So you [are] weary to see me? After all this is over you'll have so much of me that you will wish me far away again. Or will you? (Ha ha.)

Your letter goes on to describe your visit to the Livingstone Memorial at Blantyre and you tell your story very well indeed. You know dear for all the years I have been near that place I have never been to that memorial. You can take me round with you some day eh? And tell me all about it.
Cheerio, good luck and God bless you all.
Yours always,
Alex
Xxxxxxxxxxxxx

5 August 1943

My time today is very short so it won't be long before I am saying cheerio again. There you are, that's a fine way to start a letter!

As you have heard for yourself on the radio etc. there is only a very small part of the 8th Army in Sicily, so where we go next is a bit of a mystery. Candidly, we would much rather be on the move again and get away from all these old brass hats with their drills of very old vintage. Pre-Boer War I think. Also we are not used to being stuck in the one place and the idea of perhaps being more or less stuck for a long time to come is more than I can bear. Or for that matter all of us can bear.

Well dear my time is up.

6 August 1943

So the weather is fine and sunny in Glasgow eh? Who knows, I may be with you next year to enjoy it all. You have been very patient and always that cheery wee wife I left behind. Still dear our time will come and we will make up for all the anxiety and worry. Mind you dear, I'm afraid that most of the worry has been on your side, because I look upon this period as just another of my travelling adventures and only a chapter in my life. The trouble is however that it's a longer chapter than I expected! (Ha ha.)

Still, only a few months was enough to clear Africa and it is rather a big place. As for Italy, I don't think the Eyeties themselves have much heart left for fighting now, although the large German forces in Italy will cause a lot of trouble. You will notice that it's Jerry who is holding in Sicily.

It's becoming darker now Nan so cheerio meantime.

8 August 1943

Well dear, we have had a move to a rest camp. We are not on a site now and the guns are laid past and it is a return to the days of Arbroath and Edinburgh. Just drills etc. with plenty of foot slogging and square bashing. You could call it a change but I'm afraid not a very welcome one. All of us are hoping for a move very soon. The sooner the better as I was never meant to be a soldier. Oh no, not me! (Ha ha.)

Now dear, I have a surprise for you as I am enclosing a snap which was taken a long time ago on our way up to Tunisia. It was taken just outside Benghazi and when we had a halt for the very favourite job of making tea. We don't need to be told twice to halt and 'Mask'. More than often we make the tea and it's not the first time we then have to move with the tea in our hand. It may not seem much to you but you just try and jump on to a moving lorry with a cup of tea in your hand and also try and drink from the cup when the lorry is moving! It is very interesting (ha ha).

I'll finish now dear, good luck and God bless you.
Yours always,
Alex
Xxxxxxxxxxxxxxxx

25 August 1943   *Central Mediterranean Forces (Sicily)*

My dear Nan,
Yes, Nan, after all these long and weary months I have at last finished with Africa and its everlasting sand and heat.

My new address is Central Mediterranean Forces (C.M.F.) and that gives you a good idea of where I am. Somewhere on the other side of the Med. And I am sure it's this reason that has caused the 'powers that be' to allow us to tell our people at home that we really are here in the 'Vineyard of Europe' namely the island of Sicily.

I am a little step nearer home.

I know it's a long way yet but I always was rather an optimist (ha ha).

I'm not sorry to leave Africa with its sand. The main change between here and North Africa is the countryside. Here we have no sand but hills, trees and believe it or not running streams of water. It is very rocky in parts. There are all kinds of fruit, apples, lemons etc. and of course miles upon miles of grapes. Grapes may be alright for invalids but too many are not quite the thing (ha ha). Anyway the Eyeties are to blame for running away and leaving their vineyards full of very nice grapes (ha ha).

27 August 1943

I have had no word from home since I wrote last so I will continue with some talk of Sicily. It is certainly an island of contrasts. Mountainous barren country and green fertile valleys. The highest mountain is of course our friend Mt Etna which is always smoking. Let's hope she doesn't become angry while I'm here.

As you can guess, Nan, it's in the valleys that the fruit grows. I mentioned the hilly regions already where the trees are, although I may add to the lemons etc. also tomatoes and almonds. Frankly, Nan, it is a land of plenty so far as fruit is concerned. Every known kind grows here and as for the methods, well they are rather primitive and not much farther advanced than Egypt. The same can be said of the living conditions in the villages too, where the roads are very narrow and full of holes. Walking on the pavements is quite an interesting job because one never knows just when a basin of water or other unwanted fluid will come down from an upstairs window (ha ha). This is not intended for anybody in particular and it's just your bad luck if you happen to be there at the time. I have seen quite a few near misses! The last one was when I was passing through one of these villages and a 'young thing' made eyes at me. Of course, perhaps I winked first but that is neither here nor there (ha ha). Anyway, to get back to my story this young lady was doing her very best in my direction when something came from above in her direction (ha ha). Sort of cooled her ardour (ha ha).

To sum up my impression it is of closely packed houses, in some of them the street door opens on the bedroom (embarrassing eh?), unshaven men, untidy women and dirty kids. I don't give the people much praise do I Nan? Well, I'm afraid I really can't as I must just write of what I see myself. I always have done up to the present and I don't think I have really closed my eyes to any good points due to prejudice. Or have I? I haven't much time now. As you can guess, I have a wee bit of work to do now and then (ha ha).

I must tell you that in these valleys there are millions of mosquitoes, which make life just hell as soon as the sun goes down. We sweat all day and when the cool of the evening comes instead of being able to take advantage of this we have to 'dress up' usually in overalls with our sleeves down. The only parts we have uncovered are our hands and face. Even this we have to cover with mosquito cream, which makes us sweat something awful. Life at night is very unpleasant.

I do hope I have some word from you very soon. It does not matter how interesting I may make my description of the places I have seen, a few words of our own affairs just makes my letters a wee bit more worthwhile.

Cheerio dear wife.

28 August 1943

I really don't expect any of my letters from home for a few days yet. You see Nan, they will still be marked M.E.F. (Middle East Forces) and so instead of coming straight here, they will all go to North Africa first.

I have looked around here and there is plenty of room for various improvements in Sicily with regards to getting the best out of the land and our one time boss of Italy had no need to send colonists to Libya. But he didn't want that. His idea about the northern Africa colony was to feed his army when the time came for his attack on the Suez. He certainly looked a long way ahead and at that time our dumb leaders thought he was a fine man.

The people of Sicily seem to be quite friendly towards us, although I do believe in watching my back. Seems a favourite pastime of the Sicilians, to wait until the night is dark. This, by the way Nan, is not my personal experience, but just what has been said by other people. Probably, I'll find it a lot like the desert tales, just a lot of Old Wives Tales well loved by various authors.

Yours always,

Alex

Xxxxxxxxxxxxxxxx

2 September 1943: Allied forces invade mainland Italy

13 September 1943

My dear Nan,

I am going to say a few words about my letter cards. I just don't feel like letting myself go when I know the 'Temporary Gentlemen' will be reading it before you do. And another thing. I am not so able to put in my (ha ha) quite so easily on letter cards. The 'Temporary Gentlemen' wouldn't understand!

Another subject I'm going to deal with is the lecture you gave me in number 113. About the drink question.

Now Nan that is a long story. Just try and imagine what happens when men who have had to go without water in the desert for many months apart from a water bottle a day, which in the majority of cases didn't taste too good. When it was a case that no man would even give his mate a drink, unless on a promise of getting an equal amount back. Well, just imagine the feelings as I have said of these men going down out of that environment to one of the towns of Egypt, where drink of all kinds is plentiful. Here they can quench their thirsts to their heart's content, not because it was beer, just because it was liquid and they could sit down and drink as much as they wanted, can you possibly blame us?

As for the habit forming part of it, well that doesn't exist at all. I'll just give you an idea. The last beer I had was at Port Said and that's almost a year ago and we have had very little since. On one or two occasions we have had a few bottles from the Naafi and the amount has usually worked out at roughly half a bottle a man. Now who wants half a bottle of rather poor beer now? The confirmed drinkers usually have it all. You see dear, the thirst and the sand are only memories and apart from these few chaps who drink for the sake of it, the rest of us have no interest in the stuff now, which a year ago would have been looked upon with awe. It can all be put down to the desert and as one of its many evils.

A few more words about drink. You mentioned that you know the unhappiness drink can cause. But Nan, do you really know? Have you had your own home and chance in life ruined through drink? No! Nan you have always had a good home. But now take what I have actually experienced myself through drink. I won't go into details Nan because you know my story, but do you honestly think I would ever start the habit? After the life my sisters and myself had through it? No! Nan, don't you worry about the habit. I like a glass of beer, but just when I'm thirsty and I don't like the taste when I'm not. Besides, the habit isn't hereditary either (ha ha).

And now a few words about this business 'upsetting' you.

You worry about me when you hear the news. Nan, you mustn't do this. I just don't like it. It's all wrong to my way of thinking.

Quite a number of men have gone home from here on compassionate grounds including some lads I knew personally. What is happening is that their wives are having mental breakdowns through worrying and imagining the worst of things always. Now Nan, can you imagine just what the chaps feel like? Like myself, they were looking forward to going home to what they had left behind and now what? Now dear, I know you keep cheery but I have noticed that you also worry about what's on the news etc. Now an Army is a big thing and you must understand that although the news may say that the 8th Army is having heavy fighting in such and such a place all the 8th Army isn't actually there. The same men don't fight all the time you know! 'Silly lassie' (ha ha). Units are always going in and coming out. If you remember, it was given out on the news that the 8th had landed in Sicily and then later said that only three Divisions took part. Understand Nan?

So dear, don't worry about me. There's every chance that chaps at home are having a lot of action also, isn't there? And look at the advantage I've got. The more planes we see over here the less there will be going over Britain. And so long as he doesn't manage to drop his stuff on the place we may be defending we don't worry.

No dear, it would please me very much if you made up your mind not to worry about me no matter where I may be. You see our worst job is trying to catch up with Jerry now. A big change from the days when the boot was on the other foot and Jerry was in <u>our</u> present position of the 'hounds' (ha ha).

Well dear, it looks as if what I have written today takes the form of one long lecture. You'll be saying that I'm getting a bit of my own back (ha ha). I really am not Nan, but I thought I would get this off my chest, because I had the time and I was in one of my fatherly moods eh? (Ha ha.)

Well dear, here's to the next time.

14 September 1943

And now for some gossip Nan. You will notice that I am now in my fourth year in the army and I have another increase in pay. I'm not sure but I believe it all comes to me this time. How nice! (Ha ha.) I also understand that, being a tradesman, the amount is another 9*d* a day. I'll soon be a bloated capitalist. Well, perhaps not, but at least bloated anyway.

My time is up for today, Nan. Cheerio.

15 September 1943

Once more the scribe returns to his pen for a few words to his lady (ha ha). You know Nan, if I stopped making all these (ha ha's) I could do a lot more writing couldn't I? More ha ha.

The Old Bull only lasted a few days. Here is the reason, Nan. At that time we were attached to the 1st Army in North Africa so therefore came under that Army's routine. It was the first time we had gone 'out of action' since we came out here. By 'out of action' I mean lay up our guns etc. and just go in for the old time parade ground. But the best part was that we had resigned ourselves to a fortnight and it only lasted two days! And were we pleased? Well, what do you think?

Suddenly one morning, the 8th Army claimed us again and everybody cheered and we lived happily ever after!

17 September 1943   *Stage debut*

Nan, I am sure this will interest you. The debut of these great stage artistes 'Macintyre and Dalton'.

We gave a sort of concert and the new act was well received. Dalton had the mouth organ and Macintyre had the ukulele. Yes Nan, a ukulele or perhaps I should add 'of sorts' as I used telephone wire for strings and had ordinary nails to use as pegs which meant tuning with the aid of a screw driver (ha ha). But mind you Nan, it sounded good and we had to give a repeat performance the next night.

I've just remembered something else. I had the chance to see a concert by George Formby out here, and although it was said that I got the chance to go only so I could hear how a ukulele should be played!!, this was nothing more than a display of jealousy (ha ha).

I really enjoyed it. Mind you he was good but I wish I had his instruments (ha ha). So much for my stage career which by the way has been interrupted due to the scarcity of telephone wire at the moment (ha ha).

You know Nan, you shouldn't flatter me so much. Reading out my letters to other girls who say they are very good. You see it means I have to keep up to that very high standard, which I'm sure in time will mean me becoming a nervous wreck. Especially when my pen lets me down and you get the idea I am losing interest in you!

18 September 1943

And now for another few words and of course another day nearer the end. Before I started today I have done some work on my pen and also managed to get some different ink. Everybody has a good name for it so perhaps I am lucky after all. Perhaps you are not interested in talk of pen ink but when you understand that writing is one of our favourite hobbies, or rather the <u>only</u> one for most of us, it is quite a big thing. Dear, imagine not being able to write my long letters? I'm sure the neighbours would be very disappointed if they couldn't enjoy parts of my letters (ha ha). And I always make a point of pleasing the neighbours you know (ha ha).

Well Nan, now I've started on this new page I really don't know what to talk about apart from the weather. Ah yes, the weather! The people who live at home in our temperate climate are very lucky indeed. Just think of a nice mild summer and a not very cold winter and no flies, mosquitoes etc. Certainly that is the most healthy climate. I don't think I'll come on any more lovely cruises to the Mediterranean after this experience. Mind you it would be nice to pay another visit to the desert later on, travelling of course in the lap of luxury (ha ha). I believe I have mentioned in my letters that there is something about <u>our</u> desert that sort of gets one (ha ha).

Here's something I haven't mentioned Nan.

When I was in Catania I saw plenty of instruments such as ukuleles etc. but they had no tone so yours truly didn't buy. They were certainly very nice looking being inlaid with mother of pearl etc. but I wanted the tone. I was offered a ukulele for £4! I'm not joking. I don't think he was very pleased when I told him it was an instrument I wanted to buy and not the town hall!

There is another point about this shopping business and that is the number of Yanks in town, who being paid much bigger amounts than us can buy these articles and this keeps the prices up. So long as they pay the prices they will never be reduced and we don't stand a chance. The British soldier is still the poorest paid and the poorest dressed and gets all the dirty work to do. S'funny?

Still, I won't do any grumbling as I am in a good mood as the pen is working. I won't finish this letter just yet in case more mail comes.

19 September 1943

No Nan, no more word so I'll say cheerio until I write again. I'll try and write again soon.
Yours always,
Alex
Xxxxxxxxxxx

PS I had a fire this morning. God bless you dear wife.

23 September 1943   *Gracie Fields concert*

My dear Nan,

What a feast of mail I have to answer. Just listen. In front of me I have eight letter cards! There are five from yourself!

Last week I had entertainment of a real good sort due to the efforts of our new C.O. who gets all the new acts out here. The first one was the show by George Formby and the latest one by a band led by 'Waldini' and the appearance of Gracie Fields the same evening. The new C.O. says that every man who can be spared from the sites must be allowed to go. I'm thinking it's a case of grabbing all when the going is good and that they don't expect us to be able to see many shows in our next campaign.

I'll tell you a little secret Nan. It was only because our equipment was the worse for wear that we didn't go into Italy at the start. However, we have some new stuff now and by the time you get this letter we will probably be a step farther than Sicily.

Now back to the concerts. They are all performed in the open air with a lorry as a stage. We run the lorries round the stage to make a sort of amphitheatre and while some of the audience sit on the ground, the rest have a view from the tops of the lorries. For the Gracie Fields show we had a platform about 8 feet high with a large tent as the background which also served the purpose of a dressing room and a stage curtain. I felt sorry for the band who sat on that stage for almost two hours in the sun. The band included six girls and when the show was almost over they gave every sign of being exhausted by the sun to judge by the red faces! It was a very good show. The leader Waldini is a first class cellist and a first class comedian. Gracie Fields was a surprise item and I believe she had given a show to factory workers a few days before. As you can guess Nan, we had a right close-up view being only a few feet from the stage. By the way we made the 'Temporary Gentlemen' move their seats to both sides. She gave us almost half an hour and although she is older and does look a little that way her voice is just the same as before. I enjoyed myself thoroughly.

24 September 1943

Is it warm! I am sitting here in my birthday suit and am sweating like the proverbial bull. The last three days have been the same. Remember I told you that I had managed to give a show with an old ukulele? Well I have managed to get a fine guitar here so I have something to help pass a few weary hours especially at night. Of course, I don't play a guitar but I will learn through time, providing the instrument lasts long enough. You see, Nan, travelling in lorries filled with ammo etc. it may get a few knocks. Still, here's hoping that it is able to last at least a reasonable amount of time. By the way I can almost play 'Nobody's Darling but Mine' already (ha ha).

I am sorry to hear you have lost your little budgie and I am sure he will be missed as according to your letters he was such a pet. And from one Joey I go on to another one, the Joe who seems to find May's company worthwhile. Well, I hope he makes the most of the time while I am out here because if he leaves it until I get back home he has lost. I shall carry May off like the knights of old!

It was real funny to read of how you had to trim the edges off one of your letters to make the weight limit!

And now I'll let you into a secret. I have managed to save and put into Certificates the sum of £20 so far and that is good going. Am clever amn't I?

25 September 1943

I am expecting a move any day now. But right now I can write to my heart's content. I have in front of me your long letter 113 of August 1st. There was a snap inside of you at Dunoon and wearing what I still consider the nicest dress you have. It's a fine snap and very much like you, but aren't you a trifle thinner?

Well dear, I was intending to continue for a while yet but I hear someone wanting to know where that fellow Macintyre is (ha ha) and I suppose I must show myself in about half an hour or so (ha ha). They can manage along without me fairly well I am sure.

Sorry Nan, I must go now as the voice has changed and is now very quietly yelling 'Gunner Macintyre'. When I am called anything apart from Gunner it is usually alright but when I am given my rank it means that the man who shouts on me has a mind to use <u>his</u> rank!

Cheerio dear and good luck.

26 September 1943

Well Nan it is all strange here. We have all the stuff we need and yet we are still here in Sicily. You know Nan, we have never had such a nice time before although of course we still have the flies and the mosquitoes. Look at the concerts and the fact that we have as much water as we need. I have a bath (in bits) every evening just before the sun goes down and the mosquitoes get busy. Everybody is like myself and just wondering what is the matter and Nan, you ought to hear some of the rumours. Glorious ones!! You know the idea? So and so heard so and so tell so and so and so on and so on (ha ha).

Well dear, this is Sunday morning and I have finished the usual jobs for every morning and now it's a case of standing by for Jerry if he comes. I will try and finish this letter before midday as I am finding the heat of the day too much and writing at that time of day is a real task and very fatiguing. I know you will say 'Why is the job of writing a hard one?' It is Nan, and in this heat it's even an effort to think. That's why I don't (ha ha).

I've also done my washing this morning and a very small one by the way – only a vest and a pair of socks. These vests seem so unusual in shape etc. that the general opinion is that they were made for the Women's Army. Imagine us wearing women's underclothing? If this goes on I can see us wearing 'unmentionables' before long (ha ha).

Well Nan, I have answered all my letters and now I can have a few minutes practising my guitar if it doesn't fall apart before then. There are two other guitars on the site and already they are starting to crack with the heat and of course the sweat from the body doesn't help either. However, I use my hair oil on mine every night and it hasn't cracked yet. My hair oil, by the way, is a mixture of lubricating oil and paraffin (ha ha). I can thoroughly recommend it – keeps the hair fine and clean and oily. That is if you have any hair (ha ha).

And so ends another letter and one nearer the end of all this talking to you with paper and pen.

Yours always,

Alex

Xxxxxxxxxxxxxxxxxxxx

11 October 1943   In Italy

My dear Nan,

No doubt you have had a long wait for this letter but perhaps you will understand why. Yes you are <u>right</u>. I am here now and dear me what a change in conditions for your wee man. The weather is so much cooler now and with a lot of rain. You know it has rained every day now for the past two weeks.

By the way dear you will notice that I am not having any pen trouble. And do you know why? The answer is the much cooler weather, which gives the pen a chance, and lets the ink run without drying it before it reaches the actual pen nib. Imagine me blaming the poor innocent pen all these months too? (Ha ha.) Still, there you are! Even us O/FC's do make mistakes at times (ha ha).

Your letter goes on to tell me of how you are still following your map. Yes, Nan, I am always a little nearer home each time, but I have come to the conclusion that all authors are liars. I used to believe that although they did write a lot of nonsense of the so-called Romantic desert etc. there were such things as 'blue Italian skies'. I have seen blue skies all the way from Palestine to Sicily, but no one ever wrote songs or poems of these places did they? Oh no, it was always blue Italian ones and yet all I've seen has been rain and is it cold? Dear me, I can't even use my original desert bath. Soon I'll have no sunburn left and I so much wanted to arrive home like a browned off desert rat too (boo hoo). By the way Nan, they tell me that the desert rat is now very scarce in its own country and seems to have gone further afield and have become wanderers searching for blue skies. This may be a bit vague to you, but put it down to my sense of humour.

12 October 1943: Italy changes sides and declares war on Germany

12 October 1943

Nan, I've never felt so cold in my life. We all have the same complaint of feeling the change in the weather very much. After all these months of the desert and of warm Sicily our blood must be very thin so we suffer a wee bit more than usual. However, we are told we are having battle dress soon and extra blankets etc. At present we have the usual thin tropical kit of shorts etc. and two blankets, one of which is used for lying on. We use our overcoats too of course but to give you an idea of the cold and how an ordinary autumn day and night affected me, I woke up this morning at 3 o'clock with the bitter cold. So putting on all my available clothes I went for a walk, and to my surprise I found plenty of company. Everybody was up for a stroll before dawn. What you may call working up an appetite for breakfast.

We have spent most of our spare time today carrying out major repairs to our small home. A few bricks and stones here and there and all the bits of canvas etc. that we can find have all been tucked into spaces. Another thing is that I have found a few bits of timber and made a bed (a smasher) so I shouldn't feel just so cold being able to sleep off the ground tonight. Our desert home was never like this (ha ha).

I suppose that today's news will interest you. Dear me, now we have our gallant Italian allies. I suppose we will have to give them some respect now and even salute their officers. Imagine the old 8th Army sinking as low as that. Still no doubt the same thing will take place as was the case with Jerry in North Africa. The French people there told us that while Jerry would salute all his officers he never saluted his allies the Italians. If I were to salute <u>my</u> officers apart from Pay Parade they would probably advise me to report sick so I don't hold out much hope for Italian officers somehow (ha ha).

Still, there is one good point to this declaring of war by Italy. It means that we can take up with the local girls now and I can assure you that they really are very pretty (when young only I should add, ha ha). Perhaps one day when I have permission I shall give you another long special letter on my journey through Italy – of the mountain passes, of the miles of vineyards and of the people of these mountain villages, the men with their velvet jackets, and the women with their picturesque costumes. Just imagine a whole village where every woman is dressed exactly the same even to colours? And where, by the way, the women do all the work. Gathering in the grapes and making the vino. As I said, dear, some day I'll tell you all about it.

I've just been outside to patch up one of the holes where the wind was sort of creeping in, so now to continue my talk. But is it cold? Still, there are no flies or mosquitoes now.

Well dear wife it is now late and time for supper. Which is the old time-worn feed of biscuits soaked in water and warmed up. We call it 'biscuit porridge'. A long time ago I made a small stove out of various bits and pieces so I am a bit more fortunate than some of the others. I can even have a hot water shave in the mornings too (ha ha). That is when I decide that I have gone long enough without one (ha ha). So dear wife it's good night until I can manage a few more lines.

18 October 1943   *Turkey meal*

Matters have improved or perhaps we are becoming more used to the climate. We have been given another blanket with the result I don't get up for a walk before dawn and I'm fairly snug until 5.30. Good eh?

And here's something else that will shake you up! Nothing less than a description of my dinner last night. Here it comes Nan (ha ha).

I had roast turkey, roast potatoes, peas, beans and gravy, followed by rice and fruit and then tea. And now I suppose you will want to know how it came about, eh? Well you know this is good farm country and where one has farms, one has chickens, turkeys, etc. See? So I wandered down to a farmhouse one day and bought a huge turkey for 10/-. Yes, Nan, I actually bought it. And of course as I seem to know a little of everything I was also responsible for the rest of the job. I never killed or plucked a turkey before or for that matter any sort of bird, but the job was done with everybody satisfied. I had already spoken to our cook and he had said that he would cook anything I brought so everything in the garden was lovely. By the way, Nan, I also had some fresh spuds and these we cleaned also. So there you are Nan. What a feed we had that night. I should mention that the peas and beans were the usual issue from the cook house. So we stood in the queue as usual and took everything that was going apart from the bully. Instead we removed <u>our</u> roast spuds and turkey from the oven. Perhaps at this point I should mention that the 'WE' I am referring to was four of us, so you can guess the feed we had with a really big turkey. However, we didn't finish it all last night and kept a piece for today's lunch, but here I come to a very sad incident (ha ha). You see, Nan, I put what was left outside for the night but as I woke up this morning I heard a queer noise outside and being very brave (oh yeah!?) I went out to investigate and I was just in time to see a couple of dogs finish our expected lunch (ha ha). Of course, as I was the man who put it there for the night, I got all the blame. Poor, poor me (ha ha). Still, we have decided on another bird if the chance comes again and this time it will be a case of letting tomorrow look after itself!

Because of the great mail I will have plenty to read. Many thanks. And what about the guitar I bought in Sicily to pass my spare time with? Dear me it never rains but it pours. Still, once I get passed this extra busy stage I should be alright and able to squeeze in my few lines every day. Alright then, nearly every day (ha ha).

And now a reply to your most recent letter.

You ask if I have received certain letters numbers 98, 104. Well Nan, I haven't received 98 which had the snap of Margaret and I'll just check my wee book and let you know. Yes dear, I find that although 103 and 106 arrived after each other, 104 and 105 both came about a week later and on the same day. I know I answered the letter but of course at that time we were continually moving about North Africa and with the packing of kit etc., not to forget that we do move guns and equipment too, being a war on (ha ha) that fact that number 104 contained a book of stamps must have slipped my memory!

My next great effort will be from 'North Africa to Italy via Sicily' that is when I have permission to do so, which will probably be a long time yet by the look of things.

Good luck and God bless you all.

Yours always,

Alex

xxxxxxxxxxxxxxx

29 October 1943

My dear Nan,

It seems funny that whenever I have rather a busy time and very little to spare, bags of mail always arrives. Since I finished my last letter all my spare time has gone on making my Xmas cards. You see Nan, cards are rather hard to get in this part of Italy so I thought it would be a good idea to try and 'manufacture' a few (ha ha). What I have done is to get hold of old cards from anybody who had them and copy the designs or part of them on to my paper. I have some coloured pencils so altogether I have managed rather well. I am making four and it takes me at least a day to make one. I have drawn plenty of flowers but for goodness sake don't ask me what kind they are supposed to be as I don't have an idea. What I have done is just to think a bit of blue would be nice in there, and perhaps maybe some red here (ha ha). Still, I've done my best and I certainly hope they reach you safely.

Here's another thing Nan. As you know when we were coming to Sicily, I gave a sort of 'turn' at a very impromptu show with another chap called Dalton. He had a mouth organ and I had a bit of an old ukulele which had been found dear knows where. Well since then as you also know I got hold of a real good guitar in Sicily, in Catania to be exact. A few of us gave a concert last Wednesday night on the gun site and now that the chap Dalton can't be had it was a case of Macintyre by himself with the guitar (ha ha).

To my surprise I got a very good reception and here's the sequel. I have just been told that I am wanted to do my stuff at Headquarters tomorrow night and that a lorry will be sent to take myself and the others who performed to H.Q. Now's my chance to get some hard knocks at the Big Noises up there. Must try and think out some eh? (Ha ha.) I'll let you know how I get on Nan.

Margaret is certainly having a tough time with boils and as you say it may be due to a lack of fresh food. Still, on the other had, we have been living on tins for almost three years and as for myself I have had none of these things, although at present I have my full quota of bandages. You know the usual small knocks etc. which go bad and just won't heal up (ha ha). Reminds me very much of the days of the old desert sores which are nothing else but ulcers of all types.

You mention how our rest camp only lasted two days. We only stayed behind because the 1st Army was short of good Heavy A/A (ha ha). However, that's all a thing of the past and in any case the old idiot who was responsible for our own particular 'do' has gone elsewhere. Frankly, he has gone home. The poor old soul should never have left (ha ha)!

And now Nan, my turn on duty is in about 15 minutes which means that I get to bed at midnight, so here's hoping the rain goes off. Good night and cheerio dear.

31 October 1943

Well dear, things were a great success last night at Headquarters and your wee man had another very good reception. In fact, I was congratulated by the O'C' himself. Now that we have more chances to come across instruments than ever before we should improve as time goes on. What we really lack is the brass. Must have plenty of noise you know! because as you know brass is really my own instrument not strings. By the way Nan, my part in the show is that of the funny man. I am not announced by the compere but just walk on and do my own announcing. Of course we usually make out a programme of sorts for the big noises and I am billed as 'Macintyre and

Partner'. The partner is my guitar (ha ha). The reason I am telling you all this Nan, is that it is very surprising what can be done in the entertainment line even although we are miles from any town or even a village, and even although there is a war on, a mention of a concert of any description makes everybody more cheerful, and of course the chance to join in singing. Not only that but there is plenty of help to fix up blackouts etc. We don't always have the chance of a show so when things become quiet men soon become rather browned off. Honestly dear, I think that we have become so used to a certain amount of excitement and just must always have it. It is surprising how everybody becomes cheerful whenever we have a move even though we may have only been in the position for a week. We always like to be on the move, providing it is the right way (ha ha).

I am putting the ribbons on my Xmas cards now and I will be posting them soon. I certainly hope that they reach you safely as there really is a lot of work in them and they are unusual and different. A sort of labour of love (ha ha).

The warm clothing hasn't come yet. You know Nan, troops are supposed to have a certain amount of time to acclimatise themselves when coming out to the Middle East. Needless to say, we never had it (ha ha). So we are hoping that this stay in Italy is to get the Old 8th used to Blighty weather (ha ha)!

3 November 1943

Our winter clothing arrived yesterday. Thick vests, pants, and even a spare pair of boots. Although the troops at home always have two pairs, up till now we only had one and if they had to go for repair we just wore our slippers for a day or two. But that was the desert where it never rained and everything was dry and just can't be done now. Hence the spare boots. As I said before Nan, I hope we have said goodbye to the tropical kit.

I have sent off my Xmas cards and they should arrive in good time.

My opinion is that although the war may not finish next year it should see us home if only for a little while. Now, don't build up any hopes Nan, as I have no proof of this but just a hunch. And don't tell anybody because they may think I know something whereas I know nothing at all (ha ha).

You mention the date of our anniversary and of how soon it will be our third anniversary. I know Nan, it has been a long time. I can't send you a cable or anything this year. But you are always in my thoughts and will be even more on that day. Remember how I had the photograph on show at Port Said last year? Well, I still have them and I will try and do the same again, although conditions are a bit different. You know dear, when you think where I have been when the day comes round I certainly have travelled a lot. The first anniversary was in the heart of the desert (60 miles south west of Sidi Barrani). The second was at Port Said and now the third which will be somewhere in Italy. I'll let you know the exact spot some day later on. I have no idea where the fourth will be. I love you very much Nan and God keep you safe. You have no need to worry Nan as one place is just as safe as another.

I'm pleased to know that Fred's plot is giving you plenty of vegetables. We are beginning to have more vegetables now in our meals although the main thing is still the old bully. We had Yank biscuits the other day and they are so much superior to ours that it was a shame to put the old bully on them. We could learn a lot from the Yanks so far as food and clothing goes and they could learn a lot from us in other ways. I'll leave you to guess what I mean by other ways.

God bless you all.

Yours always,

Alex

xxxxxxxxxxx

15 *November* 1943

Well dear, here I am for a few more words about the war in general before bedtime. The weather is so much colder than in the Middle East. It certainly has been a violent change from the days of no shirts etc. Now we can't have enough clothes on (ha ha). Now don't start sending me parcels of pullovers now (ha ha).

As I said before Nan, all this weather should be a good rehearsal for Blighty which is always coming a little closer every day. While I am on the subject of countries I want to say a bit about Italy and its people and all this blah I read in the papers, which by the way are arriving again. But why must Fred spoil the picture of my favourite film star by cutting out his football coupon? Did I ever tell you the name of my favourite star Nan? Well, it's Donald Duck (ha ha)

But to get back to the Eyeties. There is a lot of talk in the papers about these 'poor people'. Well, perhaps it may be wrong to talk like this but I'm afraid I don't feel sorry for them. They asked for war and they are having it. Also a few months ago they were killing our lads and treating the prisoners badly and I don't see why because they are now on our side they should have changed such a lot. What I have seen of the people in their own country they are only a little higher in intellect and living conditions than the wogs in Egypt. I'm afraid all that Eyetie culture is of the past and not the present. I'm afraid that Jerry being in their country is letting them see what war really means and that the days of their 'Beautiful Bombs on Britain' are over. There is only one way I am sorry for them and that is for some of the women. The retreating Jerry is now reverting to rape which isn't just war and it really is a pity.

Oh! Why did you start your letter by telling me that wee May is asking for me and is thinking of me ever so often? You've upset me right away and now I can't write because of the knowledge at the back of my mind that perhaps at this very moment she is still dreaming of me! By the way Nan, I still have the gloves you sent me which were such a labour of love by wee May. Tell her that I shall always think of her when I put them on when I have an extra dirty job for my hands (ha ha).

The next part of your letter Nan is all about how much you miss me and of how much you long for my return. I know just how you feel and I admire your very brave spirit. So don't ever become downhearted although at times I know you must become browned off. I do so myself so that's how I know (ha ha). Always remember that up till now I have been very lucky and that every day is a day nearer the end. That in itself should cheer you up. Now don't tell me that you never get that feeling (ha ha) because perhaps you are not aware of the fact that I can pretty nearly sense the mood you are in when you write your letters and I can always 'read between the lines'. Now don't deny it Nan because you know I am correct (ha ha). Never mind dear wife, perhaps it won't be long before I have the opportunity to make up for all these months of parting and am I allowed to say wasted time? I love you Nan and everything will turn out all right in the end.

You tell me that Ewan did mention of how perhaps he may come out here but tell him from me to stay where he is. All the advantages have gone now. No warm winters, no lovely veiled women and no cheap beer. All we can offer now is winter, women who have a large number of lice in their hair and cheap wine better known as plonk (ha ha).

Well Nan with that little piece of news I must say good night. I am going to have a bit of supper before going to bed which if it interests you is composed of some spuds and bully (the usual) and I have smashed the lot up and intend to put on the old primus stove which has paid for itself in gold and which I wouldn't part with for anything.

16 November 1943

Today I had a warm shower – my first by the way since I was at Sfax and needless to say I enjoyed it very much. The place where we went is in a fair-sized town, or to be more exact what used to be a fair-sized town before we hammered it, and the showers are in the basement of a large building which I believe was the Fascist Youth Club and had all kinds of sporting facilities such as a swimming pool, gymnasium etc.

Dear me, I nearly forgot to mention that I have given another command performance at H.Q. and as before your wee man was very well received. This is not surprising as I am a brilliant artiste! Such humour! And what a musician! Not only do I play my guitar in my own specialty act but someone bought a cornet in one of the towns and I also play that as well. You see Nan, I have promised to teach the owner how to play it, on the condition that when I want it myself I have it. What I call enterprise (ha ha).

So once again Nan, I'll finish another letter which means another one less to write before the day comes when I can talk instead of write. Cheerio until my next words.
Yours always,
Alex
xxxxxxxxxxx

20 November 1943

My dear Nan,
You will notice that the writing is much thicker than usual. This is due to the paper which is rather damp. In fact, Nan, everything is rather damp nowadays, even the jolly old spirits. Instead of warm sunshine every day all the year round, we have to grab the chance of a bath (in bits) and clothes washing on the first dry day. Certainly we have no more clothes than we had in the desert during the winter but then it was a dry cold and not dampness as it is now. We are still in our very small tents with the usual hole in the ground so you can guess how everything becomes a bit damp. The war is going well however and that's the main thing, isn't it?

I have plenty of cigarettes and you know Nan, if I have any more fags I'll be smoking myself to death (ha ha). Apart from my attempt at humour they really are very welcome. I notice by your letter that there has been an absence of a really long letter for a while so I'm thinking that my letters telling you I am in Italy haven't reached you yet. Obviously, I can't tell you the exact spot. There are towns, or rather what is left of them, and as for the shops etc., well Jerry didn't leave very much behind. He took everything he could and what he couldn't carry he destroyed. A sort of scorched earth policy. And although I perhaps say that I visited a town it really is a town only in name, and possesses none of what you would expect in towns. Most of the towns are just scenes of desolation and destruction with a few civvies here and there and more of them are returning every day. The most common shops are barbers and tailors although the tailors are only able to sew on badges and nothing else. I will write about the towns of Italy in the next volume of my travels (ha ha).

You tell me that you plan to send me a second Xmas parcel. And poor me trying to keep my kit light. We just can't carry much stuff, Nan, so you see the personal has to be kept very small. You see this is a war of movement and speed and you know the old saying of he who travels lightest travels fastest. So I am looking forward to your parcel but after that just send items to me if I ask for some supplies.

You remember I told you about the concert? Well, they have been so good that we intend to try a real show with sketches etc. at the end of the year. One of our officers is rather good at the job, having done a bit in civvy street, and your wee man has been appointed sort of assistant producer (ha ha). Already our fame has travelled wide and believe it or not we have had requests to give shows to lots of various units including the American Air Force (ha ha). The snag is that we can't just go away from our positions without very high authority but we hope to get that as well (ha ha). The biggest worry is the band because although we have a good variety of instruments now including violins, cornet, clarinet etc. they are all various pitches, no two being the same, with the result that what may be 'C' on one instrument just isn't on the rest (ha ha).

What a worry! Still 'where there's a will, there's always a relation' as the saying goes (ha ha).

21 November 1943

Sorry Nan, but I had to finish rather abruptly last night without the chance to finish my usual way. As usual things are rather uncomfortable and we had the job of baling out the tent last night. Who the hell said 'Blue Italian skies'? I've never felt so cold, wet and miserable since I left home. Still it could always be a lot worse, so why grumble?

I'm sorry I wasn't able to send a telegram to you on your birthday. But you know that I haven't forgotten you, as if I could. As always you express the wish that I am home soon. You know Nan, I'm probably wrong, but I have a hunch, just a hunch mind, that I will be home next year some time. I have no real information, nor have I heard any rumours so don't go around telling anybody and don't build up any hopes.

You say that you long to hear me sing my wee song and play my ukulele again. Dear me! Nothing so common (ha ha). I have a vast selection of songs now and I play the guitar. I am taking the best possible care of the guitar and I intend to try and fetch it back with me if at all possible (ha ha). At first the trouble was the heat and now it's the damp. What a life!

In your letter 121 you mention me swimming the dock at Sfax. The thought of that water is enough to make me shiver. Imagine swimming now? I couldn't even bear the idea of undressing nowadays (ha ha). Only a few months ago the sweat was running down my back and now the cold water is running down my nose (ha ha).

And now I come to the subject of feet (ha ha). You worry about your cold feet Nan, but if I were you I would ignore it because wait till you feel mine in cold weather. Fact is you should feel them now (ha ha). I can't! Of course this weather makes everything damp including the boots and of course they are much colder than usual. By the way Nan, it's still raining very heavy although so far the rain hasn't managed into the tent. I spent some time this morning preparing 'defence in depth', otherwise called a trench, all round our little home (ha ha).

Well dear, I want you to have this letter as soon as possible so I'll say cheerio for the present and God bless you all.

Yours always,

Alex

Xxxxxxxxxxx

24 November 1943

My dear Nan,

Another day nearer the end of all this parting. Yes dear, I'm afraid that I have had my fill of adventure and of travelling in foreign lands. The novelty has worn off. You know Nan, I have come to the opinion that all authors are liars. First of all until I saw for myself I did think that there really was a certain amount of truth in the 'Romance of the desert'. However, my own experience bursts that bubble.

And now this 'Blue Italian sky business'. Another lot of nonsense because I have had nothing but rain, rain and still more rain since I have been here. As we still live in our little tents you can understand that conditions are a bit trying at times. At the present it is raining (as usual) with quite a wind blowing and I'm fed up (ha ha). On the other hand I am well at present and suffering from no ill effects of the weather. But still, I am fed up (ha ha).

Well dear, I have answered all your letters and I am beat for something to write about. I could of course read some of your letters over again as I have done before but I have had one of my fires last Sunday and the only word I have had since then has been a letter card from Ewan! I sent you a registered letter last week Nan and it contained a few grips for your hair. They look awful long to me but I suppose they are fine when they are in the hair.

I'm looking forward to the arrival of my Xmas parcel and of course the extra 'lucky bag' also. I have plenty of cigarettes right now so I am exchanging some of them for chocolate. Imagine Nan, there are people who don't like plain chocolate! Sometimes I make a bar of chocolate into a hot drink. Nae bother at a' (ha ha).

And Nan with that example of my business sense I'll say cheerio.

25 November 1943   *Bandaged hands*

Nan, you must excuse my writing. Remember I told you I was well but had my full quota of bandages. Well so far I had them all on my left hand. But now I have them on my right hand, the thumb to be exact, and have you ever tried to write without using your thumb? Try it some day (ha ha).

Now Nan, I want to explain these bandages as I don't want you to start worrying. The least little knock or breakage of the skin and it becomes septic right away, an occurrence which has never happened to me before. I am not alone in this respect as a good number of us have the same complaint. Most of us in fact. You can judge the extent by the fact that one man has a full-time job looking after us. Yes Nan, I agree with you that it is time we were back home for a spell. No one knows the cause of these sores although two of the reasons are firstly the food we get and secondly our long spell in the desert is telling on us now. Whatever the reason I think it is a !!!! nuisance (ha ha). In any case I am not as bad as others. However, one bad effect of this thumb is that I can't play my guitar, with the result that there will be no concerts for a while. Me being the big noise has sort of stumped the whole idea for the time being. We are 'resting' (ha ha).

The weather is much better today, blowy and cold but dry. I washed my clothes three days ago and if all goes well they should be dry today. Gone are the days of washing and drying clothes in a few hours. Instead of just saying that 'I'll have a bath tomorrow and do some washing' sort of careless like, it is now a case of grabbing the first good day which comes.

I enjoyed reading of your trip to the farm at Bridge of Weir and of the very pleasant day you had there. But you know Nan, you shouldn't tell me about big cosy fires, fresh eggs and butter. Making me feel sorry for myself (ha ha).

I certainly will sing your song for you dear wife on our anniversary when our day comes around again. If all goes well and the conditions are in any way decent the photographs will be on show once more similar to my 'display' at Port Said last year. Here's hoping that I have all these bandages off by then and [am] able to do justice to the guitar as well as it sort of makes up for my very poor voice and, like the painter's brush, covers all the flaws!

Well dear wife, my time is up for today. Always another day nearer the end and another two pages less to write.

Good night again dear wife.

28 November 1943

Well dear wife, here I am again by sheer luck (ha ha). There has been a real gale blowing tonight and it was only the fact that I have a good size in feet, and therefore a good grip, that I am here at all. By the time you get this letter you will know that the fun started in earnest again this morning, so here goes for the next defeat of Jerry!

I had a letter from Ewan and he said the general impression at home is that Jerry will only last a few months. I don't share that view and the truth is that such talk is sheer nonsense. And very dangerous talk too. I admit that Jerry is on the run but he is a far different proposition from our 'poor Italian allies'.

It may be that Jerry will crack soon but not in two months. Fighting in Italy is vastly different from what we have had before what with all these rivers, mountains and of course the rain. Still, the Old 8th will do the job (as usual). We will probably end up by invading our own country through force of habit (ha ha). No doubt they are waiting for us to invade France eh? (Ha ha.)

I've just had a phone message which means that I am up all night (ha ha). And what a night! Just my luck (ha ha). It means that I must try and have a few hours sleep before my turn of duty comes.

So dear wife I must say good night and good luck.

Here I am again.

I want to send this letter on its way so I'll finish on this page. I was on duty and it certainly was a rough night. However, today's weather is fine and we have been able to put our blankets out to dry. After the duty last night I had permission to go to bed so yours truly took advantage of this opportunity. As it was fine and warm I slept through the whole morning and just got up for lunch. Can't beat it can you, eh? (Ha ha.)

My hands are much better today. I am still writing without the use of the thumb but even though I say so myself I am becoming quite an expert at the job.

And now dear wife I must say cheerio meantime.

Yours always,

Alex

Xxxxxxxxxxxxx

30 November 1943

My dear Nan,

Your bumper letter 123 written at Troon has not arrived yet. Perhaps they will require a special heavy lorry to fetch it and that is the reason for the delay!

Before I deal with my 'fan mail' a word about myself. The weather has been good the last few days. Another thing to help is that we have lost the small desert tents and now have large ones. These are thickly made and are just the job for holding eight men. So at least for the present no more crawling into wet holes and a small tent. It does look as if we have our winter equipment, even to heavy woollen underwear. A long time since I wore them eh? (Ha ha.) Beginning to feel like a home soldier already with all this warm clothing and large tents (ha ha). Dear me, I'll soon be polishing boots and saluting officers (ha ha).

Your letter 121 tells me of your trip to Hamilton and of how I am to expect a piece of shortbread in my parcel baked by Aunt Nell. I am certainly hoping that this parcel arrives safely as you have spent a lot of time and labour with it. Not forgetting that extra parcel! Let me thank you, Nan, for your kindness.

2 December 1943

I have a little gossip for you about the weather and this is a momentous happening. It was very cold yesterday and when we saw the dawn this morning we saw snow in the high ground. Yes Nan, <u>snow</u>! The first I have seen since the winter of 1940 at Southend. I was up most of the night and I certainly felt very cold.

6 December 1943

I had to finish abruptly, Nan, but here I am again. I am sure you will understand. Yes dear, another move! And not for the best either. We have been up to the neck in mud ever since we reached here and it's still raining too. I think we left Egypt too soon! However, I am well and not grumbling and I am still receiving a good mail from you. I wanted to let you know that my Xmas parcel has arrived.

I've enjoyed all the contents although you will have to tell Fred that it may be a while before I can solve the puzzle. This weather is not ideal for sitting still and only using one's brains. Provided of course that one has brains (ha ha). I have managed to sort it all out and squeezed into my pack, even to the box of shortbread which I am intending to try and keep until the New Year.

Yes, dear wife, we are almost at the end of another year and another year of parting. I do hope that the next year of 1944 means that we are together again. That is my wish dear and I know you agree with me in that respect. However, let's be patient and all will end all right, of that I'm sure.

I was interested to hear of how trying your job in McDonald's can be, but never mind dear perhaps I'll be able to take you away from all that worry soon. At least I hope so (ha ha). And as for the wee ones, well being a man (I hope) and very proud, I'll see what I can do for you (ha ha).

I almost forgot to tell you that my hand is almost free of bandages and the thumb which was the most awkward of all is healing up nicely. Covering the hands with all this mud etc. seems to have helped towards healing rather than the other way around. Just my luck and me after my 'ticket' home too (ha ha).

7 December 1943

Just another few words. Today I have received another small parcel from you and it was posted in June! Now don't blame me! The weather is still very cold and the mud is still here and I suppose will be around until the end of the winter.

Good luck and God bless you all.
Yours always,
Alex
Xxxxxxxxxxxx

11 December 1943

My dear Nan,
You know that I am very busy and you will have to excuse me if I perhaps seem to write things which you don't understand, such as at times repeating items of news. You see, Nan, we are a lot busier than we have been, so between moving here and there, sometimes up for two or three nights and days at a time, my mind just can't settle on my letters. However, we seem to have stopped for a while so I will try and make up for lost time.

Dear me, so you are now thirty eh? Soon have to change my terms from 'dear' to 'old woman' or perhaps 'my old dutch' (ha ha). I wonder if I will be with you when your next birthday comes along? Still looks like being a long war in my opinion. As for where we are now the country is all very mountainous and all in favour of the defenders and Rommel is making full use of that fact. However, we are going ahead and Jerry is still on the road back.

I agree with you Nan that we have missed a lot these past three years but we have been lucky and we will have plenty of time to continue where we left off. Yes Nan, I have my wee fire as usual on a Sunday morning when I find that my lot of letters have started to become large and taking up too much space. And as usual I have my thoughts during that period and as usual they are all with you and the folks at home.

You state in your letter of how you picture me opening the parcel. Well dear, I had to carry it for over two days unopened due to running all over Italy, still I managed to keep it fairly dry and there wasn't really such a great deal of mud around it anyway. I can assure you that I will have a sort of celebration on the 20th. Mud or no mud!

13 December 1943

Here I am again. You mention your birthday and of how much you would have enjoyed my company during your celebrations. I feel this parting dear just as much as yourself and I hope I gave the impression that I was with you that day. Perhaps circumstances may be different next year. I have had all the travelling in foreign lands I want now and before I go from the subject Nan, it may surprise you when I say that my most pleasant thought goes right back to the desert. Must be something in that 'Lure' they talk about.

Did you ever receive the shields I sent you? They have quite a history Nan as we had them before you people at home ever heard of Alamein and the 8th Army and when we really were desert rats and lived in the sand for nearly a year. The 51st Division are only a mob of rookies compared to us old 'Rats' (ha ha).

I almost forgot to thank you for the threepenny piece from your dumpling. I can't get at my other little pieces of money, cloth patterns etc. So until I do I am carrying it in the little wallet which you sent me in my Xmas parcel.

I must tell you that I am receiving better food at the moment. We have had fresh meat for dinner for almost a week now. And in this cold weather we certainly enjoy the hot stuff.

You remember Nan that I had a kitten at Port Said last year? Well, at present my left arm is being held down by the head of a dog! It isn't my dog but it always comes with me and leaves its mark behind (ha ha). So as it is now dark and I suppose the dog is tired, it has come up and sat down in front of me when I write with its head pillowed on my arm and has now gone to sleep.

Well Nan I will try and write soon

Yours always,

Alex

xxxxxxxxxxxx

20 *December* 1943   *Wedding anniversary*

My dear Nan,

Yes! The 20th December again, and here I am sitting in my tent somewhere in Italy. There is green grass near me with trees, bushes etc. Although the day is dull there has been no rain. Everything is quiet and everybody is also very quiet. Either reading, writing or perhaps just resting. The only noise is of planes of which there are many, but they are going from us, not for us.

I am sitting as usual on the edge of my bed. A board on trestles believe it or not, which I find very comfortable. Beside my bed is my pack and today, pride of place on top of the pack, are our two photographs. I have no cupboard or box or anything as I had a twelve month ago at Port Said, but I have done the best I could with what I have got.

Before I started to write you these few words, I played my guitar, and sang your favourite tunes. 'I'll walk beside you' and 'Nobody's Darling'. By the way dear, my guitar was a wee bit damaged but I spent all my spare time yesterday doing my best to make it serviceable for today. You have no idea of the remarks which are passed about the guitar, and of how I've carried it from Catania. But they just don't understand, do they Nan? You asked me to sing your songs for you today so that was why I hung on to the guitar. Understand dear?

And so Nan, you have a picture of where I am and how I have sort of made this day ours. Yes dear, three years ago and we were together although perhaps I have been a husband in name only I have not been sorry, because I know that sooner or later our day will come when what we have missed, and what we both long for, will be really ours. At times during these years of parting, perhaps I have been a bit low in spirit, first of these months of heat and sand and thirst, then the mad days when we went back to El Alamein, and now the cold, wet and mud of Italy. Still, in spite of all that, I have a lot to be thankful for. I still have my health and you, my wife, have also had good health and the same can be said of all my people at home. Up to the present, I only have a few scars to show for my campaigns out here so as I said I have a lot to be thankful for.

I was intending to finish at this point Nan but I must go on to thank you for the cable which I have just received. Isn't it remarkable? It has been delivered to me right bang on the actual day.

Well dearest wife I will say cheerio with the wish that I am with you when our next anniversary comes round. Meantime good luck and God bless you. All my love,

Alex

Xxxxxxxxxxxxxxxxxx

23 December 1943

My dear Nan,

As you say Nan, it is a long time since I left you but we have been very lucky. Candidly Nan, I think that we have now got over the worst part of this war and perhaps soon you will be able to, as you say, thank me 'the right way'. Although why you are under the impression that you require to thank me I don't know!

You ask me if there is anything you can do for me. Well Nan, the first thing you can do is to look after yourself and be your usual cheery self. When you are well and happy I have all I require.

So the fashion now is for short skirts? (Ha ha.) Because practically all the photos I have had from you recently have been leg shows. But very nice legs thank you (ha ha). These snaps show me how happy and cheery you are. That cheerful smile of yours Nan is the only present you need give to me. Not forgetting, of course, the legs! (Ha ha.)

Must finish now and get my beauty sleep.

26 December 1943   Xmas day boss – Captain Macintyre!

Nan, you will want to know how I spent my Xmas, so here goes.

We have been very fortunate in being in Italy this Xmas as we were able to have tons of apples, oranges, nuts and gallons of wine. No! Nan we had no turkey. We must have eaten up all the birds during our first few weeks in the country (ha ha). Instead we bought three pigs a long time ago and have been carting them all round the country with us until yesterday. So the main food yesterday was pork.

Here is our list for yesterday.

Breakfast was porridge, pork chops, Spam, jam, bread and tea.

Lunch was pears with custard, cheese, jam, mince pies, Naafi cake and our own fruit cake and of course bread and tea. Hardly anybody finished the whole lunch (ha ha).

Dinner, we had roast pork, spuds, peas, cabbage, apple sauce, Xmas pudding, custard, tea and of course apples, oranges, nuts.

As you can see Nan, we had quite a day. And now I am going to do a spot of boasting again.

All the arrangements for the whole day were due to me!

It was decided that the Site Commander for the day would be Captain Macintyre!

I was therefore duly promoted. I had supreme command for the day and was the Boss. All the other ranks became Gunners and the Gunners all became Sergeants. But I was the Orderly Officer, complete with shoulder pips and of course the revolver around the waist. As you can guess I made sure that the real Officers fell due for all the dirty jobs. I detailed sergeants for cookhouse fatigues etc. including the dishing out of the food. I organised Parades, times of the various meals, received all the messages, signed answers etc. as 'A. Macintyre Captain R.A.' and in short I had the time of my life (ha ha). I had my breakfast and lunch brought to me in the Officers Mess (by one of the Officers). I told him to fetch my breakfast and as he was a gunner for the day all he could say was 'Yes Sir' (ha ha).

The dinner was, of course, the main 'do' of the day and I must say that everything went well. Every man had a good warm feed and the guns were still ready for action. It took a bit of planning! We put up a tent and made a long table and instead of having mine in the Mess I took my place at the top of the table. By the way, I had a good Orderly Sergeant (about as daft as me) who carried out my details to the word.

I ordered a parade at 9.30 am and told him that if I saw any man <u>properly</u> dressed he would be put on a charge! What a parade! There were all kinds of dress. Soft hats, bowler hats, one-time football jerseys etc. The drill was a real one with the sergeant drawing the men up to attention and then I came along and I had a real inspection of the ranks. There were a few drunks on parade but the best laugh was when someone decided that I should be led around by a chap with an old Eyetie accordion. Talk about laugh! By the way I had one of my identity discs in my eye as a monocle (ha ha).

To put the finishing touch to the proceedings the Major of the Battery came from H.Q. on a visit and poor me had the task of meeting him and showing him the site on his tour of inspection. However I got that job done to everybody's satisfaction and all that remained was the usual singsong which went on well into the night. As my old guitar is still in one piece I had to perform there too!

Candidly, Nan, I had a very tiring day as I had been up since 3 a.m. on duty before I took over as 'Officer Commanding'. Perhaps this may be strange to you Nan, but although it was a busy day I was quite proud because being chosen as the 'Big Noise' is a sure sign of being popular with almost everybody. And again, they know that I can cause a laugh of some description (ha ha).

Still Nan dear, although I enjoyed myself very much I hoped there and then that it would be my last Xmas out here and away from home and you. The discussion after the dinner between us Officers (ha ha) was all on that subject and the general opinion was that we would be home some time in the New Year. Of course, we are only a few men in the army out here, and we know as much about what is happening as you people back home, although we do smile a bit at certain items of 'news' which come over the radio. By the way Nan, I had the honour of reading Monty's Xmas message out to the chaps when I was on my parade yesterday, and as usual it was all of the struggle ahead, and of our great achievement since last Xmas. Then we were attacking El Agheila, North Africa, and now we are in the centre of Italy, with the Italians out of it.

Well dear, I hope you have enjoyed my talk of Xmas day – my fourth in the Army, let's hope I don't have a fifth.

I'm sorry Nan, I seem to have mixed up my pages. Put it down to the effects of the morning after, because I did have quite a variety of drink. I must have a remarkable capacity for a usually sober man. There was whisky, gin, vermouth, muscatel, vino, piscato and the plonk (ordinary wine). Apart from a rather mucky mouth this morning, it had no effect at all (ha ha).

Well dear wife, I have just been told that the lads have brought in a piano on a lorry. Now don't ask questions where it came from. We don't (ha ha). At the same time I am now wanted to join the crowd with the guitar. However let my 'public clamour', I intend to finish this letter tonight as tomorrow looks like being a very busy day for your wee man.

Yours always,

Alex

xxxxxxxxxxxxxx

31 December 1943

My dear Nan,

Here I am to start my last letter of this year. The end of another year and another day nearer the end of all this war. Not of course forgetting another day nearer the time when I will be with you once more, with all these days of parting over and we are living our own lives, to the best of our ability that is (ha ha).

Well Nan, we have seen great changes since last year. Then, I was in North Africa and we had visions of only requiring to go as far as Tripoli, as we were at that time expecting this new force to come east as far as Tripoli. But what happened, they just couldn't do it, and we had to go up all the way to the town of Tunis ourselves, through such obstacles as Mareth, Akerat, etc. which had been built just to stop troops coming from the east. The result was that instead of catching Rommel between the two armies in the desert, he was able to prolong the campaign by fighting in the mountainous country of Tunisia.

The same thing is happening in Italy. It is very mountainous country which lends itself to defence and makes advancing a long and laborious task. But we are advancing and Jerry's days are now numbered. And he knows it too. Remember Nan, this is the time when Jerry will use gas, when he finds himself with his 'back to the wall'. I am sure he will try and use gas sooner or later. You know Nan what I mean, don't you Nan. You can't be too careful.

However Nan, I'm not going to give a talk on the war situation (ha ha) but, mind you, without mentioning the war how can one talk of what has been happening?

As for myself, the greatest change this year has brought is the new country and new climate. Last year I wrote on the last day of the year of the usual sand, wogs and warmth. This morning, I woke up to find everything white with frost and feeling very cold myself. As I said Nan, that is the greatest change of all.

Then there are the people round about. The difference there is that instead of rogues who were so ignorant that they could neither read nor write, we now have rogues who can and according to themselves are very 'civilised people'. The superstitious and ignorant mob. And then there are the Yanks whom we have made close contact with. They are a bit bombastic admittedly but their chaps who have seen a bit have lost all their own importance and think that there are no troops like the Old 8th Army. Even their air force which came to us at Alamein have stated that they would rather stay with the Old 8th Army than go back to their own army. The only ones who think themselves the 'salt of the earth' are, as I said, guys who haven't had any 'excitement'. When it comes to that we have the same 'heroes' in our own ranks.

Well Nan, it's now coming near bedtime so I must say goodnight but if all goes well I should be able to add some more tomorrow. And of course tell you about my New Year Eve. It won't be much because all I have for a celebration is a bottle of plonk and of course your tin box of shortbread which I haven't yet opened. However, if all goes well I should have my small drink and piece of shortbread tonight. At the same time I won't be wandering far as it doesn't give any promise of a decent night, being very blowy with a strong suggestion of rain. And I don't like rain.

By the way Nan, I saw an American film tonight. The film was lousy and was called *I'll be Waiting* or some name similar and featured Gable. Something to do with the Yanks and Japs. The only part I enjoyed was the battle scene, meant to be dramatic and yet so unlikely that we all laughed!

Sorry Nan, but I must say goodnight on this New Year's Eve of 1943. I ask God to bless you all at home. Goodnight dearest wife.

⥱1944⥲

Electric light! – trip to Bari – hospital and another leg operation – Rome trip
– disbanding of the 276 Battery – Pompeii – posted to new unit – radio course
– rumours of leave – wedding anniversary

January – May 1944: Allied troops fight north through the Italian
mountains. One target is control of Monte Cassino, a strategic
'gateway' to Rome

1 January 1944

Well dear, another year and who knows what it may bring us. My New Year's
Eve passed very quietly as I had one or two glasses of wine and of course a piece
of the shortbread you sent me and which I enjoyed very much. I was surprised
when I opened your tin box to find another two bars of chocolate. You know,
Nan, although I do appreciate your action, I would rather you kept chocolate
and sweets to yourself, as I am sure you will have much more enjoyment than
I. At present we are very fortunate in being able to have at least one bar of
chocolate each week, which we have with our fags. Of course, we pay for the
chocolate but some weeks the 'powers that be' soften their hearts and supply
the bar through the rations. When we were attached to the 1st Army for a few
weeks in North Africa we had a bar of chocolate each week as issue! I have
enjoyed the chocolate you sent, but at the same time I felt sort of criminal and
as if I was taking one of your very few luxuries out of your mouth so to speak.

To get back to my New Year's Eve. I had some wine and shortbread, or
should I say we all had wine and shortbread and afterwards we boiled up some
milk from a farm. I'm afraid that the milk, wine and shortbread didn't agree
with me because I felt rather unwell so I went to bed shortly after 10 o'clock.
However I didn't have much rest, as I was awakened shortly after 12 by a few
drunks looking for me to wish me the usual New Year greetings. And of course
I had to get up and 'go the rounds' with them. And it pouring down cats and
dogs too (ha ha).

I should mention now that it wasn't the milk or the shortbread which
took effect on me but the wine, which was very sweet and sickly. You see

Nan, it was never meant to be swallowed by the gallon as we do but only sipped now and then. We go and bring back a two-gallon can of it at a time. Terrible isn't it (ha ha). You can tell Aunt Nellie and Mother that the shortbread was very much enjoyed. As for today Nan, well nobody has done anything of any interest. Everything is very quiet and the reason? (Ha ha.) Rain and mail. It's been pouring all day so this means practically no activity anywhere. We are all out of the rain and only crawl out for meals. We have a fire in our tent which gives off plenty of smoke and very little heat (ha ha). But the very little heat is better than none, believe me (ha ha).

Two men from our site can now go on four days' leave to Naples. As you probably know this is Fifth Army territory and very few 8th Army men have been there. They have at last opened it up to our men from this side of Italy. The fairest way was to put the names in a hat. One of the names was that of your 'wee man'!

So I should be making my way to Naples in a week's time.

I should explain how leave works. It is vastly different from leave at home. Take for instance this concession to Naples. When I go there (if ever, ha ha) it means taking practically all my kit, including my bedroll or four blankets and a groundsheet as we won't be living in hotels or things like that but probably in some camp. All very different from home isn't it? And then of course there will be nearly a day's journey to Naples by lorry. Mind you I am not grumbling Nan, but just trying to let you know what leave here really means. Do you know that when some of the chaps had leave from the desert they had a journey of nearly 700 miles and that most of the journey was on the desert railway goods wagons? That was to get to Cairo. Then some of the chaps took nearly a week to get back to us (ha ha).

One place I won't be and that is home (ha ha).

19 January 1944 *Electric light!*

My dear Nan,

Here I am again for a few words to you before I go to bed. I won't be able to say a great deal, but I will continue until the rest of the chaps in the tent start to ask a few gentle questions as to how long before the <u>light</u> goes out. The sooner I finish the more gentle will be the questions. You will be interested to know that it is genuine electric light!

You see your wee man thought it would be a good idea to try some of the Eyetie mains which are to be found all over here – even cables leading to the remotest small farm. Well, to cut a long story short we were very fortunate to find current, so hence the fine light. By the way, Nan, I have had to use all my spare time putting lights into all the other tents now, which I take a very poor view of. Of course, maybe I have the wires in such a mess that nobody else can make head or tail of them (ha ha).

I had your letter telling me of how Margaret was now a Lance Corporal and I can assure you that I never slept all that night. Upset myself through envy, I did (ha ha). Imagine me in the Army all this time and still a common Gunner. Perhaps I should say uncommon Gunner. The name by the way is 'Mad Mac'. And I used to be a very quiet man too. Well that may be quite a good reputation but where are my stripes? (Ha ha.) Still, Nan, perhaps if the war lasts another ten years or so I'll be at least a Lance Corporal too?

The reason for the very uneven writing is the fact that I have tried four different nibs in my old pen and each one seems to be worse than the other. I still have the pen you sent me a long time ago but the war is telling now and Eyetie pen and nibs are like themselves: 'No bono'. Now Nan, I am not dropping you any hints because I do know that pens are scarce at home, but just giving you a bit of gossip and also letting you know that I have had very good service from your present. I think of all the letters I have written since I got the pen in that parcel and of how often it has been praised and of how often at times it hasn't. Yes dear, it has been one of the finest presents you have sent me. Dear me, here I am talking of presents instead of answering your letters, just like me to go on romancing, isn't it?

I'm afraid I must say goodnight now. I am being asked if I put on this light so that I could write all night and of course a lot more questions on the same lines but not quite as polite (ha ha).

25 January 1944

My dear Nan,

Firstly the weather. Fact is, it's been a lot more unpleasant than today. Now for myself, which is the easier subject to dispose of, well all I can say is that I am well at present and have felt older at times. And that is subject 'Number 2' disposed of. Aren't I a clever man? (Ha ha.)

Your letter 131 gives me the impression you are becoming a bit fed up with my long absence from home and frankly I don't blame you, especially as you know that a good number of the others have gone home. And the majority of them came out at least a year after I did. That also includes the 51st Division who didn't come out until the 'do' at Alamein. Still Nan, there is nothing I can do about it (ha ha).

You say that you would be pleased if I were home if only for a short time. Well dear that may be all right, but have you ever thought of the second parting? Do you honestly think it would be worthwhile? I very much doubt it myself. Now don't get the idea like what one of the chap's wife's did, by thinking that he had actually volunteered to stay out here, while the rest went home to Blighty (ha ha).

My time is up for tonight but I must thank you for the photo you included in the parcel of papers and also for the soap. I was under the impression that it was scarce at home and that you needed coupons. By the way Nan, I am able to buy soap out here so don't you think that I am going without a wash. If I do, it's not because the soap is scarce but because the water is too cold (ha ha).

26 January 1944

Well Nan, the weather has gone back to the old ways again and we have rain and very high winds. At present it is blowing a gale outside the tent with a lot of rain. But I am inside and dry so why worry (ha ha). So I will just try and continue from last night.

I hope I have the chance to enjoy Mary's baking soon. Do you think I could have a piece of sponge cake some day? I'll give her my recipe for bread (ha ha). You know Nan, I'm sorry I didn't meet Mary a long time ago as I'm so fond of my 'tummy' I could have fallen for a good baker. I had a great notion for a cook once up in Lochgilphead because she always made me some nice pancakes for my 'tin tea'. Of course perhaps she was practising out the old adage of 'the road to a man's heart etc.' (ha ha). Of course, I also had a number of other flames. As I was never very handsome I put it down to my personality. What a blether!? (Ha ha.)

And then when I was of the age to know a lot better I went and fell for you and I didn't have time to rise again. Before I knew what had happened I was 'collared'. But the funny part was that I didn't care whether I managed on my own feet again or not. S'funny isn't it? (Ha ha.)

To get down to 'brass tacks' Nan, the fact is that I really love you an awful lot. Dear me, going sentimental again. Mustn't do that you know. Must be the tough man I am supposed to be.

By the way Nan, the reason for the very faint writing on this paper is the fact that it has come into contact with diesel fuel which you can guess I am always working with.

The fuel is very useful but at the same time destroys practically everything which it comes into contact with it and it looks as if my pack has had a drop or two over it. I should tell you, Nan, that we always put a certain ointment on our hands before we start working with this fuel, as it has a habit of causing any cuts to become septic. No! Nan it isn't nice stuff. But Nan, you don't want to read all about fuel do you? (Ha ha.)

Your letter goes on to tell me of Margaret's stripe. She is now an N.C.O., otherwise a member of the Gestapo, a person with a stripe is also like 'the whip bearer of capitalism' and lots of other such remarks (ha ha). No, Nan, I am not jealous but really very proud of my little sister. Of course, if the war lasts long enough, say ten or twelve years, I may have a stripe too (ha ha).

2 February 1944

My dear Nan,

I will answer the one long letter of yours which I still have left, number 132. I did say a few words about this letter before but you see I always like to answer your letters thoroughly. You see I may forget to answer a certain small incident and then I receive a request from you asking me if I had ever received a letter with a certain number. And then I have to make all my excuses and try and say that I was surprised that you hadn't read that in my letter number so and so (ha ha).

I must thank you for the snap you sent. So far as your appearance is concerned I don't see any great difference in your looks. I could of course mention the matter of clothes but then on the other hand I could say that you would look good to me without any at all (ha ha). So you see Nan, I can't make the matter of your smart coat and hat an excuse for a few more lines. There is only one point which I really must say a few words on and that is that you are looking very well and that these glimpses of home make me realise just how much I really do miss you.

Dear me, I must be very careful. Would never do to become sentimental again. Or is it the case that you do like a bit of it now and then? (Ha ha.)

Well Nan you tell me of how you know that a lot of the 51st Division are at home now and of course naturally you are wondering why they are already home while chaps who have been out here much longer are still in the line. The whole trouble seems to be that there has been so much talk in the papers of this 51st Division that people are labouring under the impression that they were the 8th Army. Whereas the truth is that the 8th Army saw more real fighting many months before the 51st were ever thought of and were still at home doing things such as polishing boots etc. Out here there were more of this division <u>behind</u> the line than ever stayed in. While a few did the actual fighting the rest were taking over the administration of towns etc. and wherever one went one saw the sign HD on walls etc. Hence their name of 'Home Decorators'. No! Nan this HD was not the 8th Army by any means and the majority of the old 8th are still out here in all parts of the Middle East now, having been scattered all over the place.

I can see you enjoyed the story of the turkey feed and of how the dogs finished it off for us. Well Nan it wasn't long before we had finished all the turkeys within a radius of a few miles, so we decided that as we must have a change from bully the supply would just have to be pork. So we fed on pork until that gave out, and now we just have to be content with what the army lets us have, and after such high feeding we naturally don't take very kindly to the usual army idea of a balanced diet. Still, we have had a lot worse, so I mustn't grumble.

Well Nan I still have my guitar, although the shape has altered a little from when it was bought back in Catania. I have also had a bit of a do on a cornet so I do let my presence be felt very much nowadays (ha ha). Their sneers and jeers etc. when I give a lovely solo say about midnight don't even upset me in the least. I always stop just before the extreme stage of violence is reached – not that I am in any way afraid but that my lips become sore. At least that is my excuse. Doesn't do to show fear at any time you know (ha ha)!

Nan, I had another jag this afternoon – this time for typhus and boy did it kick (ha ha).

It's cheerio for the present.

3 February 1944

Before I go on to any other news I have something which is going to give you a real shock. And this time no kidding. Nan, I have stopped smoking! I have managed past the first few days and that is all the battle. And believe you me the first day was some battle, especially during the night when I couldn't busy myself with odd jobs but just had to sit and imagine all the fags in my pack going to waste. But still Nan I got over it and so far I have no sort of craving for a fag. Another item is that everybody around me in our tent smokes and that first night was a little trying (ha ha). It won't be necessary to send me any more cigarettes now. The fags already on their way here I can always exchange for something else like chocolate. Just you leave it to me (ha ha).

You ask me if my hands have improved, so you will be pleased to know that they are all right now, although between you and I Nan, I intend to take more care of my hands from now on. I forget there is still a war on (ha ha).

The period after the war seems to give me more room for thought than anything else. Just what is in store for us after all this fighting is over no-one seems to know, even with all this talk of post-war planning etc. Well so far it hasn't gone past the talking stage. Yes Nan, one does wonder what will happen in the future. Still why worry? I always remember the old advice of never crossing bridges until one reaches them.

4 February 1944

Your recent letter starts by telling me that you dream so much of myself and that you find it hard to realise that I have been away the best part of three years, and Nan all this reminds me about <u>my</u> dreams and of the fact that although I have often been back home I have never had you in my dreams. I seem to have had all sorts of other people. You see dear if I find you often in my dreams the thrill of actually reaching home and you would lose all that edge, wouldn't it now? Never mind Nan, we will have all our wee times to ourselves when our day comes again. I know that although at times you will probably feel as if you are receiving the 'heavy end' of things, you will always keep the chin up and look forward to the day when I will be home and the days of parting and uncertainty are only a memory and of the past. Yes Nan dear, these days will come again as they must and then you and I will share all our moments with each other. Understand, Nan?

You thank me for the hair clips, which seem to have caused quite a sensation (ha ha). And then of course the arrival of the razor blades for Fred. So now you can tell Fred just why I sent them. You see in one of your parcels you sent me a few blades from Fred and they were so poor that I felt sorry for Fred and sent him these Eyetie blades which in my opinion must be better than what he was using.

I reached this point by a process of logic (ha ha).
Yours always,
Alex
xxxxxxxxx

17 February 1944

My dear Nan,
Now you must excuse my scribble. As you can guess, I have been a little busier than usual for almost two weeks and together with the present conditions one hasn't the spirit to sit down and write letters. Believe it or not the only place for a seat would be the cold snow. Try and write yourself some day when you are feeling cold and wet (ha ha). Where oh where are those 'Blue Italian skies'? Candidly Nan, these are the worst conditions we have experienced and a lot can be said for the desert after all. At least we had no snow and mud there. Dear me! Never content! However in spite of all these trials I am perfectly well and so far have had no ill effects from the weather. The rum which we get is a big help!

I will try and answer at least some of that mail today. You tell me of how much you enjoyed my Christmas card 'effort'. This gift of mine seems to have caused quite a sensation eh? You didn't know I was an artist did you? (Ha ha.) All my own work (ha ha).

Yes Nan, I still have the guitar but the shape is a little altered now. However, it is still playable and that is the main thing. But how long it will remain so is another matter. Still I'll plonk away until it falls to pieces (ha ha).

You mention our savings and you know that if I am still in the present circumstances of not being able to spend the proverbial farthing I should manage my target all right (ha ha).

It has been snowing more or less steadily for the last three days and at the same time thawing, so everything is just mud and slush, and as some of the ruts caused by lorries are almost two feet deep, you can guess the walking conditions. The ruts were made before the snow came, so you can see the conditions on the ground. Now we know why we were given an extra pair of boots a few weeks ago. The powers that be knew something (ha ha). The snow has stopped now and the ground is rapidly thawing. What a mess! I wonder how long the Italian winter lasts.

I enjoyed the story of the Christmas party which our friend Mary held for the kiddies. You mention my guitar, but at present we have no wee shows, as the idea is to avoid crowds, as Jerry may send out a visiting card any time, and the only cards I like are the ones made of paper (ha ha). There is some consolation, Nan, in this weather, and that is the fact that Jerry is getting the same snow and mud, and also more visiting cards from us than he is able to answer. As for my concerts, well you see I make up most of my own songs, and at the present time I have no fresh verses. Who the h ★★★ <u>can</u> find inspiration from cold feet?

19 February 1944

I have been kept a bit busier again. I was sent to perform with my guitar at the camp of a Canadian tank mob. You see Nan, we had to have the use of their tanks to move our guns through the mud, as our own lorries, which by the way never let us down before, just couldn't move. I suppose our officers had mentioned a sing-song at a later date, which resulted in our going across there last night. Well Nan they enjoyed our little show very much. I don't suppose you will grudge missing out on a few lines for these fellows, who don't have any entertainers or instruments of their own. It's a great thing to make people laugh and forget things for a few hours. Perhaps a lot of my stuff is fit only for barrack-rooms, but if you could hear them laugh, Nan, you would understand.
Yours always,
Alex
xxxxxxxxx

23 February 1944 (Sorry Nan, some mud on the paper)

My dear Nan,
Another letter for you, and another letter nearer the end. The weather is the cause of all the trouble out here. There is still snow lying around, but it is now disappearing very slowly. As you can guess, there is plenty of mud around, and it is a case of drying boots at every chance. We have two pairs now, and believe me we do need them. We may be given rubber boots soon, which will be very welcome. I now also have a leather jerkin in my kit, which does help to break the edge of this very cold wind. I've never known such mud, and when a Russian envoy says that the mud in Italy is worse than in Russia, then it makes one think.

26 February 1944

I haven't been able to write for the past three days – very busy and under very bad conditions. We now have a gentle rain, in fact it has been raining for the past three days, and conditions are rather damp. However Nan, things could always be worse, and I have no reason to grumble. I will try and answer your letter 135 if all goes well tomorrow. It was a real novel – 28 pages!

While your letters are becoming longer, my letters are becoming shorter, and also more of a scribble. Blame it all on the weather. Thank you for the small pocket calendar which you enclosed in this letter, and where you have remembered my own birthday. For that action dear, many many thanks. It was real nice of you. Your letter tells me of your feelings at the New Year time, and of how much you missed my company. My thoughts were the same and I missed you very much.

You talk about your Christmas parcels. I laughed at the description of the clothes when you termed them 'unmentionables'. If I remember correctly it used to be a pet word of mine in the days of long ago, in the days of civvy street. Now that I am in the army for such a long time I don't use the word. I don't require to (ha ha).

Sometimes I wonder who has the hardest job, we out here or you folks at home. Still Nan, this is war, and I suppose all we can do is try our best, and at the same time hope that the war with all its various trials will be over soon. I am becoming rather tired of it myself now (ha ha).

Our letters are our only link with each other, and it does make a big difference when they arrive in good time. In fact all the difference in the world. Won't it be fun when we can write and actually know that it will be delivered at a certain time the next day? Such fun (ha ha). Or even better still, when we are in the very enviable position of not having to write letters at all? Just talk. And to judge by the length of your letters it looks as if all I will be able to do is listen (ha ha).

Well Nan, I'll finish now.

Yours always,

Alex

xxxxxxxx

20 March 1944   Trip to Bari

My dear Nan,

Provided that nothing out of the ordinary happens, this should be the letter about my visit to Bari. Well Nan, here goes.

The first stage of my journey was from camp to Termoli. I have all my kit packed up so I get on our lorry to H.Q. The weather is wet and I am naturally covered in mud. Still, a leave is a leave, and I am hoping that Bari is a lot drier!

Well Nan, at H.Q. we pick up the rest of the chaps and proceed to Termoli. There's not much I can say about that trip apart from the fact that the lorry was packed and it is pouring of rain. It is quite a long journey to Termoli and we reach a camp in the late afternoon. Everything is wet, cold and very muddy but as we are the first to arrive we are fortunate to be able to sleep on the tables and off the ground. However as the tents are flapping about in the wind and rain, conditions are still a bit unpleasant. However, I am not grumbling as the chaps who arrived after us had no tables etc!

Our first job is a walk into town just to see what's doing. Making a few enquiries here and there we find a free 'tea and bun' shop run by some Canadian organisation. The town by the way isn't very badly damaged, at least compared with the others further up. Quite a number of civilians in town and the usual one or two shops selling the usual collection of rubbish.

The next stop is the ENSA theatre. The show was a programme by the Band of the South African Force. It was a change to sit and listen to a real military band of 24 players and I enjoyed it very much. Then we had another little cinema show which was a film featuring the Andrews Sisters. In fact a most enjoyable evening. And that Nan, was my first night!

The next morning I was up about 7 o'clock and queued for my breakfast. This was fried bread, sausage and beans. Then I queued again for sandwiches and two cakes for the journey to Bari. It is still raining heavily as we make our way to the station so it is a case of slipping and staggering all the way there (ha ha). However, I do reach the train and manage to find a seat by the simple method of throwing my kit through a window and clambering through after it and leaving the door severely alone. I got this habit from my days in Egypt and the Wog trains (ha ha).

The country is all wet and very misty. At this point a few words on the trains. Naturally, they are Eyetie and had been very nice and comfortable before the war. Now instead of cushions, the seats are made of strips of wood. All the leather has been ripped up and removed. My guess is that Jerry did this. At last we reach the first real-sized town which is Barletta and here I experienced one of the most pleasant happenings of my leave, because at this station there is tea and buns waiting for us and did we enjoy the treat? However, the best part of all was the smiles and the few words from the two Salvation Army girls who dished out this surprise. What a difference from the dark Eyetie girls with their painted lips and most awful shoes and legs (ha ha). They were real nice and fresh-looking girls from our own country. Perhaps this may seem strange to you Nan but girls like these are a real treat for us. Again you might say 'What about the nurses etc?' Well Nan, between you and me the majority of them are on the 'hard-faced' side (if you know what I mean). Oh dear, I wish this pen would behave. Well Nan, now that I have raved about my two girls, I'll proceed on my journey to Bari.

We reach Bari in the afternoon. For once, the army has some organisation and we are soon on lorries on our way to the camp. This same very good organisation (most unusual) is still in force and we are soon booked in, settled ourselves in our hut and on our way to dinner.

Our sleeping quarters are long huts holding about twenty men and every man has a real camp bed. You know! These canvas ideas? Everything is fresh and clean so that is the main worry settled – where to sleep!

The dining hall is one of the finest parts of the camp. We just sit down at a table and the food is brought to us. By the way, Nan, all the labour here is done by civilians who were at one time in Jerry concentration camps. They are mostly Yugoslav and they do work very hard indeed. It was a very nice dinner.

I must stop now Nan and see if I can repair my pen.

21 March 1944

To tell the truth Nan, I really haven't repaired my own pen, but made a new one from various bits and pieces which I collected from the chaps round about. So far the 'job' seems to work and that is all that matters.

I want to give you some idea of what is in the camp in Bari in the way of entertainment. There is a Music Hall, a cinema, Club Rooms, Naafi, Library with all kinds of games etc. Also a good dentist and a Medical Officer where chaps can have a new set of teeth in two days. You see Nan, as this is a rest camp all these cases of teeth are treated as emergency as the men are only out of the 'Line' for a few days.

I finished the day by going to the Hippodrome and seeing an ENSA show called *Airs and Graces*. The show by the way was very poor and hadn't one item to grace it. I had a good night's sleep on my camp bed. However, I would have enjoyed it much better perhaps if I had a 'partner' for that night. Otherwise if I had you my wife. Still never mind Nan, perhaps we will have that 'pleasure' some day soon, who knows?

The next day was started by going for a shower and changing my clothes etc. Following that, the next thing was a visit to the Naafi, for the usual tea and buns. After lunch I had my first visit to Bari. The town itself is showing very little damage apart from around the docks. The shops have very little to sell in the way of any gifts for you and all I could see was cheap jewellery.

We went to an ENSA show in the Garrison Theatre, which by the way is the Opera House, and is a lovely building inside. A real continental building with large stage and five tiers of seats. The roof is domed with large paintings of events which took place in the 'Arena' in these days. Above the stage is a tableau of figures with wings etc. in the middle of which is a large clock. The most interesting part was the fact that the clock worked and kept good time (ha ha). The whole building of course is the usual red and gold colour scheme with an abundance of mirrors. Then I returned to camp and had a very good dinner and finished my day by going to the cinema. The stars of the film were Laurel and Hardy.

22 March 1944

Well, Nan, I do remember that this is my birthday, and that I am very well, and that the weather is very wet (ha ha). I have just sort of realised that if I continue my story at the same rate I should be writing about 60 pages! (Ha ha.) To avoid this problem it would be as well for me to cut a long story short, because each day in Bari was a repeat of the previous one.

I should mention that all the various roads in the camp had names of London streets. The main office was called Lambeth Palace. In the whole camp there is one street placed 'out of bounds', and that is called 'Petticoat Lane'. Yes Nan, you guessed correctly. This is the place where the Naafi girls live. They even put a lot of barbed wire around here (ha ha).

I should tell you of a little incident which should interest you. I was talking to a Yank and he told me that planes could reach home from Bari in six hours. Imagine, Nan, six hours! Yes, Nan, I did make enquiries, but it was 'no go' (ha ha). Still, it is very interesting, isn't it?

I returned to camp by the same method as I went – by train to Termoli and the rest of the journey by lorry. We have a lot of Canadians here now, and candidly, they are not liked at all. As you know Nan, I have had experience of all the colonials out here, and although perhaps some of the others have been at times a bit rough, they were real good company, and real genuine fellows. The Canadians are different. They keep to themselves, are very poor 'snipers' and always out for trouble. Needless to say, Nan, they get it, and slowly I believe they are beginning to realise a few home truths. What we think is that they have had too good a time in Britain, and too much of their own way, with the result that they don't understand why it shouldn't be the same out here. Yes, Nan, a poor lot.

In the meantime I'll say cheerio. Good luck and God bless you all.
Yours always,
Alex

26 March 1944

My dear Nan,
You know that my pen gave up the ghost, and it may decide to go on strike any moment. Just like the poor hard-working fellows back home (the rats!). My time is very short at present and I am feeling rather cold. The weather is very blowy with rain and sleet, not ideal for writing letters. Still, dear, if I don't try at least a few lines I'll never catch up. I have been moving around since I came back from Bari, and now I'm going to my bed. Yes!

27 March 1944

What a life! In Egypt we had the hottest summer for 40 years, and now in Italy we must experience the worst winter in memory. The best place to go is under the blankets!

Thanks very much for the fags Nan, because although in one of my letters I told you that I had stopped smoking, it only lasted eight days. On the ninth day I felt so cold and miserable that I had a smoke, and that was that. Still, I'll have another try when the weather becomes warmer.

Thanks for the story of the christening robe, Nan, as I know just how you feel about it. It won't be my fault if the robe isn't used (ha ha). You speak about the cold weather at home, and I used to feel sorry for you all while I was enjoying perpetual sunshine, but times have changed (ha ha). Now, instead of feeling sorry for you, I feel sorry for myself. Cheerio until the next time.

28 March 1944

Now Nan, in all your recent letters I have perceived an undercurrent of 'fed-upness' as the one and only subject is of how long I have been away, and of how much you are looking forward to my return home. And Nan I don't blame you the least bit. I know that our three years is a long time away, and that others have managed home with less overseas service than myself.

By the way Nan, I have written down the phone number of McDonald's just in case I do have the chance to surprise you (ha ha). That's the spirit Nan, you make all the money so that I can come home and live like a gentleman (ha ha).

Give my regards to all at 85 and my best wishes to Torchy. Poor little girl, stuck with all that old bull. Remind her that all my buttons are very dirty and that I don't even shave every morning!
Cheerio, good luck, and God bless you all,
Alex
xxxxxxxxxx

4 April 1944

My dear Nan,
Thanks very much for the birthday card. The words are very nice, and like yourself I hope the day is not far distant when we will be able to celebrate these anniversaries together. This reminds me that it will soon be four years since you received your ring, and since I received my watch. The watch is still going strong, although a bit battered about. Of course I am fortunate that one of my mates was a watch repairer in civvy street, and he looks after

all our watches rather well. I wish he could do as much with fountain pens. I can see myself being reduced to writing in pencil soon. You know, Nan, when I am a very rich man the first thing I will do is buy a real good pen (ha ha). Just for the job of writing my name on cheques etc. (ha ha).

I admired the snap of the girls which you enclosed, although it would be just like you to be talking all the time. Are you never quiet? (Ha ha.) The girl in the centre of the snap seems to be down on her knees. Now I must come to the point. Well Nan, a friend of mine, a Sergeant, wants to know about the girl with the knees!

I was up the poles again in search of 'knowledge' after my last 'electric light' job. However, I couldn't find any and it wasn't until afterwards that I found out that the main supply came from Pescara, so as the saying goes, 'we've had it' (ha ha).

14 April 1944

My dear Nan,
The news from this part of the world is that the weather is now ideal for us old Desert Rats. In fact today I had a bath in bits outside and in the old Western desert style (ha ha). The only disadvantage of this idea is that nowadays we have the Eyetie women to contend with although they seem to keep away from us rather well. I shouldn't worry about the Eyeties, Nan, they have no sex appeal, and you have no reason to be in any way jealous (ha ha). And that's that!

The war is just going on and we are kept busy putting over a few shells and Jerry lets us know that he is still there by putting a few back – just to be polite you know! Cheerio and goodnight.
Alex
xxxxxxxxx

15 April 1944

You said in your letter 144 of how cold it was in Glasgow. Now dear, it is better here now and soon I'll be moaning about the heat! Though I don't suppose it will be so hot up in these hills as in the plains or farther north. We can though expect plenty of flies and also, I understand, mosquitoes of the malaria variety. Not a very rosy outlook really.

You describe details of life at 85 very well though I don't suppose there is much point in my sending you hairpins when there are so many down these armchairs! Still dear, it's good to know that 85 is the same cheerful place and that life seems to carry on in the same way. We have a lot to be grateful for, haven't we?

It looks as if big things may be expected this year and who knows what may happen? To finish with Nan, I can assure you that I am looking forward to that special day coming every bit as much as yourself, although perhaps I treat the subject in rather a flippant manner and as more of a joke than anything else. I really think it is the best way Nan, at least until I really have definite news for you.

17 April 1944

I have just received your card from Troon and I am pleased to read that you enjoyed yourself on your welcome break from the selling of shoes. Your relatives seem to be very nice people and I hope I have the pleasure of meeting them soon. Yes dear! That will be the day. When my 'doings' are in that blue case too. You paint a nice picture of the spring morning at Troon, Nan, but why spoil the hum of birds by mentioning the hum of planes? Out here we are still wondering when the war is going to start again!
God bless you all,
Alex
xxxxxxxxxx

23 April 1944

My dear Nan,
As usual during these last few weeks I haven't a great deal of time to myself so I have to revert to my old habit of 'letters to be continued'. So you see, if I only manage, say, two pages at a time, don't be getting the idea that I am neglecting you or forgetting you and instead of writing letters having the time of my young life in the company of these seductive dark-haired senorinas (with and without lice).

24 April 1944

Goodness lassie, you are spoiling me with these stamps (ha ha). Now Nan, your letter is a real love letter dealing with how much you miss me, how you worry about me and of how you look forward to my arrival home.

However Nan, I am disappointed in you, because when you devote so much to the thought of your 'wee boy' I have a sneaking feeling that you only want me home as a 'means to an end' (ha ha). My dear girl, when I am back at 85 again it's rest I want and a lot of sleep (ha ha). And I mean sleep (ha ha).

Perhaps if I spoke to Fred in a very nice way he would let me share his bed (ha ha). Still Nan, to forget this nonsense, I have no intention of sharing

Fred's bed. I know just how you are feeling, and my earnest wish is that your dreams come true. Meantime, Nan, cheerio and good luck.

25 April 1944

Here I am, Nan. Now give Ewan my best regards but ask him if he can't fly to Italy instead of where he is going to and I could maybe get a lift (ha ha). You never can tell can you?

Your letter goes on to tell me of your dream about that house, furniture and the wee fellow. You say that I may have the impression that you are a blether. No, Nan, I don't think you are a blether. I think you are an <u>awful</u> blether really (ha ha). I just hope that your dream comes true and very soon.

I am pleased to read that you have these wee nights out and that you usually enjoy yourself thoroughly.

Here, it is just a case of waiting for something to happen. Mind you we keep fairly busy popping a few over to Jerry. Sort of breaks the monotony you know (ha ha).

Until I write again dear, good-bye and God bless you all.

Yours always,

Alex

Xxxxxxxxxxxxxx

3 May 1944

My dear Nan,

Well Nan, I am in the mood to write and the sole reason is that I received two letters from you tonight. It was one of the most pleasant surprises I have ever had when I found your photograph in your 150.

I would like to write a few lines about this photograph before I go under the mosquito net and to bed. Yes dear, mosquitoes are here again and we have the usual drugs etc. But to get back to this photograph. In my opinion Nan, you are looking real well and should I say 'positively stout' (ha ha).

Perhaps it is the art of photography! You remember the first snap you gave me? I do believe it was the first because it is practically yellow now. It is a snap taken at some coast resort. You were very round of face in these days but of course that was before you had the misfortune to meet me and have all the cares and worries of marital bliss. Well Nan, this latest photo is just like you were then. In other words you are growing younger than ever (ha ha).

Before I finish I should say that I like your style of dress and neckwear. I refer to the row of pearls. Yes, dear wife, you are something worth coming home to and I hope that day comes soon.

And now dear goodnight.

4 May 1944

You thank me for the very good mail you have had recently but dear why thank me? A poor man it is who can't write home to his wife now and then (ha ha). In any case, letters are my only contact with you aren't they? So why neglect it? And yet you thank me. No! Nan, the thanks should be from this end.

You haven't had much of a married life Nan but if all goes well I will try my best to make up for all you have missed. Perhaps I shouldn't say this dear in case you think me rather sentimental, but you know Nan, you are really worth living for (ha ha). Well, I'll leave my loving business for the present. Anyway, I'll wait until the time comes, and perhaps even then I won't do much talking either, you never can tell (ha ha).

I am glad you enjoyed the tale of my Xmas day but I can assure you that you couldn't enjoy the story half as much as I enjoyed my Big Moment (ha ha).

And now I come to the part of the letter which shook me. That was the story of how you have applied for a <u>house</u>. You know Nan, the thought of a home of our own really thrilled me and I certainly hope that we have the good fortune and health to enjoy what some day may be ours. But why didn't you tell me before? Surely you didn't think for one moment that I would object? Anything like that is alright with me.

Sorry Nan, I need to finish now. So 'Here's to the next time'. Cheerio Nan.

5 May 1944

Your letter is wondering if I had stopped smoking the fags. I did manage to jilt Lady Nicotine for a period of 6 days and then I felt so cold, wet and hungry that she vamped me again and poor me fell once again. But Nan, I'll have another go soon.

No Nan, I don't think you're crazy to enclose the Women's Own. Indeed, I rather enjoyed the stories. Must be that sloppy part in my make up (ha ha).

And now dear wife, it's goodnight.

7 May 1944

Yes Nan, it is Sunday morning here and as I have been on duty practically all night, I have my day off today. By the way, a 'day off' doesn't mean that I can go to town or pay a visit to 85! All it means is that I am not wanted in case of action (I hope) and I can go to bed if I wish. However, I don't feel like sleep so I will take the chance to do a few odd jobs and a spot of writing. I have some socks to darn and of course a bit of spring cleaning. I am Mrs MAC this morning (ha ha).

A little later this morning, I will have one of my little 'fires'. I know that this action seems strange to you but it is one of my many peculiarities. Of course, I have a great number of other strange habits. In fact, I am a very odd fellow altogether. Aren't I? (Ha ha.) But there you are, it takes all kinds to make a world.

Yours always,

Alex

Xxxxxxxxxxxx

11 May 1944

My dear Nan,

What do you mean by your remark that a dirty face adds to your glamour? Who's been filling you up with this glamour stuff? If I didn't know you I should say that you will end up a 'fast woman' (ha ha).

I am surprised to hear that you have been taking pills which were rec-ommended way back in 1941 as I thought that incident was all finished with. But perhaps I am misunderstanding it all. I should hate to think that you were still feeling the effects of that day. Let me know for sure will you Nan?

I was interested in your habit of taking flowers to Mother and I know she does like flowers very much. It's a pity I can't send flowers from here as with the warmer weather they are beginning to appear in the fields now. I don't know much about flowers but I do know that there are plenty of tulips around me and just a few yards from where I am now there is a large rose bush with hundreds of roses just beginning to bud. A great change from the barrenness of the desert. The fig leaf which I sent Margaret came from the tree just outside my tent – my washing line by the way (ha ha).

So you keep all my letters eh? If I kept all yours I'm afraid I should need a lorry to myself and I can't get that. I just devised the method of allowing them to gather for so long and then having my small fire. The fire, of course, must be on a Sunday morning. But then I was always a queer sort of chap wasn't I? (Ha ha.)

12 May 1944

Well dear, as I finished yesterday on the subject of flowers I would like to say a few more words. As I can't send any flowers home I am going to attempt to dry and press them and then enclose them in my letters. I don't know anything about this but as I said I'll give it a try. I have collected a few of the flowers around here and I am endeavouring to press them, so that I can send them home to you.

This morning I found a rose after a long search, so I thought that instead of pressing it, I would try to keep it as it is by <u>waxing</u> it. I should add that I had heard of this idea and as I like to try anything at least once, I thought I'd do a spot of waxing. I melted a candle in a fag tin, and dipped the rose into it. The result was that the flower just disappeared!

Maybe I didn't do it right (ha ha).

Still, I am pressing some other flowers right now, by the simple method of sitting on them (ha ha). If they do turn out, I'll send them on to you, but if they don't, forget I ever attempted this job!

You should also know that the 'fun' has started again here in Italy so here's hoping that we go a long way this time before we call a halt. This 'Do' will go well, as the old 8th Army are having the first go. Perhaps you will hear my loud knock on the door this year yet, eh?

And now Nan a few words about your 151 and all about that wedding. They certainly took a long time to make their minds up. Perhaps of course they believe in that old saying of 'marry in haste' etc. which is a very good saying too. I wish I had taken longer myself now, when I see the opportunities I am missing of having such pleasant times with the glorious Italian girls. It's terrible, being tied down to a wife (ha ha).

I was real interested in your story of Monty, and of how you had a smile and salute from him. You go on to tell me of how you have read a lot about him. You will also be reading about General Leese, who is a very good mixer. He has a habit when he comes across any unit, of throwing a few thousand fags out to the men. Monty doesn't smoke himself, so he never thought of such an act. I don't wish to detract from Monty, but you must remember that the man who was behind him in the desert and right into Italy is still in charge here. The planning of all the battles from Alamein to Cassino was done by Alexander. All Monty did was carry these plans out. Of course, with such men as the Desert Rats, how can he lose? (Ha ha.)

I now have a taste for foreign food. What is meant by the words 'sausage and chips'? Now, if you said to me it was a dish of macaroni, garlic and olives then I would understand (ha ha).

And now dear wife good luck and God bless you all.

20 May 1944

My dear Nan,

I haven't received any more mail from you, but the fact is that I'm not with the battery at present. The letters will probably all reach me at once, including that lucky bag you mention. You hint at the contents, and something tells me that you have sent me a pen.

Now, Nan, I know that pens are very hard to get back home, and that was why I told you not to try until I actually asked you. Nan, perhaps these last few lines may give you the impression that I am a bit angry with you. Don't you believe it, Nan.

Frankly, I love you for your action, but being a man (I hope) I must show my authority. Never do for my wife to get the idea that she can just do what she likes and not bother one little bit about what I say (ha ha). You may even boss me when I reach home again (perish the thought) so I want to give you some idea of what I can do when I put my foot down with a firm hand (ha ha). Now let that be a lesson to you, and don't you dare disobey my wishes again. Oh! What's the use! I suppose I will just be the loving husband and really very pleased to think you have been so thoughtful in managing to find me a real pen. Aren't I clever? (Ha ha.)

And now Nan dear God bless you all.

4 June 1944 – Fall of Rome to British and US forces

6 June 1944 – Allied troops land on the beaches of Normandy, France – D-Day

10 June 1944

My dear Nan,

I've been away from the unit for a few weeks, with the result that I have been without any mail from home. Please Nan, although this may appear very mysterious, you have nothing to worry about. You will find that all your fears have been groundless. It is rather awkward having no word from you, and I shall certainly ask a few questions! When I get back I shall threaten to give up my stage career, and that will shake them! As for my guitar, it was left with the Battery, and I am just hoping it is still in one piece.

You would smile if you were where I am now, and listening to these chaps moaning about going home. Some of them have been out here for nine weeks (ha ha). Cheerio, and God bless you all.

18 June 1944   *Hospital*

My dear Nan,

Now I can tell you why I haven't been able to receive your letters. It really amounts to a confession on my part, because the fact was I've been in hospital these last four weeks. I didn't see any reason why I should tell you, and if I had been able to receive my mail, there would have been no need to make any excuses at all. Knowing your nature I couldn't dare mention the word 'hospital', so I left that part out. I can honestly say that I am well now, and I returned to the Battery this morning.

Cheerio and good luck.

Yours always,

Alex

xxxxxxxxxxx

20 June 1944

My dear Nan,

There is a possibility that I will be attending a medical board soon and no doubt lose my A1. Now dear the trouble isn't serious and as for de-grading well I will probably receive A2 which in itself proves what I am saying. Now if I was to be placed C3 or anything like that it would be a different matter.

I am still really very fit. The thing is that the heat didn't help matters and as I don't expect to be out here for years it's quite on the cards that the leg will give no more trouble. I will still give you all the waltzes you want (ha ha).

You mention of how pleased you are at the new attack. As for ourselves Nan, we have come back out [of] the line now and are A/A once more, which is looked upon as a rest after acting as Field Artillery. We have been up for over four months including the winter so we haven't done too bad after all.

I hope I don't have another Italian winter.

I will write again soon.

Yours always,

Alex

Xxxxxxxxx

20 June 1944

My dear Nan,

I had about a dozen letters from you to catch up on after my stay 'in Dock'!

I will start with 149 and gradually answer them all as I go along. First of all, I must say thanks for the very nice card which was enclosed with this letter. You know, Nan, after reading this card I have a sneaking feeling that you maybe do like me a bit. What about you and I getting together, eh? (Ha ha.)

You mention that you would like me to try and play 'Blue Heaven' on the guitar for you, so I'll see what I can do. When I returned from dock I heard the Battery are intending to form a band of sorts, as there is a possibility of being able to get instruments now that we are out of the line. It looks as if I will have to play both the guitar and either a cornet or trumpet. Some people are just born great, others achieve greatness, while some have greatness thrust upon them. To which of these categories I belong it is hard to say (ha ha). Perhaps the penalty of fame, eh? (Ha ha.)

I had to laugh at your description of the spring cleaning episode at 85, and at how it was likened to an attack by the Fifth and Eighth Armies. As it was a success, the main attack must have been by the Eighth! Funny, the Fifth tried to take Cassino for four months, then the Eighth go across and Cassino falls in four days. The Fifth are given the job of taking Rome, otherwise just walk in, but the taking of Cassino meant the fall of Rome. I should add that the Fifth is practically an all-American outfit. 'Nuff said!' Some of these days I shall be able to speak my mind (ha ha). In case you get me wrong I should perhaps say that we have no Yanks in the 8th.

21 June 1944

I haven't yet received your parcel posted on April 27th. However, there is ample time yet. Speaking of parcels, a few of our new friends the Eyeties have been caught pilfering our mail. Still, I don't think for one minute that the Eyeties have my '<u>pen</u>!' I know you only said, 'A certain thing', but am I right? I will look forward to the arrival of that shoe-box.

You tell me that Margaret and Ewan intend to marry after the war, and tell me to keep this secret. If I remember correctly, Ewan told me that was his intention the last time I spoke to him, which was in December 1940. But perhaps he didn't have Margaret round to his way of thinking at that time (ha ha). I hope that they have their wish very soon, and that they have much more time together during the first years of marriage than we have had. I don't think I could wish them much more than that, could I, Nan? I just keep hoping for the best. At the same time I don't think it should be too long now.

In one of your letters Nan you tell me of your 'True Confessions', and ask me if I know of any myself.

Well dear, perhaps I should say that the one happening which is ever in my mind is the day when I arrived at 85 in February 1941 from the boat at Glasgow. I had left you as I thought for a few years, but even on the ship I had the funny feeling that I had not really left you, and that I would see you again. You met me at the door, and I practically carried you into the bedroom, with Mother hovering in the background, and I believe going 'Tut tut!' (ha ha).

I often wonder what my next homecoming will be like.

26 June 1944

I have not managed to add any more for the last five days.

You say in your letters Nan that you would like to pay a visit to London, and you can call it another of our remarkable coincidences, but I was going to tell you that if all went well after the war we would go places and do things. London naturally is one of the places. I have been there before, but London is a very large town, so clever as I may be (ha ha) I could not honestly say that I knew London. But then, after finding my way for over three years out here, surely finding my way round London will not be such a big job.

You tell me of your homecoming from Troon, and the welcome you had. Yes, dear, it would be a great pity if this war brought any unhappiness to 85.

I am pleased that you enjoyed the news of the fall of Rome. I may have the opportunity of a short visit there myself.

Good luck and God bless you all.

Yours always,

Alex

8 July 1944 [in green ink]   *Rome Trip*

My dear Nan,

I know it's a funny colour, but there you are. I don't understand the Italian language, so how was I to know the ink I bought in Rome was this most unusual colour? I have a lot of mail to answer, but I wanted to tell you the story of my visit. However, there is a snap in one of these letters of yourself with a book on your knee, and a lovely leg-show. I couldn't sleep all night with the thought of how young and desirable you are, and of how long I have been away from home and you. Dear me, now I am becoming lecherous (ha ha). But honestly Nan, I do miss you very much, and I don't mean just your legs either. Still Nan, it may not be too long now, although the old story of scarcity of shipping has been changed now to the shortage of manpower. I think myself it is all a 'racket'.

But Nan, you don't want to hear my grumbles. What you want is my story of Rome. So here is my description of my day in the capital of Italy.

I had a good long road to travel and we parked the lorry in a part of the town reserved for us. We were near the Coliseum, which was our first point of interest. It really is only an old ruin, although it was very interesting to see a place which I had heard so much about and seen so many times in photographs. I can't describe it, Nan, to be fair, as it is just a very large open space surrounded by the old pillars which I am sure you have so often seen yourself, if not in photographs, then portrayed by the magnates of Hollywood. The fact is, Nan, that about all I can say about the Coliseum is that I have actually been there, and visited the spot of these actual happenings. And Nan, so much for the great Coliseum.

Well, Nan, the morning is now very short, and we finished by just walking around the town itself, examining the shops. The town itself is very clean, and undamaged by war, and life for the people hasn't changed very much. That was one part of my visit which made me really mad, when I saw the very well-dressed men and women parading the streets, with no knowledge of war and what it really means. There is plenty of material in the shops, but the prices are well beyond the range of my purse. I hunted the shops for something for you dear, but I'm afraid I was out of luck. There are plenty of stalls on the streets, but the most common articles were crosses on chains and photographs of the Pope, which I don't think would interest you, as I am sure you have no great desire for such things.

Oh, dear, I almost forget to tell you that after all my worry about pens, and after all the trouble you had sending and finding this pen for me, I found thousands of them in the shops in Rome. It was because of this and all these other things which I saw here which made me realise that these Romans were really enjoying the war, and having a much better time than my own folks at home. Still dear, damn their pens etc! (Ha ha!) I look upon this pen and anything you send me as really a part of you, and it means more to me than all the so-called glory of Rome. Here I am becoming sloppy and forgetting all about my story of Rome. All I bought in Rome was a torch for myself, which came without batteries. If I told you what I paid for it you would say I was absolutely mad (ha ha).

All that remained was to return to the car park and have a bite of lunch. You see, Nan, we brought our own grub with us, the inevitable bully, as for us Rome isn't a town full of cafes etc. where one can have a real feed. There is a Naafi in the town, but they only have tea. However, Nan, there was a restaurant in town for us chaps where the Army supplied the food and the Eyeties did the waiting. We received tickets for this place at the car park from the officer there, who used to be at the Bari rest camp. Fred will no doubt remember one of the famous 'Wembley Wizards' named Alex Jackson. He is actually the officer I am referring to, who looks after the sports end of the 8th Army rest camps.

9 July 1944

After our lunch we made for the Vatican City, not I assure you to pay homage to the Pope, but to visit St Peter's church, of which everybody has heard so much. Well, Nan, perhaps I am prejudiced against this religion, but I found St Peter's similar to other churches, although on a much grander scale. It has all the pomp which is a part of the R.C.s. You know, the usual big paintings, pillars etc., and big lumps of brass. The best part was the view of Rome from the top of the dome. This meant a climb of over 400 steps, and this feat nearly finished all of us, but the view was well worth the very stiff climb. I spent an hour or so here, and I should mention that a good number of what at first looks like paintings are really very small mosaic work. No doubt about it Nan, very clever indeed. Everybody was enamoured of the view from the dome, but for myself Nan the whole thing left me cold, because one only requires to climb the hills of Scotland to get a scene of much more grandeur, not just an imitation, but the everyday work of nature herself.

So much for St Peter's in Rome. By the way Nan I had to pay 9d to climb these awful stairs (ha ha). It was now three in the afternoon and very hot indeed, and so we made for the Naafi where we had a cup of tea. As all the walking and climbing had made us rather weary, we looked out for a show of some sort. Eventually we found an open-air theatre not far away, although we didn't know until we were inside that it was an all-Italian do. Still, we had a seat, and plenty of laughs, most of them of course at the wrong time, but then what can be expected when a tall and not too-bad looking girl walks on, very lady-like, wearing the least possible attire, a long 'browned-off' expression on her face, and her jaws working overtime with the chewing-gum. Then a singer has a row with the conductor and blames him for not keeping time properly. What a show!

11 July 1944

Now Nan, you know that I have been in dock, and I now think it was only a waste of time trying to keep that news from you. That's what I get for telling lies. You worry about my leg, and I should give you a little more detail. I must go right back to the time my legs were bandaged due to what may be termed an accident. As you remember, it all healed up apart from a small spot behind the left knee. This became rather serious, and I had nearly four months in the Aussie hospital at Kantara in 1941. It was found necessary to remove a piece from behind that knee. Well Nan, seemingly a vein was cut then, with the result that there was no passage for the blood. Now you see, after these years, as the blood couldn't go through, it had to go somewhere, so it tried to come outwards. A swelling came on my leg, between the knee and the ankle. I reported sick, and had a month in dock. The swelling was removed and everything now is all right. Don't let the thought of a medical board upset you dear, because it is just the way of the Army.

Cheerio, good night, and God bless you all.

23 July 1944

My dear Nan,

I have sent off the photographs taken inside the Coliseum. I also have some other photographs, but I must warn you that I really don't feel as old and miserable as they make me appear!

Well dear I have received your 158 and the 'leg show' will be enough to keep me going meantime. And what's all this talk about sleeping with me? To judge by the tone of most of your letters, it seems to me that I will have to enjoy my sleep in the afternoon, and by myself too. Still, it may not be very long now.

And another thing, Mrs Macintyre. What do you mean by 'tea in bed' eh? Where did you get these fool notions? I am the one who has the tea in bed. The Big Boss, see!? And I shall expect sugar, and plenty of it. Apart from my so-called wit Nan, I am pleased to read how much you look forward to our home, and of how happy you are gathering all these odds and ends.

I also have another number for your list of my savings. The value is £7-10-0, and the number is LG621303.

By the way Nan, I heard the news of the landing in France while in Dock at Vasto.

I was interested in your story of how you paid a visit to Hamilton. Perhaps I will remember that hint of Uncle Bob's to play up on the limp, but perhaps I won't.

I must say cheerio Nan.

Yours always,

Alex

xxxxxxxxx

30 July 1944

My dear Nan,

I had an idea that something was wrong as mail was reaching the unit and there was none for yours truly and well that was rather unusual, so like yourself I put two and two together and made the usual answer.

I'm afraid I haven't given you much sympathy on the trouble you had with your throat. What you want is my company and not a few words of kindness.

Whatever you do Nan, you must take care of yourself and one of the best hints I know for good health is to avoid worry. I still think you worry too much and you also walk too fast. Be like me and grow fat by just taking things nice and easy and letting every day take care of itself. Still sometimes it works and sometimes it don't (ha ha). Now just don't worry about your wee man, now fat wee man. You know Nan, I am the owner of such a tummy that I must ask my mates if my boots are clean before I go on my day's leave to Rome. Of course, once I am in Rome I am always looking in shop windows and seeing for myself (ha ha).

Like yourself we out here are very interested in the landing in France and no doubt you will know that the first full Division to land there was one of the old original 8th Army.

I am pleased to know of you receiving the box of chocs. And perhaps I may say that I did enjoy the one you let me have (ha ha).

Now I know what makes you so fat (ha ha).

I must say cheerio meantime.

Yours always,

Alex

Xxxxxxxxx

PS I had a fire today.

3 August 1944

My dear Nan,

I'm well at present and the weather is very warm, and it should not be too long before we have the harvest of fruit again. You know, the grapes etc. Shades of 'Dysentery Rides Again'.

I am still doing well with the savings, and that is even with the chance of visiting Rome with its very high prices. I couldn't find anything useful for you in Rome, Nan, as anything small was rubbish, and anything large was also rubbish. I couldn't even find any hair-grips, so, Nan, I am afraid that you have 'had' your gift from Rome. Of course, I could send you a photograph of the Pope, but I have a funny feeling that you wouldn't appreciate it.

7 August 1944

My dear Nan,

It seems that the spotlight has now moved from the 8th Army to the forces in France. But we keep on plodding away and doing the same job as always, and that is making Jerry move back. I see by the news that the British Army in France is now doing the 'Cassino Polka'. Holding the main enemy force and giving the Yanks the easy road. Still, so long as it helps the war effort why worry? Here things are going well, and the only 'fly in the ointment' is that dread of another Eyetie winter, as the last one was pretty tough.

I suppose at this stage I should say a few words about myself. The main thing is that I am well, and what my thoughts are you can guess. For that matter dear I don't think you need go any further than your first choice.

Yes! Nan, you are correct. It's the old cry of 'I wanna go home!' (ha ha) Still, as I said I expect big things these next few months, so the spirit is still very high.

I have your card dated July 29th, and I am so pleased to read that you are now up again, but a bit weak on the pins. I know you will be all right Nan, but once more I must say that whatever happens out here you must on no account worry about me. I will be home safe and sound eventually.

Now I'm afraid I must do my small part for the war effort, so once again good night and a good awakening.

8 August 1944

Well Nan, I have heard no more news of the de-grading business, and in any case it won't make any odds to my army service. No doubt the army will remember the case about the year 1950, and then discover that I am still in the Middle East!

I'm sure you must have enjoyed yourself at the Empire. Mind you, Nan, I am not saying anything against the show you saw there, but it can't be near so good as myself and 'Old Faithful'. Yes, Nan, I call my instrument of torture 'Old Faithful' as you suggest, but maybe it would be as well to name it 'Old Faithful 2', as I have another item of the same name at home, which would in any case be a more welcome sight than my guitar! You know who I mean!

You will be interested to know that I heard a pipe band in Rome, but it happened to be an Irish mob, and the tunes were all different from what I expected. This performance was just under the balcony which Musso used to make his speeches from, and no doubt the same idle rich of Rome listened to both the performances. 'Sfunny! (Ha ha.)

Yours always,

Alex

Xxxx

14 August 1944

Today I am writing to you during the afternoon, as the weather is very warm, and everybody has gone back to the old idea of the desert by crawling into the shade, and either reading, writing, or lying down. Needless to say, the majority are lying down. Where we are at present there are miles of grape-vines but the trouble is that we are just a bit too early. Terrible state of affairs! There are a few tomatoes around and these are a little help.

I am a little surprised that you are still away from work but the news that you will soon be off to Oban for a well-deserved break makes me feel a lot easier in my mind.

You know Nan, the mention of Oban brings back a lot of memories of my push bike days. My passion for travel, I'm afraid, has cooled quite a lot since these days. Still I suppose that after this spot of bother is over, I will be wanting to drag you to some other strange countries. I always had a funny nature which, after noticing for a while, you decided to change, so you run me off my poor old feet and before I had recovered my sense of balance I was truly 'hooked'. Oh, the wiles of women!

And now my poor friend Ewan is having a few nibbles at that self same hook!

Yours always,

Alex

Xxxxxxxxxxxx

19 August 1944

My dear Nan,

I am well and just the same as I was when I left you such a long time ago. Well Nan, perhaps I have changed a little but then you would be better able to judge that. After all I see myself every day and I don't make it a long study. It takes a strong heart to put up with my appearance every day so instead of grumbling at my long absence, perhaps you really should be very thankful that you have had almost four years less to 'put up' with me!

In your letter 159 you enclosed a cutting dealing with service abroad and I certainly agree with you in that matter, as it is time I was home again. It would be a lie if I said I wasn't fed up. I am, and right up to the neck too, but still, being fed up doesn't get anybody anywhere, so I just keep myself going by a few odd jobs and the time passes much quicker.

To give you an idea Nan, a long time ago I picked up an old scrap engine, very small of course, and after a lot of work I have it running, so that I also get electric current and run a small radio set which I also built up from scrap. We get the news at night but I always have my fingers crossed as the whole affair may blow up at any time (ha ha). Still Nan, it has kept my mind occupied for a long time now and for that I am thankful.

Naturally, I have had a lot of teasing as it is a miracle that it goes at all but then even that passes the time and helps to keep the mind off other matters. Among other remarks I have been told to 'send the engine home to a museum of wonders' (ha ha). And the wireless with it (ha ha).

And now I must get a few hours sleep, being on duty all night.

20 August 1944

Here I am but I won't have as much time as I expected.

I see in one of your letters that you remarked on my idea of pressing flowers. I did have quite a bookful at Lanciano but when a man goes away to Dock like that, he can't have all these items taken care of until he comes back. So that's that.

I have had quite a few snaps taken of myself recently and I hope I can send these to you soon. Still, I won't be satisfied until I have my picture taken with my grey suit and as you say my 'clean collar and tie'. To judge by the recent news I am of the opinion that Jerry has had it and this is the time when, not being satisfied with flying bombs, he may use gas, especially on towns. These flying bombs came as a surprise Nan, so don't let the gas catch you the same way.

And now Nan I come to your 161. How do you expect me to answer a novel of 25 pages? It takes me all my time to read these pages, far less answer them all. I hope you have repeated a lot of items of news in this letter or else I shall be answering this one letter for the duration!
Good luck and God bless you all.
Yours always,
Alex
Xxxxxxxx

25 August 1944

My dear Nan,
I am so pleased to read that you are now a lot better and, although you are only working part time, you are more or less back to normal. I just thought to myself, 'Och, it's a sore throat and nothing to worry about'. But it must have been more serious. So, I'm afraid you are up to the same trick as myself when I 'hold on' to news when I go into Dock, just in case you worry too. You know Nan, we are a very curious pair and you can guess what my thoughts are at the present time and for that matter all the time. Yes Nan, the time when I shall be home again and we shall be together, I hope for all time. We have been apart from each other a long time now Nan but the news is very good from all the various fronts so perhaps it may not be for very long now. And no more fast walking and selling shoes! But then as you are the boss, I can only do as you say and dear knows what plans you have for poor me!

Things have changed, Nan, and now instead of a bad-tempered young man I am an old hen-pecked individual and young Miss Smith is now old 'Mrs Mac'. I must have my little joke you know. Knowing that you have no sense of humour I always mark them thus (ha ha).

I see you received the photograph taken inside the Coliseum. So you think that I am looking well and that I have a sunburned body. My skin is certainly brown but it is surprising how my body can become pale after a winter such as last year. I'm afraid that it shouldn't be long after I am home that I become my usual pale-looking self. My, my, how I hate myself. I think I will grow another mouser as it suits my personality.

I have an item of news for you. When we came abroad Nan, the maximum period of service was four years overseas. Since we have been out here it has been extended to five years. Not a very pleasing prospect eh? Well, Nan, we have just received word that it has been reduced to <u>four and a half</u> years, which if we have to serve the maximum means our time being up next summer. Now that things are going even better, we are hoping that the period may be reduced still further. Who knows?

Yours always,

Alex

Xxxxxxxxxxx

29 *August* 1944   *Disbanding of the 276 Battery*

My dear Nan,

I'm afraid that this letter will not be very cheerful, as I'm not in a cheerful mood. So I will get down to brass tacks and give you the bad news. Yes, dear, the news is very bad for myself and the rest of the lads. Things have been a bit quiet for us since Jerry started going back, and we have really had very few enemy aircraft to bother us. Well Nan, to get back to my tale of woe, we were reviewed by General Alexander himself yesterday. After presenting a few medals he gave us the news. In a few days the whole regiment ceases to be. <u>In fact we are being disbanded entirely.</u>

You see, Nan, when we came out here at first there were plenty of Jerry planes, and we were needed, but now, as Alexander says, the Jerry air force has had it, and that leaves us with too many A/A guns. Now instead of these guns we need mainly infantry, and the place to get them from is in the A/A regiments. Another thing he said was that he had decided to be very fair and start disbanding the younger mobs first, and that so far he had disbanded 20 A/A regiments out here, and that it had now become our turn.

The old 276 Battery has had its day. At the present time no-one knows what will happen to the various individuals. We are all very vexed at the breaking up of the Battery. Although we may grumble at times about the old bull, the fact remains that it's not a bad old mob after all, and although it may seem a bit funny to you, it is a fact that a number of the chaps were near breaking down after this news, and that included the Sergeant-Major.

Yours always,

Alex

xxxxxxxxxxx

29 August 1944

My dear Nan,

The disbanding of the Battery means there is a lot to tell you. I am sending the measuring instrument which I have made and a few other personal items. The meter has taken me a long time to make, and as it is my own idea and circuit, made up from bits picked up here and there, I do think a lot of it. I have proved it dead accurate apart from one position, and that can be easily fixed when I have plenty of time and leisure.

I have also enclosed my old wallet and a few old letters which I have carried for a long time now. You should not be worried about this, Nan. The items are sentimental possessions. The reason is that after the Battery is disbanded it will mean passing from depot to depot before settling down, and as I am an old soldier I know what depots and transit camps can be like. Also, instead of travelling in our own lorries we may have to do a spot of walking etc. and so I am reducing my pack to the bare minimum. I am taking no chances. Of course, my original intention was to bring them home myself but I don't want to take the chance of losing them after looking after them for so long.

I am a sentimental old fool. Still. You married him, didn't you? No! Nan, I don't know why.

I don't know yet what will exactly happen to me, but my address will be changed very soon. I have two choices, which are posting to either another permanent field battery, or to the Infantry. Frankly I have no choice. The sad part is the breaking up of the old battery, poor old 276. It is very hard parting from ones' mates, especially as there are still about half of us originals who left home together back in 1941. It is a sad blow to the old mob. I am wondering where I will eventually 'land'. However, it makes no difference and the only sad part is the breaking up of the Battery and the destroying of old friendships, but then this is war, and although we grumble there isn't much we can do apart from that.

You must not worry and start thinking all sorts of things as to my future, because I am an old soldier, so the new life will make no odds. I will just take it in my stride.

I don't know what the future may hold, so there isn't much to be gained by imagining things. I will write again soon.

Yours always,

Alex

xxxxxxxxxxxx

3 September 1944

My dear Nan,

I can't settle to write long letters with so much uncertainty in my mind.

We know nothing at all here about any changes. I am sure that our days as an A/A Battery are very few. Of course, we are still on an A/A site but no one is really bothering very much.

We had what may be our last concert together last night and of course yours truly was there with his old guitar. And that reminds me of another piece of news for you. I shall have to sell the old instrument, as it will be rather awkward to carry when the change takes place, and I am afraid that last night was its 'Swan Song'. However, it has lasted well and all of us have had a certain amount of entertainment since I got the guitar in Catania. This may be a bit sloppy Nan, but perhaps you will be happy to know that your favourite songs have been sung and played for you on many occasions.

I am afraid you must forgive me if I keep on the subject of the 'changeover' as it is the thing uppermost in my mind and no doubt in yours also. We are all a bit upset and the only cheerful aspect left to us is that the news from all the fronts is good and it may not be too long before the war is over. At least, the war with Jerry. And this brings [me] to our subject of conversation out here. What is wrong with Jerry? Imagine the Afrika Corps surrendering? In these days we were told that this was the cream of the German Army and it certainly seems to be true because to judge by the way they are running away in France, the troops there are not of the same calibre as the 'Afrika Corps'. No doubt of the fact – the pick of the German Army was lost in the desert. Still, as that sounds like boasting, I'd better change the subject.

Well dear, today is the start of the 6th Year of War and my memory goes back to five years ago, which was also a Sunday. You were Nan Smith then, and the young lady whom I had decided even before then would one day be Mrs Macintyre. Of course, perhaps you had the same idea in mind but then I wouldn't know (ha ha).

Yes dear, I had fallen in love with you the first night we met, not in the Albert Ballroom, but when I walked down Hope Street with yourself, Torchy and May to the tram. Perhaps I had a strange way of showing it at first Nan, but when you made me realise my mistake, I know myself that I did change a lot. Just put it down to the fact that I hadn't met any woman like you before. Dear me, aren't I sentimental?

Before I close perhaps I should mention that I will have my little fire today.

Good luck and God bless you all.

Alex

xxxxxxxxxx

6 September 1944

My dear Nan,

It was very funny to read of your experience with the bulls?? at Oban. And although you must have been a bit excited I'm afraid that I must give you a lecture on farm stock as the beasts which you believed to be bulls couldn't possibly have been.

I know you have good eyesight Nan, and you say that they weren't cows, but bulls are not allowed to roam about in the way you met them. Remind me to tell you all about it some day (ha ha).

Your latest card was posted from Largs and naturally the name brings back many memories of sirens, maiden ladies and of course those most awful twin beds. One thing I will never praise even for hygienic reasons. A terrible invention, no doubt an idea of some disappointed old lady (ha ha). Well Nan, it is a very short letter but until I write again I must say cheerio and God bless you all.

Yours always,

Alex

xxxxxxxxxxx

12 September 1944

My dear Nan,

I have been real worried about your health and the news of your illness really shook me. So please look after yourself. I know that is not in your nature, and neither is it mine, but I have been four years in the Army and my outlook has changed a little. In the future Nan, your main purpose is your own health and to judge by your illness, you haven't been avoiding dampness enough.

Of course again things are different at home and you are surrounded by all your own folks and well perhaps it would be better if I just let you carry on your own sweet way after all. It was, and of course still is, your nature which 'got' me at first and I shouldn't like to see it change whatever happens.

Dear me! What a man? Says one thing and than calls himself a fool and says the opposite? Blame it on the sun (ha ha).

I am sorry if the news of the break-up upset you, Nan, because I always say that things are never so black as they first appear. I have received my first interview, and for the moment I'm being allowed to keep my trade, and stay in the Royal Artillery. This will mean that the first place I go will be to a base camp. Oh dear, what a failure (ha ha)!

Yours always,

Alex

Xxxxxxxxxxx

16 September 1944

Well Nan, it's surprising the number of jobs 'they' can find for you on a camp such as this (ha ha). My news is that we are starting to form a sort of concert in the mob, before the final break-up, and, as we intend to be rather ambitious, I am having a very busy time. No! Nan, I haven't got my old guitar. It went away a few weeks ago to a Yank at a base camp. The same thing happened to the radio and a small engine, etc., but there you are, Nan, it had to happen. However, where we are now, instruments can be had, and I have been promised one for my show.
Yours always,
Alex

19 September 1944   *Trip to Pompeii*

Today I had a trip to Pompeii, where I spent quite an interesting day. I visited the old ruins, and after what I saw, well, I am not surprised at the destruction of what must have been rather a vile place in its day. Perhaps I should add that the present inhabitants of the new town of Pompeii deserve a similar fate. If you remember Nan, in all my letters from Egypt I spoke of the wogs as the lowest form of life in the world. Well, I have changed my mind. The Eyeties of Naples and district are even lower.

You know, Nan, you folks at home really have a very hard task to perform, and to judge by what I hear from chaps who have just come out here, you must find life very strange and trying. Most of us 'old hands' (ha ha) think that the behaviour of the girls back home leaves a lot to be desired. Candidly, they should be very roundly smacked where it hurts most.

For the first time since we came out here we are classed as 'out of action', and instead of the usual rough camps it's all the old bull once more, and nothing to do between times unless preparing for the <u>next</u> appearance of the old bull later on!

I was looking through my snaps today while sitting in the ruins of Pompeii, and I seem to have one or two missing. I must have left them in my wallet in my hurry when I posted that back home to you. However, in my pack I still have the two big photos of our wedding, in a strong case which I made myself.

Now Nan, I won't send you anything from Italy for your birthday as it is all pure rubbish but I will try and let you have a few shillings.
I will write again soon.
Yours always,
Alex
xxxxx

20 September 1944

I am so pleased that you are once more your usual self. Now that you are again well, Nan, you should take that little more care of yourself, and go a wee bit slower. Mind you Nan, just that wee bit, because I like your smart walk, etc. (ha ha). Of course I could say that I like everything about you, but then that would be 'sloppy' (ha ha).

By the way, Nan, at the present time it is raining cats and dogs here, and we had to bale out this morning. Visions of another Eyetie winter. Oh dear! (Ha ha.)

In one of your cards you say that you love Largs, so maybe I will take you there, or perhaps, you being the boss, you have already decided where you are taking me!

You asked to know the story of my radio. Well, another unit near us bought a radio for £40. After a time it went wrong and nobody could repair it. So I went across and offered to buy it. A few of us clubbed together and after a lot of visits and fags etc., I got it for £12 (ha ha). After that I wanted electricity, so I built up a small engine and dynamo from scrap, and after a while, with a lot of patience and bad words, I ended up with a good radio and enough power to light our three tents as well.

We carried this around with us for a while, until the bad news of the break-up. So out I go again, and end up selling the lot for £20. Business is, as you know, business (ha ha). I also sold my guitar, and I really was sorry to part with it, but it had to be done, and that's that.

You are vexed about the changes, Nan, but all this changing around will help to shorten the war, and that is all that matters.

Now now, no wet pillows (ha ha).

You know, Nan, sometimes I wonder whether I really made you as happy as you say, because my meeting you has brought such a number of tears to your eyes at various times. I never thought I would be the cause of sadness to you. All I can say, dear wife, is that I will do my best to make up for all this, and keep that nice and cheerful appearance on your face.

Now Nan, it's cheerio and God bless you all.

Yours always,

Alex

xxxxxxxxxx

21 September 1944

My dear Nan,

I received the news last night about you losing your teeth. You certainly are having a hard time, dear, but please try and keep your spirit up. You mentioned the 16th as 'The Day', so I suppose by now you will be over the worst of the job. I didn't expect you to be losing your old smile. However, if the gums are bad, Nan, I really suppose it is the best thing. It won't be so very long before you have another smile, that is of course providing that you do keep them in (ha ha)!

There's nothing I can say which can tell you how I really feel about all this trouble you have had these past few months, but I do feel for you dear, very much. I can't even keep myself going in fags now (ha ha). I really am surprised at you letting yourself go so low in health, and all the time telling me of how well you were. Still, Nan, I understand your nature, and why you kept quiet. I really believe that your main trouble has been worry about me. Candidly, Nan, you have no cause for worry about me at all. I am well, and have every hope of being home quite soon. Now, Nan, don't get notions (ha ha). I am sure that after waiting years a few months can be termed 'soon'. So once more Nan I must say cheerio. Good luck dear wife.
Yours always,
Alex
xxxxxxxxxxx

PS How ya, Gumsey?

23 September 1944

My dear Nan,
You have had a very hard time these last few months dear but all I can do is say that I am sorry, and only hope that I was there with you because no matter what I say on paper it doesn't really express my feelings. Still, I do know, Nan, that you will be alright and perhaps your great patience will be rewarded very soon. When that time comes I will try and make up for all these weary years you have spent, and, if my guess is correct, all these wet pillows. I do love you Nan and when you are unwell, well I don't feel so good myself. Still Nan, good days are ahead I am sure and no more partings. We shall be together always in everything.

I have just had my lunch which wasn't too bad as army grub goes. Well Nan, I'm sorry but I must start my Old Bull so it means cheerio until I write again.

23 September 1944

Well Nan, many thanks for the stamps enclosed in 166. I keep on telling you that you spoil me but it just doesn't make any difference. A poor lookout for a man who intends to be master of his own home isn't it? I never marked my usual (ha ha) there as the joke is so obvious.

I had to smile at the bet which Ewan made about you fainting when we meet again. For myself, I don't know, but in any case, I have sort of planned our meeting and if you do fall you should fall on something very soft I hope (ha ha).

So you don't think very much of my idea of the afternoon siesta, but that you intend to make sure that I don't even have that little pleasure. Such selfishness! Well, I never did!

Speaking of Burns' poems Nan, reminds me that I still have the small book of poems which you sent me such a long time ago. I have a little read now and then in my spare time. I have quite a bit of spare time nowadays but with things being so uncertain, I just can't settle to anything. I'd rather have a handful of spanners in my hands. At present we have no equipment so there is no chance of anything like that. We just sort of hang around with a lot of the Old Bull annoying us.

Good luck and God bless you all

Yours always,

Alex

xxxxxxxxxxxxx

26 September 1944

My dear Nan,

I haven't had any letter-cards from you for a day or two, so I don't know how you are feeling after your visit to the dentist.

Would you believe it? You can ignore what I have just written, as I have just received a letter-card from you <u>this minute</u>, and now I can carry on writing without any worry. To be truthful, dear, I was worried, because my last word from you was the 14th, and some chaps around here have had mail of the 19th. Coupled with the fact that I knew you were at the dentist on the 16th. You see, Nan, after preaching to you not to worry if my letters become scarce, I go and do it myself. What a funny man (ha ha).

You say that you are feeling grand, but honestly I don't believe you, because how can any woman who has great difficulty <u>talking</u> be feeling grand? (Ha ha.) I just hope all your troubles are over. Also, you will have to contend with my coming home some day, and you will have to be ever so strong, as you will have an additional worry. Me! Pardon my very poor wit.

Now for my news. I have had a medical board. For the time being, instead of being my usual A1, I am now classed as B2. This is a big drop, but the Army works a very funny way, and it says that a man with any feet or leg complaint becomes 'B' category. And now I'll tell you a secret. If it hadn't been for the disbanding of the Eighth, it would never have happened at all. So this board will probably mean a good chance of a real rest.

Now Nan, I'm sending you some money after all for your birthday. Maybe you could buy some toothpaste eh? (Ha ha.)
Yours always,
Alex
xxxxxxxxxxxx

27 September 1944

Here I am again for a few words before I go to bed. The light is very poor, but I will do my best. I have another day in Naples tomorrow, and to tell you the truth, the only reason I go is to get away from camp. Candidly Nan, Naples and its people are a combination of the lowest form of life I have ever come across since I left home.

I hope that your dentist episode is now over, and the end of what has been a very unfortunate time. I hope you take it all in your stride and come up smiling, although I don't expect you will be very keen on smiling with no teeth. But dear me! What a position for a woman to be in? I bet 85 will be much quieter these days (ha ha).

Nan, I'm sorry, but the light is going out. Goodnight, dear.

28 September 1944

My dear Nan,
Here is my enclosed map of Naples. The red line through the centre marks off the 'out of bounds' area, which is quite a goodly part of the town. As you can see, we more or less stay in the one main street. There is no telling what may happen to a chap who wanders off by himself, especially in darkness. A fine race, are our friends the Eyeties!

Your letter continues with the tale of how you are preparing for your trip to Oban, and like yourself I am thinking of how fine it would be if I was with you preparing for the same holiday.

There was a remark in your 168 that I look upon with great disfavour. Ewan and Margaret want me to be there when their wedding comes off! I should think so too. They can't do without me! (Ha ha.) I can't have Ewan married while I am out here. What about all the good advice I can give? Being an old married member of the Smith family, think of all the tips I can give him.

I am very sad, Nan. First of all, wee May, my number one passion, goes on a holiday with a 'guy named Joe'. Now Torchy, who I thought was at least true to me, is also lost. Woe is me! Ah well, I will go for comfort to one of those very beautiful Italian girls, with dark hair, dark eyes, and dark hearts. Well, Nan, with no good beer around, I must seek comfort somewhere.

Oh dear, I almost forgot, I have a wife, haven't I? My bad memory again (ha ha).
Cheerio and good luck.
Yours always,
Alex
xxxxxxxxxxxxxx

29 September 1944

I had a day yesterday in Naples and as I told you it is only an excuse to be out of camp. There is a very good Naafi in what was once the Royal Palace and the whole day could be spent in the building which has everything, even to a cinema inside.

I had a card from you this morning and I am so pleased to see such a different tone back to your usual self. I am surprised though that you are able to have a temporary set of teeth so soon. I thought you had to go many months until the gums became hard.
And now dear cheerio once more.
Yours always,
Alex
Xxxxxxxxxxx

7 October 1944

My dear Nan,
Well, I have been very fortunate in getting a direct posting to another Unit instead of going to Base to be chucked around from pillar to post.

If all goes well I should be there in a day or two. As things are now, it seems as if I am being kept at my own trade in the R.A. and that I am not alone, but still with a few of the chaps I have been with these past years. About 20 of us.

Many happy returns for your birthday and I only wish that I could be with you in person.
Cheerio, good luck and God bless you all.
Alex
xxxxxxxxxxxxx

11 October 1944

My dear Nan,
We are going to move to a new camp in a matter of days. The weather is now very wet and unpleasant and conditions are not too good, although

I must say that the food is not too bad, when one considers the conditions under which the cooking is done. I am in a sort of Transit Camp and although there is not too much of the 'Old Bull' we are kept fairly busy with a variety of different jobs. You see Nan, we move this and then we move that, then we dig trenches to drain off water. I don't mind the work, but it is very uninteresting so naturally the sooner I am away from this camp the better for me.

Still Nan, I don't want you to get the impression that I am grumbling, because really I am not and so far I have been quite fortunate and there are a lot of chaps who are a lot worse off than I am, and if they don't grumble then why should I? In fact Nan there is more grumbling from chaps who have done nothing and the general practise seems to be the art of getting out of work and dodging as much as possible. Naturally, in such company, I make sure I don't do the work myself (ha ha).

Now Nan, I'll give you my news as soon as I have some. Any word of the parcel I sent home?

Yours always,

Alex

xxxxxxxxxxx

153 Heavy A/A Battery   *Posted to new unit*
51st Heavy A/A Regiment Royal Artillery
14 October 1944

My dear Nan,

I have my new address for you.

I have known I was coming here for a little while now and that was the reason why I told you in my last letters that I had been very fortunate. You see Nan, although I haven't been with this 'mob' before, they are not really strangers as we have always been in the same area and under the same Brigadier.

They are another of the very few old 8th Army Units left and came abroad three months before we did, so you see it's quite a pleasant thought to still be with men who think the same as we do. I have a horror of being posted to an 'English' Unit which would probably break my heart – that is providing I didn't break theirs first (ha ha).

Another fact is that although I am still classed as O/F.C. there is a chance that I may go back to my old trade of Driver/Mechanic again.

I am so pleased to know that you are your old self again. And to make matters even better your new smile is even better than your old smile! I wonder how you look without them? (Ha ha.)

And all the time you are improving in appearance I am getting older every day. Scarce of hair, round shouldered, big tummy and dear knows what else. Fact is, Nan, that I really am the same as I was when I left you, with the addition of a few wrinkles round the eyes due to sun glare. Still a very handsome man I am. (Oh yeah?)

Yours always,

Alex

Xxxxxxxxxxxxxx

16 October 1944

My dear Nan,

I have not received your letters for a few days but to judge from my previous experience of what happens to my mail when a change such as this takes place I can look forward to a parcel of letters arriving some day soon and all stuck up with adhesive paper. No doubt you will remember the P.C. I sent you from Egypt many months ago Or was it a question of years? Another thing Nan, is the fact that it is quite possible that I will receive a reply to this card before the older letters reach me, so don't be wondering why I write of all sorts of subjects and yet seem as if I am ignoring any news which you have given me of happenings at home, which you are expecting me to say something about!

Well Nan, on orders this morning I have actually been posted to this 153 Battery so it looks as if I really am more or less settled once more.

As this has happened in a little over two weeks, you can understand why I told you that I considered myself very fortunate. Perhaps Uncle Bob can tell you of the feeling a man has when he has visions of many weeks to be spent in Base Camps etc. Of course, some chaps spend most of their Army career in these camps but they are of a different type and calibre. However, Nan, as I said I seem to have dodged most of that, so things could be a lot worse. Also in my last letter I said that I may have to change my trade, but so far that doesn't seem very likely either as the idea is to keep me on Radio at least in some form or other. To boil it all down Nan, at the present I can say that everything in the garden is 'lovely'.

You will notice, Nan, that we have another new General, making the eighth we have had out here. Must be plenty of them in fact '10 a penny' (ha ha).

Well dear, by the time you read this you will have had your birthday and I hope this is the last of these celebrations that we spend apart. Did you receive the money I sent you Nan? I know it isn't much. Still, with this new increase in pay, I should be able to let you have a few 'bob' for the end of the year also.

As for my savings, well Nan, I'm afraid I did set myself a very high target for the end of the year. Still, I did try (ha ha).

And now Nan, once more it's cheerio with my best wishes to all at 85 and Hamilton.

Yours always,

Alex

Xxxxxxxxxxxxxxx

21 October 1944

My dear Nan,
The chaps here at the 153 are a good lot and I am sure I will get on well with them. Fact is, I am getting to know them already. The actual gunners are coloured boys from Africa, and only the drivers and tradesmen are white.

The coloured chaps are a very cheery crowd and not to be compared with the Yank fellows. They keep by themselves and have their own cookhouse which can easily be understood as the food they eat is quite different from ours. They don't speak English apart from their sergeant who is the interpreter and they are very religious, having a little service of their own after every meal. In fact Nan, they are a fine crowd with no bad habits and not like the Yanks and they don't get drunk or molest women. They even go so far as to tell an Officer if they hear us using bad language and believe it or not they are also good on the guns. This Unit had white gunners but they were replaced by these chaps.
And that Nan, is all my news for the present.
Yours always,
Alex
Xxxxxxxxxxxxx

1 November 1944   *Radio course*

My dear Nan,
I have been on another course on a new type of radio instrument. I was kept more than usually busy as it was actually a course for sergeants and naturally I had to do a lot of extra thinking. I was put forward for this course before the old mob broke up. Now don't get ideas that I may be getting promotion because it is now too late for that. You see Nan, now that there are so many sergeants at Base, Units cannot promote their own men, but get the 'ready made' from the Base. So that's that. By the way Nan, I was third in the exam on the course so I consider it a very good show as the two men who beat me were two sergeants. However, it won't get me anywhere. Just my own personal satisfaction (ha ha).

I hope by now you have received the money I sent for your birthday. Also that the parcel sent in September has reached home. Oh dear, I almost forgot. I also had a parcel of books etc. from you when I got back last night and I was very pleased to receive them.

But I'm afraid I must say a few words about one of the articles and that is the <u>soap</u>. Now Nan, to get soap at home one needs coupons, while out here we now have plenty of soap, and no coupon worry. I do appreciate your action Nan but it gives me the feeling that I am robbing you folks back home of something you really will need much more than I. We get an ample supply of soap which is also [of] a quality you will find very scarce at home. The reason we have it is because it comes here from either America or Canada. Candidly, if it wasn't for the reason we can't send Naafi stuff home, I should probably have sent you some soap before now (ha ha)!

Good luck and God bless you all.

Yours always,

Alex

Xxxxxxxxxxxx

1 November 1944

My dear Nan,

I have just finished a card to you but I thought I might as well keep on writing while the going is good. Now I want to tell you what I have just received so hold your breath!

First of all 6 letter cards and 4 letters from yourself – 169, 170, 171 and 172. I also had a card from Ewan and word from Cliff Andrews in Australia. The letter from Australia did not contain good news as his brother has been killed in France. This may seem strange to you Nan, but the fact is that the young brother did not go to Australia, but stayed with his old people in England. So you see Nan, I must write to Cliff very soon. He is a fine chap and took good care of me way back in Kantara days.

Naturally, your letters are full of talk of the dentist and your new smile – which I really think is a wrong expression, as in my own opinion a person doesn't smile with the mouth but with the eyes. Still no doubt you know what I mean.

You also remark how a shirt requires to be 'let out' which as a man I do understand! (Oh yeah?) Your talk of chanters, pink jumpers, football pools, silk stockings, ladders, unmentionables. You haven't by any chance been drinking have you? Or is it me? (Ha ha.)

Still dear, I am so pleased to know that you are now past the rotten time you had with your teeth. Telling me of how brave you were in the dentist's chair. I bet you were shaking all the time! I know because I usually do a 'tremble' myself in that part of the world (ha ha).

As for the pink jumpers, well that of course means 'Torchy', the only colour-blind girl I know. I sincerely hope that Ewan doesn't do anything rash before he has a chance to hear my advice, being an old married man (of at least four days) ha ha. He should find my advice a great help before he sets sail on the sea of matrimony, I think that is the correct term (ha ha).

All this talk of ladders and stockings and unmentionables. You know Nan, you shouldn't mention all these things including 'wee cuddles' etc. (ha ha) are apt to put notions into my head. A very dangerous policy indeed and especially as I am surrounded by blue skies, a beautiful moon, dark-eyed maidens. Well, I may not be at present as it is a little dull! Also, there is no moon to be seen, it's raining again and the maidens smell!

Yours always,

Alex

xxxxxxxxxxxxx

2 November 1944

My dear Nan,

I was surprised to see the white heather in your letter. Thanks very much Nan and I will try and take care of it as long as I can.

As you know Nan, I have come to this Unit to replace chaps who are going home soon. Mind you Nan, they haven't done much longer than I out here but they were in Norway, and as they were less than six months in England before coming out here that all counts as 'overseas' and a part of their 4 and a half years. It is quite good to know that these chaps are going now and our turn is coming nearer. It is a long way off yet, but after the length of time I have had out here, it really isn't such a lot after all. Even now I can hardly realise that it is almost a year ago when I was the Battery Captain for Xmas day at Foggia.

As for Italy, Nan, I have resigned myself to another Eyetie winter, and although it isn't very cold yet it is very wet and last night we had about the worst storm I have ever experienced. It started about 8 o'clock last night and though the actual wind has dropped it is still raining and it is now midday. Talk about mud!

I was surprised at the price of grapes back home and of how scarce they must be. And to think that I have had so many out here at the one time that I have had to run for the nearest hedge (ha ha). However, all that fruit has gone now in the making of wine or as we call it 'plonk'.

I remember an incident last winter when I went up to a Canadian Tank Mob to do my 'entertaining' (ha ha) and they had about 40 gallons of plonk in petrol tins. However, there must have been some petrol or fumes in the tins because the stuff almost killed us all. Talk about drunk men! There were guns going off, mostly through the roof. Tanks running all over the place and dear knows what else (ha ha). Luckily, I had very little myself and was able to get myself and the rest of our party back to our own camp before dawn (ha ha). But oh! my head the next morning (ha ha).

And here we have another of our strange coincidences. You tell me that you had a dream and that I was there with a new 'mouser'. Well Nan, I really have another new 'mouser' which I stared about a month ago. S'funny? (Ha ha.)

Now Nan, I have a job to do, in fact bale out some water, and I shall have to finish writing as it is very dark now.

And so dear wife 'until the next time'.

4 November 1944

The rain has stopped and the sun is shining. This gives us all the chance to hang out our blankets; though not actually wet, they are of course very damp. And then there are such things as pants, towels etc. and boots. So I can assure you that the trees all around are now bearing most unusual fruit!

I am pleased to read that the lights are on in Glasgow again and that you don't have to do any more fire watching in McDonald's now. Although I never mentioned the fact in my letters Nan, I didn't like the idea of you having that job at all especially when air raids were possible over Glasgow. But now these days are all over so all is well.

God bless you all.

Yours always,

Alex

xxxxxxxxxxx

5 November 1944

My dear Nan,

So you have parted with your teeth and you now feel such a lot better in health. As I have always said Nan, when you are well so am I. And of course the same thing applies the other way round.

You say a few words about my medical board and of how the fact of my down-grading hasn't upset you at all. I was afraid it would Nan and I had half a mind not to tell you. But then I don't like secrets. So there you are.

I am pleased you have received your birthday present. And that reminds me that I may have another few 'bob' for your end of the year celebrations which I am afraid will once again be without my presence. Still I believe I am safe in saying that if all goes well I should have at least visited home before the next one comes along. Cheerful aren't I? (Ha ha.)

I have enjoyed reading of your visits to Hamilton and I can just imagine the scene at the top of the stairs when you surprised the folks there with a new smile instead of the 'gumsey' they were expecting.

I will finish my talk of your change by the remark that 'long may your skirts tighten' (ha ha). I have already asked for a few exercises to stretch my arms, just in case I may find a good long arm very handy in the days to come (ha ha).

By the way, Nan, give my thanks to Ewan for the present he brought you from Sweden. I often wish I could send you something nice but I am in the wrong country now and that is why I send a few bob instead and even at that I suppose you would be more pleased with an equal number of coupons. Still Nan, I do my best.

And now Nan, I must come to the end of my talk, and I suppose I should finish by telling you that as today was Sunday, I had one of my small fires.

God bless you all.

Yours always,

Alex

Xxxxxxxxxxxx

7 November 1944   *Trip to Florence*

My dear Nan,

The only change in the monotony of this life was a visit to Florence. I haven't much to say about Florence as having already seen Rome I have really seen all that Italy has to offer. The shops and stalls have the usual lot of bracelets etc. In other words, trash at fancy prices. The only other item of news was that I saw a very good show by a South African party. They were very clever and very clean.

I was real interested in the story of the 'debate' at Torchy's Unit and I remember how Margaret used to argue with Fred. We have had a few of these lectures out here by 'English Wallahs' who although they haven't actually called the meetings off must have wished they could do so. I remember one of them who told us that 'British ★★★★★★' had come to stay. He was doing quite well until someone asked 'What the ★★// is that?' As this meant treading towards the very 'thin ice' of overseas service he changed the subject (ha ha).

However, we had a talk on this subject a few days ago and we do realise that this 'partial release' is really quite fair, apart from the very unfair reasoning that home service counts the same as overseas. It is going to cause a lot of 'pub brawls' I'm afraid (ha ha).

One side of this 'release scheme' is very interesting Nan and that is that a good number of these 'replacements' for the likes of us chaps will be young men who have been at home in reserved occupations.

You mention how interested you were in the news of my leaving Old Faithful 2 behind and that reminds me that one of the chaps here has a real posh guitar. But between you and I, Nan, my old one has it 'whacked' for tone. Must have been because it had so many cracks that more tone got out (ha ha). Never mind Nan, I may pick up another one some day and then I'll let you have your favourite song time and time again. Oh dear! Getting sentimental again.

8 November 1944

I should like to say a few words about an experience I had last night. You see Nan, we had a show given by a guy, billed as a stage star etc. He sung a few songs and cracked a few jokes all of which were smutty, but it wasn't until he brought the A.T.S. into the conversation that we objected. Mind you, Nan, Army audiences can stand a lot of smut. No doubt you understand that; but although we have no experience of the A.T.S. ourselves, we do know that it is the same as the Army. A mixture of all the types. And we don't like a civvy telling us that these girls are more or less all loose women. We objected rather strongly and after looking at his watch a few times he said goodnight!

You know Nan, even my own 'turn' was much cleaner. I never insulted the womenfolk and I was never forced to retire early (ha ha).

So yourself and Peg have been down at the new houses eh? Sort of making our minds up for us before we get the chance to state our opinions?
Cheerio until my next letter.
Yours always,
Alex
Xxxxxxxxxxxx

15 November 1944

My dear Nan,
First of all I must ask you to excuse the scribble but the fact is that the weather is very cold and wet at the moment and that there is a very high wind. As we are in our usual tents, you can imagine the conditions under which I am trying to write. I really am in an awkward position as we do have a small fire, but as fuel is very scarce it is kept for the evening. Now perhaps you will say 'Why doesn't he write at night?' Well the answer is, Nan, that although we have a small fire at night, we only have one very small lamp which it is impossible to write with. So that is that.

Dear me! When I look back at what I have just written, I think I could have saved all that talk because the writing isn't so bad! In fact, pretty good (ha ha).

Well dear that is about all my news from sunny Italy except to say that I am keeping well and I am my usual cheery self.

I am very pleased that my parcel has arrived. You know, Nan, I often pictured how you would feel when you saw the contents under the bits of wire etc. My very precious wee items of sentimentality. Candidly Nan, I really don't know what I shoved in because I was in an awful hurry at the time and I just grabbed the various items. However I do know that one of the letters in my wallet was the first one you wrote to me as my wife and is the reason it was in there. Well Nan, I suppose that after seeing what I sent, you will no doubt look upon me as a sloppy old fool (ha ha). And who knows perhaps you are right.

The chaps who had finished their 'time' in this Unit have left and by now must either be waiting on the boat or are already on board and on the way to Blighty. We had a sort of celebration or rather they had (we did the guard that night) and the wine flowed rather freely!

Yours always,

Alex

xxxxxxxxxxxxx

18 November 1944   *Rumours of leave*

My dear Nan,

Well Nan, the gossip is that the chaps who were due for home should be back there in a few days.

Speaking of leave brings me to a remark you made in your letter about men going home from here on the grounds of starting a family.

I understand your thoughts on that subject Nan, but I'm afraid that I am very much against the idea. When I 'time' my family it will be when I or rather you and I think fit, and not a part of an organised state scheme.

If I remember correctly our old friend 'Musso' had the same idea many years ago, but of course he was a Dictator and only wanted more cannon fodder. Between you and I, I fail to see any difference in these two schemes. The powers that be should have thought of all this before they condemned men to stay abroad for four and a half years. So for the present, dear, forget you ever heard of such an idea.

There is another 'Leave' scheme which you have probably heard of as it was announced on the radio only yesterday. You see dear, if we went home under <u>this</u> scheme we would be back here again in a few months!

And now I must say cheerio.

Yours always,

Alex

xxxxxxxxxxxxxxxxx

21 November 1944

My dear Nan,

I see by your letters that you were interested in the news of our African friends. One point I didn't mention was that the Sergeants who do speak our language are actually tribal chiefs. Interesting eh?

Well Nan, the new chaps are not at all like the old crowd who left. They haven't the same friendly spirit and not being such a long period away from home one can understand why. Trouble is they have too many 'Engless ideas' and haven't been away long enough to lose them. Still a good proportion of us are old hands, so we are still quite happy. You know Nan, I'm afraid my outlook on my Army career is now changing. My only idea now is just to hang around and pass the remainder of my overseas service in the best possible way. You see with things so quiet now, life is very monotonous and I don't think anybody can blame me if, after all this time, I am beginning to wane a little in my interest. I can't even find any wee engines or meters to build either.

Mind you, Nan, don't get the idea that I have nothing to do. There is plenty of work but the trouble is that it is all so pointless. Still I suppose everybody has that 'browned off' feeling at some time or other?

I am looking forward to the arrival of my Xmas parcel, Nan. I must say many, many thanks. I really do think that this will be the last one dear that you will be required to send me. A damn bad show if it isn't (ha ha).

That reminds me Nan, that we have heard no more official word about leave to the U.K. and of how it affects us. The Army never hurries. In the meantime Nan, don't build up any hopes as I don't think I stand much of a chance. In any case, I may as well stay where I am. There may be a catch in this leave business and being an old soldier I'm afraid I have a very suspicious mind (ha ha).

Yours always,

Alex

Xxxxxxxxxxxxx

26 *November* 1944

My dear Nan,

Well dear all your latest letters are of how much you enjoyed my diary of 1943. It proves my statement that Alamein was the turning point of the War and that compared with our time before then we have had a 'Cook's Tour'. Perhaps you will say rather a long tour! But then, Nan, we are now on the journey home.

You will have heard a little more about this leave to Blighty. It applies to men with between 3 and 4 years' overseas service. Yes Nan, that includes your wee man. But I can understand the 'catch' so I'm afraid I would refuse the chance and prefer to wait the other eight months.

If all goes well I go off on another course tomorrow. I was asked about it today and naturally I accepted. It won't get me anywhere but it may be interesting and be a change from the present monotony. I know you will wish me luck Nan. Now Nan, I may be very busy and I may not be able to write my usual letters next week.

Yours always,

Alex

Xxxxxxxxxxxxx

2 December 1944

My dear Nan,

Here I am again. Now Nan, I will satisfy your curiosity as regards this present course. The Radio part comes easy but the real study is the sending and receiving of Morse. I go to bed with dots and dashes every evening (ha ha)!

Here is where I will 'shake' you. I am at present 'billeted' in what was at one time a block of flats and we have real central heating and running water! 'Molto Bono.' Pardon my Italian. There aren't any windows I admit, but central heating and water!

What's all this about your new smile being an improvement? Who said you needed an improvement? To me the only improvement would be if you get all your fat back again! I didn't say you were fat! You did! I didn't! Oh what's the use? Anyway you know what I meant. You only wasted an argument (ha ha).

I suppose dear this month will bring you many memories of 4 years ago, as it will to me. I have the feeling Nan, that we can look upon this as the last anniversary we shall spend all these miles apart. As always Nan, the photographs will have pride of place on that day no matter where I may be. You see Nan, I carry them in my 'small kit' and I never go anywhere without that. When that day comes dear I will try and give you a picture of the whole surroundings. Perhaps this will reach you long before that day but just in case Nan, let me wish you 'Many Happy Returns'.

Good night, God bless you all.

Yours always,

Alex

xxxxxxxxxxxxxxx

7 December 1944

My dear Nan,

My usual travel talk will have to be left out this time as there is nothing to tell, except to say that so far this year in Italy we have a repeat of last year in the conditions of rain and mud. 'Sunny Italy!'

Well Nan, quite often among ourselves we have a 'look back' on the various countries we have visited and always the opinion is that the Desert was the best spot for a war and the healthiest.

At present, Nan, I am well though perhaps a trifle thinner than I was on the other side of the Med and maybe a lot older looking than when I left you, which is of course perfectly natural. As for the rest of my news Nan, well, I am still on this course and the Morse is driving me crazy. (If possible) (ha ha) I'm still learning but between you and I, Nan, I wish I was 10 years younger. The brain must be growing old first (ha ha).

Nan, I will mention what you call your 'wee secret' about Torchy and Ewan. Please add my best wishes to your own. However Nan, I will say that if Ewan gets the same feeling as I have even though I am away from my wife, he won't ask for anything more. The best I can wish him is that same feeling and may he be able to enjoy it for a long time to come. You can tell him that I know how he felt when he had his talk from Dad. Yes Ewan! That's the way I felt too (ha ha).

Perhaps I may not be home for the 'Day' but I will still be there in spirit at least. One thing [is] sure and that is that he will not be moving twin-beds to the sound of sirens etc! Lucky fellow! Still again Nan, that time is a long way off and who knows what may be the state of things by then.

I have had more official word about this leave business. Chaps like me <u>can</u> apply and they will get it. That is provided they agree to do <u>another</u> 12 months' service afterwards. Not so nice is it? So I think 'I've had it' as far as this leave goes.

And now dear wife it is coming near the time when we miss each other most of all, and as you know my own thoughts, all I can say is that I am very sorry that I will not be able to greet you on the morning of December 20th as I should like to and as I would were I at home.

I do love you Nan and therefore miss you a lot. Still when we consider all that has happened we have been very fortunate and all that is required now is a little more patience and all will be well.

Yours always,

Alex

xxxxxxxxxx

8 December 1944

My dear Nan,

Today I received, shall I say? our 'Yearly Cables'. Thank you very much Nan, although I really don't think that you should find a cable necessary as all our Cards for almost the past few weeks have said a few words about December 20th 1940.

But there you are.

Both of us have that memory in mind and it seems we never are pleased unless we write numerous letters to each other on that subject! We are a silly pair, because I am sure we could write about other subjects such as the War or home leave etc. etc. (ha ha). However Nan, during this period the War takes a 'back seat' and I am very pleased to notice that this talk of leave has now gone to the rear also.

Now don't be getting the idea that another wife of one of the chaps had – she told him that as other chaps were going home and he wasn't, she had come to the conclusion that the poor fellow had volunteered to stay here and had no intention of ever coming home (ha ha). It would have upset me if you had built up false hopes and that was why I bluntly told you to forget you had ever heard of it. Sort of 'cruel to be kind' idea.

Once more cheerio and God bless you all at home with perhaps a special word for Ewan and my Torchy.

Yours always,

Alex

xxxxxxxxxx

10 December 1944

My dear Nan,

Well Nan, I'm sorry I upset you by telling you that I was 'browned off' in one of my letters. But don't let these words worry you as I am bound to get 'browned off' quite a number of times. Something had rubbed me up the wrong way and I was in that mood when I started to write. I am one of those moody guys (ha ha).

You see Nan, the whole trouble is that we have been out here too long and we think we haven't had a fair deal. And now they add to it by telling us that leave from France is starting next month. Of course these poor fellows have been away from home over six months and must be missing their usual seven days' leave! Although the France 'Do' is all the news here, the old 8th Army is having it rather rough.

Sorry Nan, it does sound rather 'catty'. Let's forget it, eh?

You will have the news that Alexander is now Field Marshal and senior to Monty. I told you many months ago that Alexander was the man behind Monty out here but that Monty just caught the public fancy at the time. The desert campaign was Alexander's plan carried out by Monty, as I've always said.

Well Nan, I was intending to write a bit more but it's cold sitting here and the pen is going where it likes (ha ha). So I will say cheerio for the present.

12 December 1944

On Sunday last I went to a football match. Yes! Nan, believe it or not a real football match. It was between the Army in the area and the Eyeties from the town and the Ref. was a chap I mentioned before, by name Alec Jackson. There was a good crowd and although we won, the Eyeties had a good team and played very well indeed. And now I come to the highlight of the match. The Eyeties came out led by the captain who to our surprise carried a large bunch of flowers!

He took great care of this until our chaps came out when he very solemnly presents this bunch of flowers to the captain of the Army side.

You know Nan, what made me laugh was when I visualised the same idea taking place at the start of a match back home say between Celtic and Rangers!

And that is about all my news. The weather as usual is lousy but I suppose at this time of year I am as well off in Italy as anywhere else.

I am still on this wireless course and we still have to learn more. The sending and receiving of Morse is a job by itself but I am getting there by degrees (ha ha).

13 December 1944

At present practically nothing is happening at all and the war is going its own sweet way, in spite of my efforts (ha ha).

What you tell me about the neighbours is just the same as we are all having in letters from home. 'Everybody' is expecting 'everybody' home for Xmas and some chaps have even been asked if it was necessary to write to them any more?
Yours always,
Alex
Xxxxxxxxxxxx

16 December 1944

My dear Nan,
I have received the parcel you sent me for my Xmas tonight. Many thanks for your kindness. The contents are all in good condition and again as usual the box of shortbread will be kept for the New Year.

The photograph is a 'smasher' (ha ha). Oh! You want me to tell you how you look? Just a minute till I have another look at your face this time (ha ha). Yes, you are very well (ha ha).

Joking apart though Nan you do look remarkably well considering the illness you had earlier in the year. Mind you Nan you do look a little thinner but maybe I am judging by these knees again eh? (Ha ha.)
Nan, we are on the 'home stretch'.
Yours always,
Alex
Xxxxxxxxx

19 December 1944

My dear Nan,

My course finished last week and I returned to the 'site' today. And what a 'sight', all covered in mud. I will probably be in mud until I leave. And no doubt find more mud where I go to. All very interesting isn't it?

I am surprised at the razor blades in the Xmas parcel, Nan, as I thought they were very scarce back home. I do hope that no one is going minus a shave because <u>we</u> are now able to have a fairly decent ration of blades from the Naafi. They are Yank manufacture and not really very good but we get a good supply.

We have got hold of an old Eyetie piano which is used for every job apart from what it was made for. In fact, I used it myself earlier today for a soldering bench. However, it can be played and is hammered by almost everybody. So now when we are asked for any article we just reply, 'Oh, I've left it on top of the jolly old piano, old boy what?!' (Ha ha.)

Still, we should manage a sing-song with the aid of the piano when Xmas comes along!

God bless you all.

Yours always,

Alex

Xxxxxxxxxx

20 December 1944   *Wedding anniversary*

My dear Nan,

Today as you can guess my thoughts are with you more than ever so perhaps the best plan would be to give you a picture of my immediate surroundings. At least, that was my intention an hour ago.

Since then however, I had word from you and believe it or not one of the letters was the card wishing me a Happy Anniversary. Another was your 178 with a snap of Margaret and yourself, and although you say it is a leg show (a remark with which I agree!) I must say that you both look very well indeed.

So you see dear, on our Anniversary I receive a photograph of my wife and an Anniversary card. This is the first time I have had such a fine and appropriate mail.

A few words about myself and then a description of my surroundings as I promised.

As usual although a trifle muddy around the feet, I am well and as I have said many a time I could be a lot worse off both in health and conditions.

Now, dear wife, 'here goes'.

Today is really a lovely day with a real warm sun. Conditions underfoot are very bad and there is quite a cold wind. However, I have planted myself down behind a large box and I am protected from the cold wind and facing the sun and I am really very comfortable. My boots are actually steaming as I sit here in the afternoon sun. It is very quiet at present and I can hear a few voices as just a mumble and the noise of trucks as they pass up and down the road only a few hundred yards away. Green shoots are already appearing in the fields which have escaped the traffic of various war materials. Reminds me of a typical spring day back home with one exception and that is the absence of birds of any description. That is one thing which I never told you of before, not because I have forgotten, but just that I have become so used to this absence of birds that it never attracts my attention now. However, as today I am trying to describe everything, I must also mention this to you. Where war has been we find no birds.

The dog from our tent has just come along to join me and is sitting at my feet with its head resting on my knee. Its eyes have just closed so I suppose it is intending to have an afternoon siesta. The only other sound I can hear is someone playing an accordion in the distance and the tune is 'This is the Army Mr Brown'. I can hear a train coming up, driven of course by one of our fellows and with the usual load of requirements.

And that, Nan, is a picture of my immediate surroundings. Oh dear! Someone has just started to thump on the old Eyetie piano. It is one finger and hammering out 'You are my heart's delight' (ha ha).

And now a few words about what you would find inside my 'home'. I couldn't find any 'furniture' so the next best thing was to build up my kit very tidy. Most unusual you will say (ha ha). The finished job has given me a reasonably flat top and you would find my clean towel (my only clean one by the way) placed on top beside my bed. On this is my leather folder I made a long time ago containing photographs. It stands upright and on one side you would find the picture of you and I taken 4 years ago. On the other side are two small ones. One of yourself taken wearing your floral frock at Dunoon and the other of Mother taken at Hamilton.

That is all my pictures dear wife and today more than any other day I say may God bless you.

Yours always,

Alex

xxxxxxxxxxxx

22 December 1944

My dear Nan,

Thanks for the stamps, Nan, which you enclosed with your 177. You tell me of how much you miss my wee cuddle as you call it and it looks to me as if I am not supposed to have very much sleep on my return home. Never mind my teasing Nan. Perhaps I won't want any sleep myself, who knows? (Ha ha.)

It shouldn't be very long now in spite of Jerry's push back in France and Belgium.

And that reminds me that today I had a form to fill in which meant giving particulars of my job in 'civvy street'. It seems to have something to do with demobbing. If I know the army I will have to fill in this form at least half a dozen times, so I wouldn't bother about it at all.

24 December 1944

Well Nan dear. This will probably be the last letter for a little while and you will no doubt guess why!

I have an item of news for you tonight. Aren't you lucky (ha ha).

Last night I gave my first concert in this new Unit and although I say it myself it was real good. In fact, everybody has been telling me today that I surprised them all and that I was 'terrific' (ha ha). Such conceit! (Ha ha.) I managed to borrow a guitar so everything was OK. The old 276 had a much better concert party but we still enjoyed ourselves very much.

Good luck and God bless you all.

Yours always,

Alex

Xxxxxxxxxx

28 December 1944

My dear Nan,

I am taking the chance to write a few lines. The weather is very cold but fine and dry which makes one feel a bit more content.

We are now over the Xmas festivities but I have not the faintest idea where I may be when the New Year comes around. It's quite possible that I may not write to you until some time after the New Year. However, I know that I will be with you in spirit and that my health will be drunk then.

Now my dear, all the best for the New Year.

Yours always,

Alex

xxxxxxxxxxx

1945

'Our wee corner' at home – Florence trips – teeth trouble – news of a boat, perhaps! – back to lorries – Venice/war in Europe over – his papers arrive – at Rome – at 'X' Special Transit Camp, Naples

2 January 1945

This is my first letter of another year. I do honestly think that we will meet again before the end of another year. Frankly Nan, it seems no time at all since last New Year when I had such a very pleasant time with the old 276. And I'm afraid that this Unit has a lot to learn from the Old Mob. Of course Nan the trouble is that practically every month now men are going home at the end of their overseas period and strangers are always appearing in our midst.

Yes Nan, it was a bad day when the old mob got the axe. Still as I always say it won't be so long now and the longest part of the road is behind us.
Well dear wife once more cheerio.
Yours always,
Alex
Xxxxxxxx

6 January 1945

My dear Nan,
First of all the weather has changed! Now instead of hard and cold we have soft and wet and of course still cold. Such is sunny Italy.

The very trying conditions are not affecting my health. I am not in my usual job and what I have is interesting and gets me a special issue of warm and waterproof togs so it naturally has advantages. I am settled in now and managing along fine with the other lads. Of course my concert 'debut' helped a lot to 'break the ice' as it were (ha ha). However another bunch of chaps are going home soon and that will mean new faces. 'Roll on that !!.*??? boat' (ha ha).

I was so pleased to read of what you termed the Xmas feeling back home.
By the way Nan, any word of my gift arriving yet?
God bless you dear wife.
Yours always,
Alex

12 January 1945

My dear Nan,

I don't have a great deal of spare time nowadays and any that I do have is taken up by the most important job of finding fuel for the fire. By the way Nan, the way of getting this fuel is the oldest method of all – chopping down of trees with any sort of old tool. One good thing is that it does help towards keeping us warm during the day as I assure you the weather is now really cold with quite a lot of snow. Still I am not complaining as things could be a lot worse.

Your mail may take a little longer than usual owing to the conditions of the roads etc. By the way Nan, I open every letter expecting to see a snap of your new self!

Naturally your letters deal with the gossip of the New Year, Torchy and Ewan. You ask me of how I spent my evening and if I enjoyed myself. Well Nan it was very quiet as you can guess being as I am among what may be termed as a strange crowd. However I managed to stay up to the New Year which seemed to be a case of firing all the guns as a New Year present to Jerry. As he did not fire back everybody was happy! My actual celebration was a repeat of every New Year abroad. A little something to drink and the passing round of your tin of shortbread. Yes Nan, I always manage to keep it intact until Ne'erday (ha ha). One of my wee strange habits of which I have many (ha ha).

It was nice to hear of your many presents and I am sure you must have been very pleased with yourself. I suppose, like myself, you will be wondering what this New Year will have in store for us?

Yours always,

Alex

Xxxxxx

14 January 1945

My dear Nan,

As you can no doubt guess Nan, I am somewhere up in these hills of Italy and I assure you the weather is very suitable for staying indoors if that were possible. However, so far I am not feeling the cold so much as last year. I don't wear boots now so no doubt the fact that my feet are more or less dry explains it. You see, I wear long-legged rubbers and they are very handy and useful as the snow is almost knee deep around us. I really don't feel the cold as during the day I keep very warm by removing some of the Eyetie scenery (in name trees) and going to bed quite early at night. You see I am on duty every second night and I must keep awake so I usually try to get as much sleep as I possibly can at other times.

It is 4 a.m. now and my relief will be up at breakfast which is about 8 o'clock. I am fine and warm as we cut a good supply of timber in the hours of daylight and it is now burning merrily. The fireplace, by the way, I made from old ammo' boxes, and is now a success even though I had trouble at first with smoke coming the wrong way. Still, I used a lot of mud and the whole job is now perfect and I am quite comfortable.

There has been a lot of grumbling about leave but for myself I don't worry. I haven't got so long until my break and if all goes well I won't be coming back to this God-forsaken country afterwards. That itself is almost worth the extra years (ha ha).

I warned you not to raise your hopes. I have been looking at the home papers and it seems to me they are a lot to blame by writing a lot of nonsense.

Yours always,

Alex

Xxxxxxxxxx

18 January 1945   *'Our wee corner' at home*

My dear Nan,

You know Nan, I have had some different jobs in the Army but I think this is the greatest change of the lot. At one time I was a rat in the desert and now I am a mountaineer in the snow. Al least I do have a variety. We have managed here to make our home very comfortable, which by the way is a tent in the snow. Last year we took over an Eyetie farmhouse but this time there aint any. After our experience of last winter, we always make sure that someone is awake during the night if snow is falling and the job is to see that the snow isn't allowed to gather on the tent too heavy, otherwise it will be another case of collapsing tent and buried men, probably including poor me. What a ghastly thought (ha ha). Alright, you can laugh but I don't think that to waken up in the early hours of the morning, to find oneself lying in snow minus pants, is an experience one should want repeated. And to crown it all I could not even find the ??!! things and I had to borrow someone else's (ha ha)! Of course, when he couldn't find his, he was a little upset. Must have had no sense of humour that guy (ha ha). Still Nan, I don't want to be telling all my stories now!

You tell me that you have socks for me Nan but honestly I do believe I can still manage along with what I still have left. I'm not hard on socks and if I find the least hole I darn it right away. One of my house-wifely duties (ha ha).

Please give Mother my sincere thanks for her idea that the bedroom is, as you say, 'our wee corner' until such times as we are able to have own home. I am sorry she hasn't been so well recently but I see from your latest cards that she is up and about again and standing over the gas ring stirring away at the pot.

19 January 1945

I have been up the hills again and believe it or not I really enjoyed it. It has been a nice day here and I didn't really feel cold during my whole day there. I came down a little early so I can manage a few lines. We only have a small lamp so writing at night is impossible.

All these rumours Nan. Now you can see why I never tell you anything which is not facts. I am one of these 'canny Scots'.
Please give my regards to all at home. Good luck and God bless you all.
Yours always,
Alex
Xxxxxxxxx

21 January 1945

My dear Nan,
I was really intending to go over this evening and visit some chaps on another gunsight, as I have been invited across for a few days now, but between you and I dear the weather tonight is not at all pleasant with a very high wind outside and where one walks there is a lot of mud and ice. So as you can see Nan, to pass my evening I have again picked up my writing pad. Dear me! I can hear the rain coming down now!

Now some other chaps have come in and as I have collared the lamp to write I'm afraid I won't have very much peace from now on until I put the lamp back up on the roof so that everybody can see (ha ha). However, so far I haven't been annoyed very much so I will just keep on writing until the really noisy individuals come in and when that happens I'm afraid that will be the end of my writing for tonight.

You tell me of how cold it is at home and of how your walk with Fred gave you rosy cheeks. And that brings me to my pet worry again. How can I imagine you with rosy cheeks when I do not even know what your appearance is like now that you have your new smile? I am waiting patiently for the arrival of that long-promised snap of your new self so don't keep me waiting any longer Nan please (ha ha).

24 January 1945

My dear Nan,
I have managed to find a lamp of sorts so here I am for one of my very small talks before I go to bed.

I was interested in the incident of the chap arriving at McDonald's back door and as <u>you</u> will no doubt know how his <u>wife</u> felt, <u>I</u> have a good idea of how the <u>chap</u> would feel himself. Mind you Nan, for myself, I shouldn't like the idea of meeting my wife at the back door. Far too 'public' for my liking. My poor wife may faint (ha ha).

No Nan, I don't mind reading of the very nice presents you receive from various people but what is the big idea of saying that 'such and such' is just the right thing for <u>your</u> wee cup of tea in bed? What is all this? My dear young lady if you have the idea that I intend to bring you cups of tea in bed! Well, to prevent any disappointment, I advise you to forget all about it. I never heard of such a thing (ha ha).

As you will probably have guessed from my other letters Nan, I am now more or less a wireless operator and it is really interesting although I do have a lot of hill climbing now and then. Quite a change from the desert days eh?

And now Nan, once more it's cheerio.

Yours always,

Alex

xxxxxxxx

28 January 1945

My dear Nan,

I have been weighing up the various pros and cons and I have decided to trust you with my hard-earned savings! You have absolutely no idea of how much thought I gave it (ha ha). Well dear the outcome is that I have posted my book off today by registered envelope but before doing so I took a note of all the various numbers etc. just in case. As you also have the same numbers Nan, we should be quite safe if by any unforeseen happening the envelope does go astray.

Now Nan, we come to the question of money and if all is well my first lot should be at the end of the month. I have counted up all my possible money and find that I should manage to send £30 by the end of the month. I should make my target by the end of March. It is all wrong 'to count chickens' but I am determined to reach my figure as soon as I can.

I have also made a horrible and terrible discovery (ha ha). No kidding though, I find that I haven't got so many certificates as I thought. I must have miscounted and it has been a real disappointment. However, I can add a few pounds right away and I am certainly having a real try to reach that target.

I must tell you however, Nan, that if a chance of leave comes along your wee man is going and 'Blow the savings' (ha ha)! If you remember my last leave was a year ago and I would be very foolish to refuse if I had the offer again before the end of March. And if it comes, the target will be missed!

I have heard that most of the old 276 who stayed at Base have now gone home on this 28 days' leave. <u>Some of them are now on their way out here again.</u> I don't think I should like the idea of home and then returning to Italy again.

Still if 'Joe' (Stalin) keeps going as he is now then he may reduce our time. Who knows?

Well Nan I must say cheerio.

God bless.

Yours always,

Alex

xxxxxxxxxx

1 February 1945

My dear Nan,

I usually have a night's sleep now as all my work is done during the hours of daylight. I told you that my job was O.P. now with radio and as you can realise one cannot observe very much in darkness! In any case, conditions would be too severe. Day time is bad enough (ha ha). Still one enjoys watching our 'dirt' landing on Jerry.

You speak about Burns day and of how Dad looks older. You know Nan, I always find it best to never let the appearance of a person worry me. Some of the chaps who came abroad with me look very much older which we never notice until we perhaps bring out some old snaps etc. and the usual remark is 'Surely that isn't you'? The same thing, no doubt, applies to myself and if you let these things worry you then you will be worried about your poor wee man. But none of us feel really much older.

I am pleased to know that you have used the little money I sent you. I am sure you will look well in the black frock you talk about. Of course, Nan, you can never take what I say as being a fair opinion as being your husband I am naturally just that little bit on your side!

Yours always,

Alex

xxxxxxxxx

3 February 1945   Cartoon of soldiers in Italy

The cartoon shows 2 soldiers huddled in many layers of clothing, scarves wrapped around their necks, sitting on the ground beside their packs. There is a blasted stump of an old tree behind them and a bleak landscape all around. It is a scene of total desolation. One of the men, bottle of beer on his knee, is reading aloud to his mate from a book.

'Here with a Loaf of Bread beneath the bough
A Flask of Wine, a Book of Verse – and Thou
Beside me singing in the Wilderness.'

My dear Nan,

I want to send you the enclosed cartoon which in my opinion is one of the best I have ever seen. So much so that I want you to enjoy this drawing as much as I did myself. Let me have your opinion, Nan.

At the present time we have a thaw and as you can imagine we have plenty of mud! Not yet at the same depth as last winter but I will let you know when it does (ha ha).

You latest letter is dated 25 January and of course deals with our friend 'Rabbie'. By the way Nan, I still have the same Burn's book which you sent me a long time ago. I know it is somewhere in my pack.

I'm really not feeling the cold the same way as last year. I think it is the fact that last year we came out from a very hot climate and it was my first sight of snow since I left home. Another reason is that this extra warm clothing is a big help, especially the boots which keep my feet always more or less dry.

Well that is all my gossip about this country and myself. I will try and let you have another card tomorrow.

Yours always,

Alex

Xxxxxxxxxx

9 February 1945

My dear Nan,

Nan dear, I have some news for you.

I will now only return home on completion of service, which should mean leaving here within four or five months provided that all goes well. I don't like talking of this homecoming Nan as it is still a long way off.

You tell me you haven't changed since I left and even with your new smile! But you forget Nan that when I left, you were rather ill and so when you tell me you are well nowadays, you are not the same girl I left in 1941! Once more it's cheerio and God bless you all.

Yours always,

Alex

Xxxxxxxxxxxxxxx

10 February 1945

My dear Nan,

First, a little of what is happening here.

Well dear today is quite nice and a change from yesterday when we had a real Eyetie winter's day. My job takes me up into the hills and as the weather didn't actually 'break' until the late morning I was caught in it. However I have good waterproof clothing and it was 'nae bother at a''.

A good number of chaps leaving us in the next few days came out in what we call the October 1940 convoy. The next convoy was the December convoy. Then the next again was the <u>February 1941 convoy which included us chaps</u>. So there you are Nan.

Can you give me any idea of a useful commodity which I could look out for and if all goes well I could fetch it home? I know it is a long time yet, but perhaps I could help if I knew. You see Nan I may be able to get certain things out here which are very scarce back home. So will you let me know? Of course, nothing is plentiful here except mud of a particularly sticky type (ha ha), so if you have no 'errand' for me I can always fall on to the mud. I do fall quite often so it will make no difference (ha ha).

Your letter 185 deals a lot with Xmas. You hoped I had as good a Xmas as last year. Well Nan, I hadn't, as I'm afraid this mob hasn't the same go or spirit as the old 276. All we managed was that one concert and even at that I only got six men who were 'game'. And believe it or not there has been no attempt to put on another show since. How men can be content to sit around up here without even trying to make their own entertainment beats me. Why, last year we had a show almost every week and there would be grumbles if we missed a week. We even took our little crowd around other units when possible.

The main reason I believe is that the older hands are only interested in home and the new chaps haven't been away from home long enough yet and are used to having entertainment provided for them.

Your description of Torchy and Ewan's engagement was so well done that I could picture the whole scene. By the way, who cried first, Mother or yourself? And that dear finishes my gossip on 85.

Yours always,

Alex

xxxxxxxxxxx

15 February 1945

My dear Nan,

I am pleased to hear about the homely smell at 85 and it seems I have to look forward to a parcel which you intend for my birthday. This means that once more I am in your debt. If I were you I should make this the last parcel unless I tell you different. Now don't get any silly ideas (ha ha).

I am also pleased to know that my savings book has reached you.

Well dear wife cheerio until the next time. My regards to all at 85. Good luck and God bless you all.

Yours always,

Alex

18 February 1945

My dear Nan,

I was very pleased to receive the memento from Torchy's engagement cake and like my other small gifts I will try and keep hold of it.

This year, dear, my thoughts are the same as your own but I should like to say a few words about one of your recent letters.

You seem to have the impression that if all goes well and I reach home, it will mean that the days of parting are over. Now Nan, this is wrong as although I should not return to Italy I may go other places so don't get any false ideas in that pretty head of yours. It will only mean more disappointments and I don't want you to have any more of those.

It was amusing to read of how you left some baking in the oven and sat down to write and then the smell of buns told you the baking was still in the oven. Serves you right for blethering away and not doing your job (ha ha).

I also enjoyed the story of how Torchy and yourself enjoyed the collecting of the Xmas gifts. I see you use the term unmentionables, eh? Stealing my thunder eh?

Now Nan, you shouldn't talk of beds and cold feet etc. Puts my mind off my work completely (ha ha). It looks as if I will have to catch up with my sleep during the afternoon eh? (Ha ha.)

Well dear, once more cheerio and God bless you all.

Yours always,

Alex

Xxxxxxxxxx

20 February 1945

My dear Nan,

I may as well let you have a few words of comfort and wisdom!

Although I am well I have lost a bit of weight especially round the waist and maybe the 'V' insert won't be necessary on my civvy suits after all. As I climb up and down hills every day even for meals the loss of the 'fashionable tyre' can be understood.

I had a very surprising parcel of papers from you. Some of the items I enjoy but others do make me 'sick'. Items such as that such and such a girl is the 'pin up' or other of the 8th Army. I have been with this Army since it was formed and I assure you that neither myself or my mates ever heard of these girls!

Well Nan, you wonder just where I am and if I am still playing the guitar. I am afraid that I only managed to borrow the instrument for the night of the concert. The man who owns the guitar is away from here and is at a camp about 50 miles down the line. However there is a rumour that he is coming up soon so I may have a few tunes some day later on.

I still seem to have another three or four months before I can tell you that it is coming near my turn. I know you already have been very good and patient dear so I am sure you can do another few months practically 'standing on your head'. I often wonder how you would look standing on your head. I should think it would be a very interesting sight (ha ha). That is of course provided that you could manage that little experiment with all that extra weight of double chins etc. (ha ha).

Thanks for the socks Nan.

Yours always,

Alex

Xxxxxxxxxx

1 *March* 1945   *Florence trips*

My dear Nan,

I am on leave in Florence and my opportunities to write have been very few.

You see Nan, when we want to go to town, we either must go by a lorry at 10 in the morning or at 2 in the afternoon. Naturally we all go during the morning and then we can only return at 11 o'clock at night. However, Nan, I stayed behind this morning and have arranged to meet some of the chaps in town in the afternoon. So you see dear, even though I am surrounded by all these interesting buildings, etc. and may I add very pretty and well-dressed girls, I have not forgotten my wife, ha ha.

The town of Florence has changed a lot since my last visit and we have quite a variety of shows and a really fine Naafi. It is a large building which was a kind of youth club before the war and has almost everything for a soldier on leave. In the building there are restaurants, games rooms, a tailor, watch repairer, photographer, shops, snack bars, theatre, cinema, 3 different bands and a large swimming pool with heated water and a spectators' gallery. Yes Nan, believe it or not, all in the one building. Nothing is small and the restaurant is as large a floor space as the Plaza Ballroom back home. I have seen a few films and the best show was *Blithe Spirit* by Noel Coward. It was an all-American cast from Broadway and I thoroughly enjoyed myself.

I am enjoying my break. Good luck and God bless you all.

Yours always,

Alex

Xxxxxxxxxxxxx

4 March 1945

My dear Nan,

Well dear, try and come with me on my first day in to Florence. The reason I say the first day is because every day following was just a repeat, except that I saw a different show or film.

I have had a look at my list of notes and the first thing that strikes me is how much the town has changed. A lot of the rubble has been cleared and the town is now more or less working quite normal. Thanks of course to the efforts of the army.

There are ample clubs in town now where meals and various types of entertainment can be had. A number of restaurants have been taken over by the army and the cost of a meal is 6d, which covers the cost of cooking and waiters. The food is supplied by the army and I must say that to sit down at a table with proper utensils and have a good meal served by waiters at a cost of 6d is very worthwhile. The meals are very good. Usually soup followed by meat, potatoes, veg and a pudding, ha ha.

In the afternoons, these places give out tea and cakes free. Apart from these places, there is this wonderful Naafi building, which I told you of in my last card. Sufficient to say, Nan, that it is the finest Naafi club I have ever seen and even better than those in either Naples or Rome. I understand the club was built for the Fascist youth before the war. Judging by the show put up by the Eyetie army, the money doesn't seem to have been very well spent!

Now dear, that was my first evening and I'm afraid the end of my little chat for today. As you can guess dear, I have now arrived back on the gun position and I really haven't much time to spare between finding the rest of my kit and sort of tidying up and all that sort of thing.

5 March 1945

The films during my visit to Florence were very poor, although I did see them all. There were also three Italian shows in town, one of which was really very good. The others are very poor and are a kind of striptease. The chorus, or rather the so-called chorus, come on the stage in various types of undress and really very scanty. They are rather stout usually and it is a common thing for the breasts to become uncovered after the first few dance steps. You can guess how we laugh when this happens, especially as I said, Nan, when the so-called 'dancers' are rather stout. Candidly, they can't dance at all. In fact, they can hardly walk, and I am afraid they must make their living at another and much older profession!

The Italians themselves flock to these very poor Eyetie shows and believe it or not, seem to enjoy them very much to judge by the shouts of 'bravo!' etc.

So much for Italian culture.

Well dear, I had my photo taken twice while in Florence, and as you can see I have enclosed one of them which was taken not far from that old bridge called Ponte Vecchio. It is a well-known bridge and very old, and is the only bridge across the river Jerry didn't destroy. My friend in the photograph is a chap from Liverpool, a big fellow who is actually 6ft tall and about 13 stone. A handy fellow to have around.

By the way, Nan, I was weighed in Florence and I turned the scales at 11st 8. Mind you, I think the scales were cock-eyed because I think I am thinner than I used to be. Of course that may be only wishful thinking. Sort of like your double chin, eh? Ha ha. All that remains is to say once again that as usual, my only wish was that you had been beside me and we could have had such an interesting time. Maybe Nan, we will have our little holiday someday soon and we will have a few walks in between my 'lounge wagging'. Because no doubt I will have to do quite a lot of talking. Such as telling you of how much I have missed you, etc., because no doubt you will be wondering if I have fallen for any of these garlic-smelling Eyetie girls. Don't you worry dear, I have never had you out of my mind, no matter where I have been or what I have been doing. I love you, Nan, and really miss you very much, and am only longing for the day when we will be together again and I can talk to you instead of writing these letters.

Still Nan dear, our letters have meant a lot to us and I am sure that you look forward to my letters as much as I wait for yours.

Yours always,

Alex

Xxxxxxxxxxxx

6 March 1945

My dear Nan,

I am now back at the gun position and there was news from you.

I am very pleased for Torchy's sake that she has had word from Ewan. Give them both my regards and to hear the news that they are 'waiting for me' for their wedding is really a surprise. I thought at first it was only Torchy doing a spot of teasing. Still, it is a lovely gesture which I appreciate very much.

I will certainly try my best to get you that purse. If I had known sooner I would have got one in Florence but never mind I may have another chance.

Now Nan, cheerio.

Yours always,

Alex

Xxxxxxxxxx

8 March 1945

My dear Nan,

I am looking forward to the arrival of my birthday parcel and also the 'smokes' which are on their way. I am smoking very few fags these days, sort of preparing myself for the price of fags back in Blighty!

I was very interested in your talk of how we may meet again and of how I may be perhaps at 85 and waiting for you to come home. You see Nan, I have had all these same daydreams myself at some time or other, and so naturally I can understand how you feel and I assure you that I don't laugh at what you call 'rambling on and on'. I know you must miss me because I do know how much I miss you dear.

Please again mention to Mother that I appreciate her lovely action in giving the bedroom to us both until such times as we find that wee corner of our own.

May God bless you fine folks at 85.

It may not be too long now Nan.

Good luck to you all.

Yours always,

Alex

Xxxxxxxxx

9 March 1945

My dear Nan,

Still down from the guns Nan and I am having to wait longer than ever for your letters from home. Some of the chaps here say that the mail arrives about once a week and sits around until such a time as there is a lorry coming down our direction. So don't be surprised if my letters are rambling on with any subject just as an excuse for writing to you and keeping in touch.

The war news is very good these days although this front of Italy is rather quiet and naturally takes a back seat to the campaign in Germany. Still, I think that the old 8th Army has done a good job and is still doing it in a country which makes movement of any kind very difficult. I think that the taking of the large dromes in this country was the main thing of the whole campaign because a large part of the bombing of Germany etc. comes from Italian-based aircraft. So although we aren't much in the news these days we really are still in the war.

10 March 1945

I have had another day in Florence Nan, and spent most of the day trying to buy you that purse but I was unsuccessful. I didn't think you would be very pleased if I only wasted money on a cheap and shoddy article. However Nan, I am not by any means finished [in] my search and I hope to have that purse for you some day.

You see Nan, this has been a static front for a very long time and the longer we stay in these towns the higher these prices become. On my first visit to Florence a certain show cost 20 lire and now some shows cost 90 lire. So you see what I am up against (ha ha). But never mind dear, I will find you that purse somehow.

The weather is fine today and some chaps even had their shirts off for a first touch of sun.

And now Nan, for a few words about your latest cards. Naturally, the only thing that interests us now is when that !!!*?? boat is sailing. The chap out here who has done two more months than I hasn't had any word yet. The sooner he gets his papers the quicker mine will come along. Just logic my dear Watson (ha ha).

I think you should have your Arran holiday.

Yours always,

Alex

Xxxxxxxxxx

17 March 1945   *Teeth trouble*

My dear Nan,

Well Nan, this morning I paid a visit to the dentist as there were a few things I didn't like about my mouth and it is three years since I had a full examination. It isn't very good news. I have developed gum trouble and the advice is to have the 'chewers' removed. However, those jobs do take a bit longer out here in the Army and so, after quite a conversation, I was told that as I should be on my way home in about three or four months, that I wouldn't suffer any harm if I waited until I got back to Blighty before having the job done.

If I had these extractions now Nan, it is quite on the cards that I wouldn't have dentures before my boat was on its way and naturally I don't want to arrive home and give you such a fright! I have no pain or bad teeth Nan just that they seem to be loose on the gums. So you see Nan, with no trouble, harmful effects etc. I do honestly believe that I won't be doing wrong by hanging on to what I now have. And that Nan, is the only fresh incident for today.

By the way Nan, in any case before I part with my teeth I will have another opinion. Being a Scot I don't like parting with anything! (Ha ha.)

Many thanks dear for the Anniversary card and I must say it was rather a surprise. Thanks for the note inside Nan. In fact thanks for everything, even for marrying me (ha ha). I am quite pleased now that you rushed me off my feet and had me married before I could collect my senses. What?! You didn't? Well anyway, that's my story and I'm sticking to it (ha ha).

I have enclosed a small guide to Florence.

My regards to all at 85.

Good night and God bless you all.

Yours always,

Alex

Xxxxxxxxxx

22 March 1945

My dear Nan,

At last, the 'powers that be' have decided to let me have one of your cards and naturally the first thing I must do is sit down and let you have a few words in reply.

I would have written to you in any case, Nan, but the card makes that so much easier. Perhaps this talk of a man who can't at any time sit down and write to his wife surprises you but you see I still have a little of that abruptness in my letters even yet, although my letters since I came abroad may seem to give the lie to that remark. It's just that I must always have some subject to talk about, even though it is only the weather. Thinking back I believe I have mentioned it in every recent letter. The weather, by the way, is warm today (ha ha)!

I have had another day in Florence and my main effort was a search for that purse. I still have had no luck dear. I have tried to attend to the request in another way which I hope will have success. More later, if all goes well (ha ha).

I am vexed at your worries about Torchy being sent overseas. I hate to think of you having any worry. I can't give you any hope that Torchy will not come overseas as being an old soldier I have a very good idea of how the army works. Frankly, I don't think much of the idea of sending girls overseas and away from their own country. It seems all wrong and especially when I read that girls are willing to go and yet they are still planning to have it compulsory. Seems Irish to me.

Nan, dear, don't worry too much about Margaret.

Yours always,

Alex

Xxxxx

25 March 1945

My dear Nan,

First of all I must explain the change of ink colour from my green ink. My usual pen has gone dry and as I cannot find my bottle of ink, I am now using a spare pen which has some ink already in it. How much, I don't know, so don't be surprised if I start to use another colour, which will mean that this pen has gone dry and that after a prolonged search, interrupted by a few choice and pointed remarks, I will have unearthed the bottle of ink (ha ha).

I suppose by now, Nan, you will have a good idea that I am rambling on just because I have practically nothing to write about. And strange as it may seem you will be perfectly correct. I haven't (ha ha)!

The mail situation at present is lousy and that tells me a lot of things which regulations forbid I put down on paper. You see Nan, I know you are writing just as much as usual. If I tried hard enough I could perhaps find something to write about but I don't want to put too much strain on my brain, especially at this stage of the war (ha ha).

There is still no word of my birthday parcel and my birthday on 22 March was just another day.

As you know Nan, I told you that if any leave came along I would no doubt have to postpone the savings target. Well dear, as you know I did have a few days in Florence and I'm afraid that's 'done it' (ha ha).

So now Nan, I'm afraid that my next 'cheque' will have to be sent at the end of April, provided of course that all goes well, and if I have any more 'leave' it will be May and so on and so on (ha ha).

Until I write again God bless you all.

Yours always,

Alex

Xxxxxxxxx

27 March 1945

My dear Nan,

I am starting to write this letter and, candidly, I haven't the faintest idea of what I am going to write about. So what can I find to write about? Oh yes, the change of writing etc.

This has been caused not by the fact that I couldn't find the bottle of green ink but that I did eventually locate it and found it broken. Now my overalls which I had wrapped round the darn bottle are a lovely colour of green here and there! So much for the colour of the ink. Now I have a few words on the reason for the change in the writing. I have repaired my pen by fitting a new nib and naturally it is rather 'scratchy' as yet.

It should improve as time goes on, that is providing the war lasts much longer (ha ha).

The news from the west is very good these days and it certainly looks as if Jerry is on the run at last. As for our own campaign here in Italy Nan, things are very quiet, at least so far as anything on a big scale goes. Maybe some day we will give you something to talk about. Who knows?! The whole thing in this campaign is the country and weather. Try and imagine country similar to the wild Highlands of Scotland and there you have it in a nutshell.

Now Nan, a few words on the subject of 'self'. By that I mean <u>my</u> self and I'm afraid it isn't going to be very good reading. Of course, I knew all this when I started to write but I kept it until near the end (ha ha).

In one of my last letters I told you of my trip to the dentist and that I planned to have another opinion before doing anything rash. Well dear, I went again this morning and I'm afraid that you have admired my strong teeth for the <u>last time</u> (ha ha). The fact was that this new chap wouldn't even let me out of the darn chair, but started to yank a few out right away. He told me bluntly that my teeth were of no use to me and although they were good looking (ha ha) and well kept it was a pity but there you are. This isn't civvy street and I can't have them all out at once, otherwise I would starve (ho ho) so it means a few out every second day and by the time you read this letter I will have 'had it'. I prefer the 'gumsey' to bad health.

And now Nan, I must say cheerio.

Yours always,

Alex

Xxxxxxxxxx

30 March 1945

My dear Nan,

Hurrah! At long last some mail has arrived and quite a feast too. First of all there was your parcel, which like all the others was intact and all the contents in good condition. Also a cable from yourself for my birthday. For all this mail and parcels Nan, many thanks.

Now I suppose you will want to read my news from this part of the world and I know I told you about my teeth in my last letter, and so, being a woman (and I should say a very nice little woman too) you will want to know more.

Well Nan, I lost another five teeth this morning and between you and I my jaw is a bit rough yet. Not only that but I have developed a lisp in my speech. A very fashionable lisp of course (ha ha).

I was told not to wait any longer but have them out <u>right away</u>. But Nan, I don't know how long it will be before my gums will be fit for a new smile and I may have to go home without any at all. And how would that shake you eh? (Ha ha.)

Still, having them out is the worst part and even if I did reach home 'gumsey' it would only be a few days before I had some new teeth. You see, Nan, all I do is report to the nearest Dental Centre and the job will be done. Simple isn't it? I have it all planned out (ha ha) and even if we went to that 'place you have in mind' for a holiday there will be an Army dentist nearby.

And now Nan, once more back to your parcel. As you will realise I can't give you my opinion on the shortbread just yet (ha ha) but I am sure it will be of the same quality as all the other samples you have sent me. The socks are just fine and I don't think it will be necessary to send me any more just yet. In any case, the socks you have at home will still come in handy as I expect to do some work before I retire (ha ha).

My mail may be a bit better now as we sent in a strong complaint as the trouble was men just not bothering to collect our stuff. A poor show.

Yours always,

Alex

Xxxxxxxxxxxx

31 March 1945

My dear Nan,

Well Nan, it won't be long now before I am completely devoid of a smile altogether. I would prefer them all out at once, but then the army says No! and that's that! As it is, I only have 10 left and by the time you receive this the total will probably be a lot less (ha ha). Still Nan, the gums are bad and I do think what I am doing is for the best. Mind you it is a pity because all my teeth are good but then what's the use of nice-looking teeth and unhealthy gums? Now dear, it is possible I may have dentures before I reach home. Even if I do come home 'gumsey' I don't suppose you will mind so much.

You can take out yours then and we can both smile for each other (ha ha).

1 April 1945

I will just go ahead with the answering of your 193.

You tell me of the cheerful voices at 85 and when you tell me you have Ewan and Torchy both at home at once the home must be in an uproar. I hope by now you have more definite word about Margaret's chance of going abroad.

I am amazed at what you tell me of the preparations yourself and Mother are making in the event of my homecoming. You talk of all these things and then you smile to yourself when I say that it was your nature which made me

234

'fall' for a certain young lady (ha ha). When you talk like that dear what man couldn't love you, and may I add the spirit of 85. My home too, by the way.

I am going to say a few words now about 194. So you are now having a go at the Pools eh? Still I must say if the best you can do is 2 out of 10 you would be well advised to leave them alone. I could do better than that myself (ha ha). Not only that, but you say that you expected 10%! Pardon my mirth Nan (ha ha).

No, Nan, I don't have another guitar. They are very scarce here in Italy and, of the few I have seen, the prices are too much for my purse. Of course, I may get hold of another one later on, depending on where I may move to. If I had known at the time what I know now, I would have held on to my old guitar. But then, who can tell the future?

I have sent a few enclosures in this letter and I am at present in the position of being able to manage into Florence about once a week. I am trying to be kept down here until I have had the job of my teeth attended to, as where I came from there is no dentist with the equipment for full dentures etc. So the longer I can stay here the better chance I have of the same guy doing the whole job.

And now dear wife I must say goodnight.

Yours always,

Alex

Xxxxxxxxx

4 April 1945

My dear Nan,

Well Nan, I have an idea you want to know all my news of my teeth trouble.

I am steadily losing them all. I lost some more today and I now very proudly possess the grand total of 4 on the top and the same number on the bottom. Sorry Nan, my mistake 5 on the bottom (ha ha). I am well although eating has become an art of concentration (ha ha) and I am actually enjoying my food. At least what I am able to swallow (ha ha). Never mind Nan, it's all for the best.

I am so pleased that you have received the photograph taken in Florence and the story of my short stay there. I was interested to read that you have a new suitcase for us. I am hoping there will be a little space for my things too! Perhaps if you packed your frocks a little tighter I could manage? After all I suppose I will have to carry the darn thing (ha ha). Please give Ewan my thanks.

Good night and God bless you all.

Yours always,

Alex

xxxxxxxxxx

7 April 1945

My dear Nan,

Here I am for another of these small chats which usually seem to start off very well and then gradually 'peter out' as if I have run out of material which after all isn't surprising as with such a static front out here these winter months one doesn't have the same new experiences to talk of or the new towns to try and describe and so I am forced to rely for my material on news from home, the weather and my own health. You can see I really have an awfully interesting time of it!

But then, Nan, who can say that a Macintyre never tried? (Ha ha.)

And so Nan, I shall say a few words about my three 'escape routes' which are very handy! Being an awkward man, and with so much overseas service, I will say a few words about the last of the three topics. In other words, myself. Maybe it's bad manners but who cares?

I am well and have now lost almost all my teeth and if you want the details I have now parted with the remaining few of my upper teeth today and all I have now are 4 on the bottom. I may have the four on the bottom to keep. Perhaps this leaving of teeth may sound strange but you see Nan the army try if possible to leave even 1 natural tooth as seemingly they are a big help to general health.

Still working backwards Nan we come to the weather and that is very good. So good in fact that you may read of some changes on the Italian Front. So much for topic 2!

So Nan, you have received the surprise packet containing the artistic effort in the making of which I used an awful lot of paper even though I had some help from a chap who is a very good artist. It was his job at home. My effort is an original and not a copy. A product of my brain (ha ha). I knew it would make you happy and I tried to imagine your feelings when you opened the letter. 'Silly old fool.'

A toothless old fool too (ha ha).

And now Nan, once more cheerio.

Yours always,

Alex

xxxxxxxxx

10 April 1945

My dear Nan,

Your latest letter was the first of the cheaper style of postage. It's about time the postage for our mail was reduced in any case as a large profit must have already been made from these letters. Now after all these years we can have our letters delivered free of charge.

Your letter tells me all about the 'Offensive on the Home Front' and the necessary 'Mopping Up' operations which followed. I really enjoyed all that news about our room. Makes me quite excited (ha ha).

I now have every hope that you won't have to put up with my 'gumsey' appearance after all. Of course a lot depends on finding a dentist when I want one. You tell me that you have finished with your own dentist now and you have paid the bill. I hope that the few extra shillings I sent you helped towards your expenses. As for myself, the army has taken them out and the army will put them in again.

Goodnight and God bless you all.

Yours always,

Alex

xxxxxxxxxx

13 April 1945

My dear Nan,

I have had another feast of mail which was there when I returned to camp last night and included three of your long letters 195, 196 and 199.

You tell me in one of your letters of a dream you had and it is so strange that I really must say a few words about it.

You tell me of how you saw me so clean and tidy and that even my <u>teeth</u> were shining. Don't you agree that remark was very strange especially when you can understand that it was just about that time when I had the trouble and decided to have treatment? You know Nan, the worst has been done, my gums are healing up very well and I have to go to a dentist again in a few weeks time with regards to a new set of teeth, so it looks as if you won't see me gumsey after all. By the way Nan you shouldn't worry about these wee things as I am perfectly well and I'm having very little trouble with food. I can manage practically everything already apart from crusts.

Don't you find that dream interesting?

The next three months should see me home if all goes well.

If not there'll be a row (ha ha).

Yours always,

Alex

Xxxxxxxxxxxxx

17 April 1945

My dear Nan,

I am enjoying my usual good health although I don't enjoy speaking too much. In fact I have become one of those so-called strong silent men. In about a week's time another trip to the dentist should be a first step towards new teeth.

The chap beside me who has served two months longer than I received his papers <u>last night</u> and that means we should be expecting ours now in from 6 to 8 weeks time, provided of course that all goes well.

It would be wrong Nan to say that I am not very pleased at this happening and not a wee bit excited at what the near future may hold for me.

Now Nan, I feel I must warn you not to take my limit of 2 months as being official because as you can see it won't be fully 4 and a half years and we may not be fortunate in having a month or two 'knocked off', say for good attendance and behaviour, as a convict would remark (ha ha)!
So now, Nan, you know as much as I.
Yours always,
Alex
Xxxxxxxxxxxxxx

18 April 1945

My dear Nan,
I told you that chap has had word of his 'Python Papers' – the name by the way which is given to this completion of overseas service. If all goes well I am expecting my papers during the month of June and that is only a few weeks ahead. Sounds rather nice doesn't it?

I'm pleased to know you are all cheery back home, even to having guesses as to when this war will end. You ask me, Nan, if I would send you my opinion to add to the others at 85 but I'm afraid that I am unable to guess, so you can just have your little game to yourselves. The more I think of this war the more puzzled I become and the less I think of it the better I feel. And that's that.

I am going in search of a dentist tomorrow and I will let you know what success I have. By the way, Nan, I am still continuing the search for that elusive purse and I'll let you know.
Yours always,
Alex
Xxxxxxxxxxxxx

24 April 1945

My dear Nan,
I am still 'gumsey' (dentists being very elusive) and the weather is now very warm. We are out of those hills now and the countryside is much more pleasant, being very flat and with a bit of green. Of course we have a lot of other queer 'plants' which tend to make our lives interesting!

That other chap should leave us next week. Yes! Nan, I agree; a very pleasant thought.

I enjoyed your very special letter of 11 April and I certainly understand how you feel Nan, on these anniversaries.

You say a lot about the drawing I sent and the whole thing seems to have surprised you very much. That artistic effort caused an extreme shortage of airgraph forms before I got the idea and even then I had to get advice on the colouring from a real artist, who offered to do the whole job as I pestered him so much (ha ha). Being as you know of a very stubborn nature I persevered and as the result made you happy, I had my reward. The little drawing served its purpose.

I am pleased you enjoyed the enclosures from Florence. I think I have seen the last of that town at least for the time being. As for Bologna, we had bad luck there and although we were in the advance there we didn't go right in. We may however go for a visit there and by that time the Eyeties will have all the prices up and have 'organised robbery'. Just my luck!

Well dear, it's getting dark now so it's cheerio.

Alex

xxxxxxxxxxxxxxxx

---

26 *April* 1945   *News of a boat – perhaps!*

My dear Nan,

Well Nan, I have heard some real good news. It is possible that we may not all go on the same 'boat' at the same time. News from very 'reliable sources' (ha ha) says that some of our convoy are actually going back in a few days' time.

Not weeks Nan! Days!

The chap I told you of actually leaves us in 2 days. He is really in the last 'draft' of his convoy to go home and if there aren't enough men to fill the ship then men are taken from the next convoy which came out. And that means us. Each group sort of overlaps as it were, so you can realise that although some chaps come out together some are bound to go home a few weeks earlier than others. Just a question of luck, that's all. This may seem a bit vague Nan, but I am sure you will get the gist of it after you have read the details your usual four or five times (ha ha)!

I should get my papers in anything from 2 to 6 weeks time.

Well Nan, it's dinner time so I'll away and sink my teeth into a nice big juicy steak (Oh Yeah). Probably the stuff the cooks call 'brown stew'. What I call it is not fit for publication.

Now Nan, I've had my dinner and it was 'brown stew'!

I have had my visit to the dentist and I have been told to wait another few weeks or as long as possible. So I have decided to wait until I receive my 'papers' and then its rush to the nearest dentist. My gums should be in really good condition by the time I go.

You ask me if the 'place' you have in mind for our holiday is alright or do I prefer any other particular spot.

Now Nan, that is what I would call an 'ambiguity' because how can I answer that question when I haven't the remotest idea of the place you have in mind? (Ha ha.)

In any case Nan, wherever it may be will suit me, as you are the 'Boss' in that matter, except of course the question of the light. I will be the 'Boss' there (ha ha) and maybe I will want an 'account' of how my money was spent and demand a very close examination of all those 'unmentionables'. And not in a parcel or box either (ha ha). Yes woman! I intend to demand full account. I have spoken (ha ha).

Well dear, this is about all for the present and all that remains is to tell you that the enclosure is one of the leaflets we put across to Jerry with our shells. They were sent over every day.

Yours always,

Alex

Xxxxxxxxxx

29 April 1945

My dear Nan,

This is just one of my usual chats about nothing in particular. Of course, I will mention my health, the weather and possibly a few words about my homecoming.

My health is its usual cheery self although what I have to be cheery about in this army dear only knows. Must be my own cheerful nature that's all. I have no teeth yet but I am not worrying at all. Different dentists have different ideas and now the next dentist will want to know why the H!!? I didn't have them out earlier (ha ha). Still, I should have a set of new 'youth' within the next few weeks.

Even if the war does end soon, and that wouldn't be surprising, I will still get my teeth.

The war is going well. The whole Jerry line depended on Bologna and the weather. The weather changed and so Bologna was bound to fall and now Jerry is on a run again.

That chap beside me does actually go away on the 30th April so there you are. Of course, I have had 'official' news from various chaps who because they are at Base profess to know a lot more than us, but I don't think it would do any good to repeat these stories to you.

Well Nan, once again, cheerio and God bless you all.

Yours always,

Alex

xxxxxxxxxxxxxxxx

30 April 1945: Hitler commits suicide in Berlin

5 May 1945   Back to lorries

My dear Nan,

I hope you haven't been worrying.

I am trying to write this while I wait for a lorry load. Yes Nan, I am back on to lorries again. Oh! And another thing, the goods I am collecting happen to be Naafi and actually <u>beer</u>. To be exact 90,000 bottles and I bet I don't even 'find' one bottle (ha ha).

However, to go on with my story. As you know the war in Italy is over and as you can guess we have put our guns away at least for the time being. At least, that's what we are told but between you and I, it will be doubtful if they are ever used again. Still I am sure you will agree with me when I say that they have done their job.

Well dear, what has happened is this. While we keep the same name of Battery etc. we are now actually a Royal Artillery service unit with a 100 or so lorries. Naturally all men who could drive were badly needed and so once more I am back on my old job. All this reorganisation meant that we had a real busy time. The task of collecting the lorries meant a journey of 400 miles. My job is taking supplies right up. For instance, this trip so far as I can make out is to dump this beer somewhere near Venice. If I can manage in to town I'll let you know all about it. Mind you Nan, I expected to be in Venice a long time ago but after Bologna our guns couldn't keep up with Jerry even though sometimes we moved twice in the one day. He certainly moved fast.

We should have some interesting journeys but it will no doubt be just my luck to be posted to Blighty when I am enjoying myself (ha ha).

Today is nice and warm but we have been having heavy rain and on my way back with the lorries I had to drive in a snowstorm. Admittedly, I was up a mountain pass, but who ever heard of snow in sunny Italy in May?

My health is very good although I am still without my new smile. My gums are becoming harder and the next time I go to the dentist I expect to have some teeth.

This is just a scribble Nan and just to explain what has delayed my letters. I will write again soon. Until then all my love.

Yours always,

Alex

Xxxxxxxxxxxx

8 May 1945: Declaration of end of war in Europe

10 May 1945   *Venice/ war in Europe over*

My dear Nan,

And now the war in Europe is over and I am sure all you people at home will be happy. As for myself out here, it has made no difference at all. Actually, I have been busier these last few days than ever before. I have returned to my first love of lorries and when I wrote I was on my way to Mestre which is near Venice and I hoped to find a few hours in that city of canals and bridges.

Well Nan, I managed two hours in Venice so here is a little description of my experience.

In the first place Nan, Venice has no signs of war, which is perfectly natural as one cannot what is usually called pass through the town. It is a 'dead end' and therefore of no use to Jerry. The town is really quite large and the first thing I noticed was the absence of transport of any kind. No, Nan, not even the old pushbike. Venice is the first place in Italy which really came up to my expectations and does appear the same as all the photographs told us.

The first part of the journey was over a really wonderful bridge from what may be termed the mainland. This bridge is wide enough to carry at least six streams of traffic and also a full-size railway.

When we reach the end of this road and railway we leave all forms of usual transport behind, and from there we must either walk or travel by gondola. The streets are very narrow and we have a job walking two abreast. I believe there are over 700 bridges! The best way to travel is by gondola and as you can guess, Nan, we all rushed for one of these boats. It was certainly a wonderful experience to go up the 'Main Street' or as it is called the Grand Canal and then take a right turning up to old Venice better known as San Marco. It was funny though to go up one street and pass a cinema and then see all the large houses with the main door on the bank or rather edge of these canals. Must be rather fun, calling for one's girlfriend and then visiting a cinema show, although pity the poor fellow who misses the last 'bus'. Mind you he has two alternatives 'Swim or Walk' (ha ha).

San Marco itself has the finest square and church I have ever seen. The square can really be termed huge, compared to which those of Rome and Florence are merely toys. I can't give you exact figures, Nan, but my own guess is that the square is almost ¼ mile across.

Well dear, I can now say I have sailed through Venice on a gondola and of course put my mark on the 'Ponti di Rialto', the Bridge of Sighs. Yes dear, quite a new experience which I hope to <u>tell</u> you all about very soon.

By the way, Nan, I told you my job was taking up beer and all went well. I brought back 40 Jerrys. They were SS men but I had no trouble at all. I was armed and they weren't, that's all.

Yours always,

Alex

Xxxxxxxxxxxxx

14 May 1945

My dear Nan,

I seem to have less time to myself than ever before even though the war in Italy is over. All I do is run up and down the country and loading and unloading all over the place. We never have two loads the same.

The weather is extremely hot. The worst of it is that we are not allowed to wear shorts as there is malaria in the Po Valley and the 'mossies' are busy during daylight as well as in the evening.

There has been no news of my homecoming. I still expect to be on my way home in June. I shall be very disappointed myself if I'm not (ha ha). We have been very fortunate so far and we can't complain.

I really enjoyed your description of your day at Hamilton and of how my shirts turned up. So you had out my grey suit eh? I wonder how it will fit. Maybe I won't need that 'V' sign after all (ha ha). And I notice that you have decided the type of clothes I must wear eh? Henpecked, that's me (ha ha). God bless you all.

Yours always,

Alex

Xxxxxxxxxxxxxxxxxx

15 May 1945

My dear Nan,

When I returned to camp I received your 204 of May 6th. I am very busy now and on the roads practically every day. I have just returned from Mestre. Our sort of permanent base camp is at Faenza and is on the Bologna road between Forli and Imola. Our job is running up and down from further north and of course over the River Po. We never travel empty either up or down and the loads always vary. For instance, we have had beer, oranges, Jerrys and scrap iron (ha ha).

However, I won't be out tomorrow as I have developed some engine trouble. Not to be wondered at as I have covered over 1,000 miles in the last few days over some very bad parts of road and we are always in a big hurry (ha ha).

16 May 1945

I do not have any news yet of my 'papers'. No! Nan not even one little rumour (ha ha).

By the way dear, although I seldom mention my 'fires' nowadays I still perform that rite as usual. Today is Wednesday and I had my last fire last Sunday, though I couldn't manage until the evening. Yes! Dear, I still have that habit.

I have your long letter <u>204</u> and also a <u>letter card</u> written on <u>VE day</u>.

Reading them both together is quite interesting as <u>204</u> is full of how you are hearing <u>rumours</u> of peace and then the <u>letter card</u> is telling me of how happy and pleased you all are at home when the <u>actual news</u> came through.

You ask me of how <u>we</u> received this news so what I am going to tell you should be interesting if not quite funny.

If you remember Nan when I told you of the change over to this work I also told you of what my first load was. Well, we were travelling for almost five days and we heard no news but plenty of rumours and so we sort of celebrated for these five days!

Oh yes Nan we '<u>found</u>' plenty of beer (ha ha). Mind you we had no real fuss. In fact, the end of the war in Europe just sort of came, and passed on, and nobody became in the least excited. Our army life is going on just the same and I suppose that was why.

In any case the old 8th Army finished their part of the war first (ha ha).

Well dear, this is a queer little scribble.

Good luck and God bless you all.

Yours always,

Alex

Xxxxxxxxxx

19 May 1945

My dear Nan,

There is no more news of these 'Python Papers' and so I can't even enjoy myself by teasing you with a few remarks (ha ha).

It has been grand to read of the sorting out of my civvy clothes and as you say dear the mention of my two-piece grey suit and your frock does bring back a few happy memories.

I am so pleased that all the folks at Hamilton are enjoying good health. However, one passage in your letter has made me think a lot. You say that Aunt Nell 'slipped you' 20 coupons for a new coat for <u>me</u> which <u>you</u> have had <u>your</u> eyes on. So from now on I have to wear what my wife has <u>her</u> eye on, eh?

Listen woman!! (Ha ha.) For the last five years I have been told what I must wear and I will see that when that day comes I will suit myself what I wear and if I even want to go 'back to nature' I'll go! Or maybe the Blighty weather is too cold eh? (Ha ha.) I don't remember much about Blighty weather but if I do want to know I can always ask the first Yank I see with a lot of ribbons up (ha ha).

Maybe I shouldn't say too much about that as there is a possibility that I may get another ribbon myself. After all the old 8th did finish it's show first. As I told you long ago, Nan, it was the country and the weather which made the Eyetie campaign seem slow. But when we moved we certainly moved (ha ha). Shall I tell you why Jerry packed up so suddenly? Well, he never expected the marshes at Lake Comacchio to ever be crossed but he forgot that was the 8th Army sector and he 'had it' (ha ha). Listen to me blowing my horn! (Ha ha.)

Our whole company is moving up north in the next few days and working a different area. Shouldn't be the least surprised if I have a trip to Austria before my time is up. This move will mean drivers having an even busier time than ever, so don't be surprised if this card is the last for a few days.

As you know Nan, I celebrated the end of the war for about five days. It would have lasted longer but the 'food' ran out (ha ha).

Well dear, cheerio until the next time.

Yours always,

Alex

Xxxxxxxxxx

21 May 1945   His papers arrive

My dear Nan,

This is the letter you have been waiting for and for such a long time. I have received word that I will be on my way home within the next few days.

I was told yesterday at Forli that I would be on my way home any day within the next week and it was quite a surprise. Then this morning my lorry was taken from me and given to another driver. The reason was that I haven't to go far away from camp in case any word does come through. The C.O. said he doesn't want me to be away up in Austria when the news comes in. Our camp is now at Mestre and the lorries have just gone up on another five-day job. The other chap has my lorry now so I am sure that although I haven't been told the exact date or actually signed any papers, you will agree Nan, that the 'powers that be' must know a lot more than I.

I can't add any more for the time being but will tell you tomorrow or the next day of any further developments.

I intend this 284 to be the last of my letters and the one which you will not answer.

22 May 1945

No more news today Nan. However, I need to tell you that I have been successful in getting your purse!

I received word today that it is on its way to you from <u>Cairo</u>. It's a long story Nan! Until tomorrow dear, goodnight.

23 May 1945

Went after some teeth today and ended up in Venice where I was successful. Will have the teeth tomorrow if all goes well. I bought a few odds and ends while I was in Venice such as brooches, beads and photographs. Raining tonight.

24 May 1945

I have still had no more news of my 'Python Papers' date and as it is a few days since I wrote to you I think it would be as well if I posted this small diary letter today. However, I still think it will be as well not to answer any of my letters from now on, Nan, as there seems no doubt that I shall be on my way to Naples before any reply could reach me. However, Nan there's still 'many a slip' that can happen so don't build up too many hopes.

I received two cards from you today and I am pleased you are enjoying yourself at Arran.

Well dear cheerio again.

Yours always,

Alex

Xxxxxxxx

PS I got my teeth yesterday.

27 May 1945

I have received word that I have to be at R.H.Q. (Forli) by the 4th of June. This is <u>official</u> but continue to be a 'canny Scot'.

If all goes well I should be home during the month of June.

A more detailed letter is following.

All my love,

Alex

Xxxxxxxxxxx

27 May 1945

My dear Nan,

No doubt by now you will have received the news that I should be on my way home in a week's time. On the first stage of my rather long journey to Blighty. In any case it shouldn't be as long as my journey when I came out here many years ago. Yes dear, it has been a long time and you have been very patient, but now the longest wait is over, and 'Today the Sun is Shining'.

My last letter to you was really a rather excitable scribble. I have to be at R.H.Q. not later than 4th June. As I am almost 200 miles from R.H.Q. I expect to leave Mestre round about 2nd June. That is in six days' time. No doubt this news came as a surprise to you, but as I wasn't expecting it myself so soon I couldn't give you any warning at all. However, Nan, this is the news you have awaited for so long now. I shall continue writing practically every day, and telling you of any fresh happenings which may occur.

I have had my teeth made in Venice, but as they hurt rather badly, I went back to the dentist today, and on my journey there with the teeth in my pocket I broke the darn things (ha ha).

However, I will get another lot tomorrow and have another 'go' at wearing them (ha ha). I won't be bringing home any presents Nan, apart from a few odds and ends.

Well Nan, another 'news flash' has just come in. <u>My 'Papers' have actually arrived</u> and I report to the Captain in the morning.

There you are now. No doubt about the matter now. Satisfied eh? (Ha ha.)

Now the story of your purse that I mentioned in my last letter. I heard of this organisation and so I wrote them after my search in Italy was unsuccessful. I enclosed the money, told them what I wanted and I have had two replies back. The first came a month ago and told me that they had received my order and would send the goods as soon as possible. The second arrived a few days ago and told me that the goods had been posted. However, the address is given as 84 Shields Road! But I still think you should receive your purse alright. After all, the postman knows you well enough by now (ha ha).

29 May 1945

I was quite busy yesterday first on a driving job and afterwards I had to go into Venice to see about my teeth again. I have got them in again, but as my mouth is a bit damaged by my 'perseverance' I have been told to remove them while eating at least for a day or two until my mouth heals up again.

While in Venice tonight I heard a pipe band performing in the San Marco Square. I don't know what the general opinion of the Venetians is towards us 'Scotzeos' but I did notice that the girls were real interested in the kilt (ha ha).

In connection with my homecoming, yesterday I <u>signed</u> the papers and now all I do is just wait.

Today the job is to go into Mestre and be medically examined, a formality which must be observed when a man is going home. The main thing is skin troubles which would spread easily on a ship and even spread back home in Blighty. However, a chap must be rather bad before it is found that he must be kept back a few weeks. I haven't heard of anybody being so unfortunate yet, as during the few weeks before a man is actually home he can be having treatment. All our chaps got a clean sheet today and that's that!

I have heard that we leave here on June 1st – in 3 days' time.

30 May 1945

Well Nan, I must finish this letter today as my journey towards home and yourself will start tomorrow morning. I leave the lorries in the morning and my first objective will be our B.H.Q. where I expect to be most of the day, as there will be quite a number of small jobs to be done, such as checking of my kit and a few other jobs.

So far as I can make out, I travel all the way down to Naples by road and not by rail from Forli as I first thought. I also understand that we aren't due at Naples until June 10th so you can realise Nan, that as I don't know how long we may be kept at Naples I can't give you any more details as to when I may actually reach Blighty.

However Nan, I do intend to continue writing small scraps of news day after day, if possible. Of course Nan, what I said about arriving during June still holds good, but at the present time I haven't the faintest idea of what day or date.

And now dear wife Goodnight.

Yours always,

Alex

Xxxxxxxxx

7 June 1945   At Rome

My dear Nan,

Here is another small instalment of my journey south from Mestre.

My last note was written from Arezzo and now as you can see I have reached Rome once again. We should have 'booked in' at the Transit Camp in Rome but once again the 'Old Soldier' took a part in such matters.

You see Nan, Transit Camps mean Guards, Fatigues etc., a really horrible thought. So we had a 'Council of War' and instead of going to the Transit Camp we made direct for the more interesting 'Rest Camp'.

The camp itself was the Eyetie Naval Academy. We sleep in the dormitories and there are plenty of baths etc. around us. There is a cinema, theatre and of course an extra large Naafi. In addition, there are facilities for all sports, such as football, cricket, tennis etc. The food is very good and we do not queue either (ha ha). We are waited upon by Eyeties and really do very little apart from washing ourselves. Breakfast has been (whisper) bacon and egg, porridge etc. and is served from 8 till 9.30 and believe it or not we were wakened at 7 with a cup of tea in bed.

Yes, certainly a big difference from the other camp where we should have gone officially (ha ha)!

We leave tomorrow for Naples on the next stage of our way home.

Before I say cheerio Nan, I should tell you my programme for the rest of the day. After I post this note I go to the Naafi for a drop of tea etc., a walk around the camp and maybe a game of billiards and then lunch. After lunch another stroll and an hour or two in the swimming pool and then dinner. After dinner, a visit to Rome, return to camp, supper and so to bed (ha ha). Yes Nan! A gentleman's life!

Yours always,

Alex

Xxxxxxxxx

10 June 1945   *At 'X' Special Transit Camp, Naples*

My dear Nan,

Well Nan, apart from the short journey to the boat my travelling in Italy is finished. I can tell you that our embarkation date is June 14th, that is in four days' time. The journey home is to take anything from 6 to 10 days. No one really knows.

The same thing applies to what may happen when we reach Blighty. It may be Glasgow or Liverpool and we may go right home or go to various base camps. The Royal Artillery Base, by the way, is at Woolwich and so we may have to go down there before going home. But then Nan, no one really knows at present.

I have the idea that this should be my last letter from overseas. The next note should be when I reach Blighty.

The camp itself here in Naples leaves a lot to be desired. Food is very poor and so are the general conditions. Frankly Nan, the army is living up to its old idea. We have done our job and now they have no time for us. Yes Nan, 'Python' personnel are treated like dirt. For instance almost 100 chaps have to go on a docks guard. And yet there must be thousands of men around Naples in the various base camps. But there you are, they must have their 'pound of flesh'.

Well dear this is all meantime so I must go in the queue for dinner (at least that's the name given to it).

I will say my cheerio now and post my note on the way there.

Now dear wife good luck and God bless you all.

Yours always,

Alex

xxxxxxxxxxxxxxxx

POSTSCRIPT

Telegram in suitcase stamped 22 June 1945

Arrived safely expect home late Sunday or Monday
Alex

Soldier's Service and Army Book

On 23 June 1945 Alex was awarded twenty-eight days' leave and two additional days to celebrate VE Day.

By 25 July he was back writing to Nan again, only this time from Woolwich Army Depot, close to London. Conditions at first were very poor and the men were wearing their same worn-out kit.

28 July 1945

We [are being ordered around by] Woolwich commandos. They have never seen a gun or a Jerry. The majority of them live around here and have been going home every night since the War. We call them the Gestapo. The surprising part is that labour in Britain is crying out for manpower and there are thousands of men like myself going around doing senseless jobs such as picking up paper and polishing brasses.

You know, Nan, I had to push an old hand-cart about 2 miles tonight with all our bedding. Not that there are no lorries but just to keep us bright and cheery. Nice experience with all the civvies laughing at us. And no wonder at it.

During August 1945, though still in Woolwich, Alex became a lot happier and had a job at the Post Office.

8 August 1945

I have no parades, Nan. I just go down between 8 and 9 in the mornings and I just sit down, sort and hand out mail and no-one says 'Boo' to me (ha ha). The papers are saying that the demob will be a lot faster now and that they hope to reach Group 32 by the end of the year. If that is so then I should be out myself in 3 months.

Alex was finally demobbed from the Army on 8 December 1945 and was present at Margaret's wedding to Ewan on the 10th in Glasgow.

Alex and Nan could not find a place of their own at first. They were forced by the extreme housing shortage to take up Mother's offer of the bedroom at 85 Shields Road until they could find that 'wee corner' of their own.

Alex had trouble finding work and did a labouring job on a building site. In their bedroom at night Nan had to dry out his overalls in front of a single-bar fire.

Nan was pregnant by this time. Alex worked every night when he got home from work on a cot in the hall of the wee flat. The noise he made caused upset with Mother and especially Dad, who went to bed very early.

In the summer of 1946 Nan had her first baby, a girl, at home at 85 Shields Road. Unfortunately the baby didn't live. Nan always spoke about 'my first wee girl' though she never had a name. Margaret recalls going to 85 and being in the house when Nan and Alex took 'the wee white coffin' down the stairs.

Margaret remembers Alex breaking up the cot.

By the summer of 1947 their lives were a little easier. They managed to rent a top-floor tenement flat in Avon Street – a two-room place with a kitchen and inside toilet.

In August 1947 they brought their son, Robert Inglis Macintyre, home from Stobhill Hospital.

How do I conclude this life of Alex? Should I focus on the years of heart trouble and the malaria which he suffered? The hobbies he continued to follow? Building a television set in the kitchen, breeding canaries in the bedroom, his wonderful photographs? Or his determination to give Nan the best life he could – buying a wee car to take us all away on picnics in the fresh air, or the caravan holidays to the east coast of Scotland?

Alex died in February 1961 of a heart attack. He was fifty years old.

Nan had to find work and went, as a young widow, to work for Glasgow Corporation as a school meals 'dinner lady'. She fought for the rest of her life to give Robert and myself the chances, especially in education, which she and Alex had never had.

She kept Alex's spirit alive in her own life. She kept her chin up and he would have been very proud of her.

INDEX